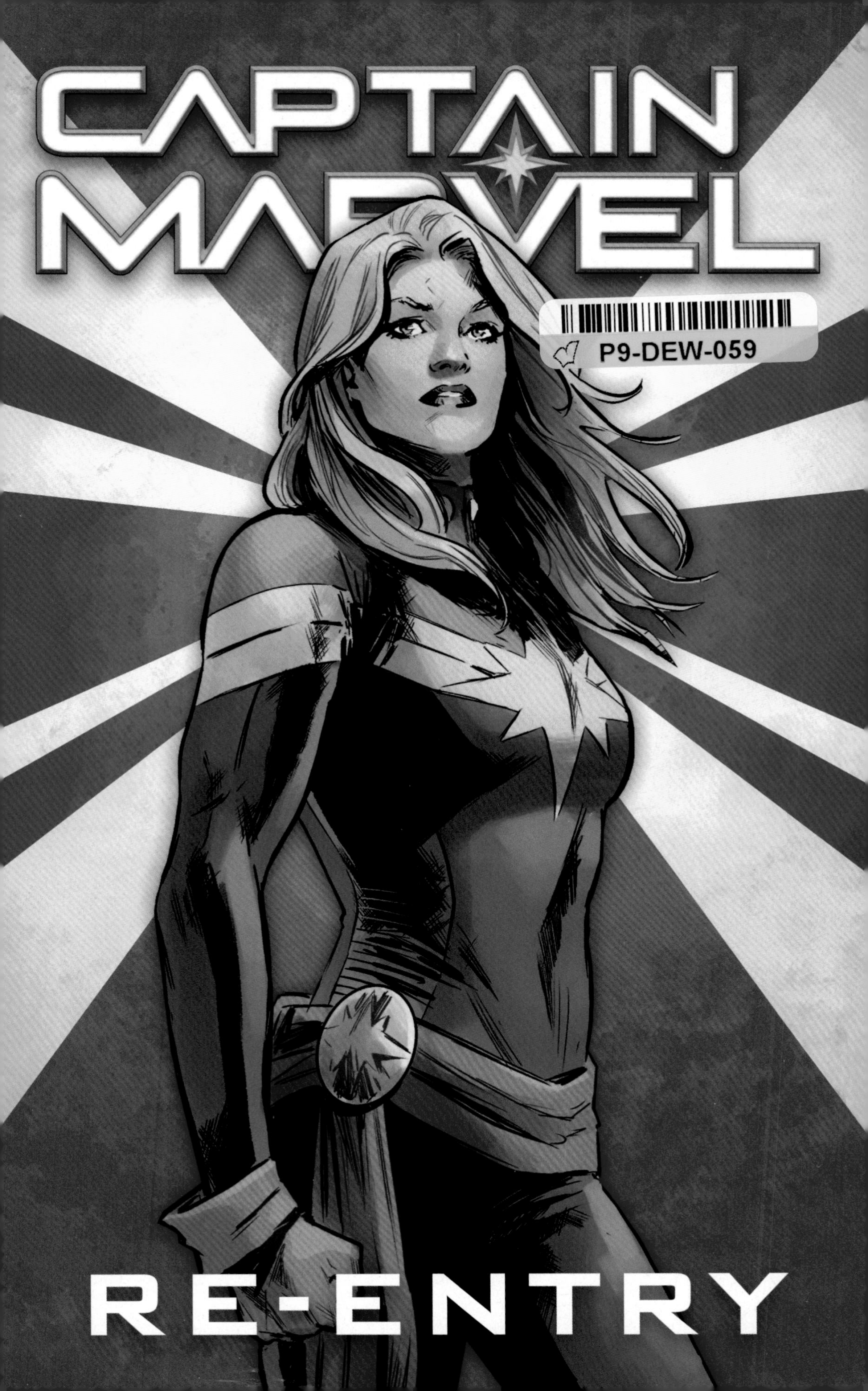
CAPTAIN
MARVEL
RE-ENTRY

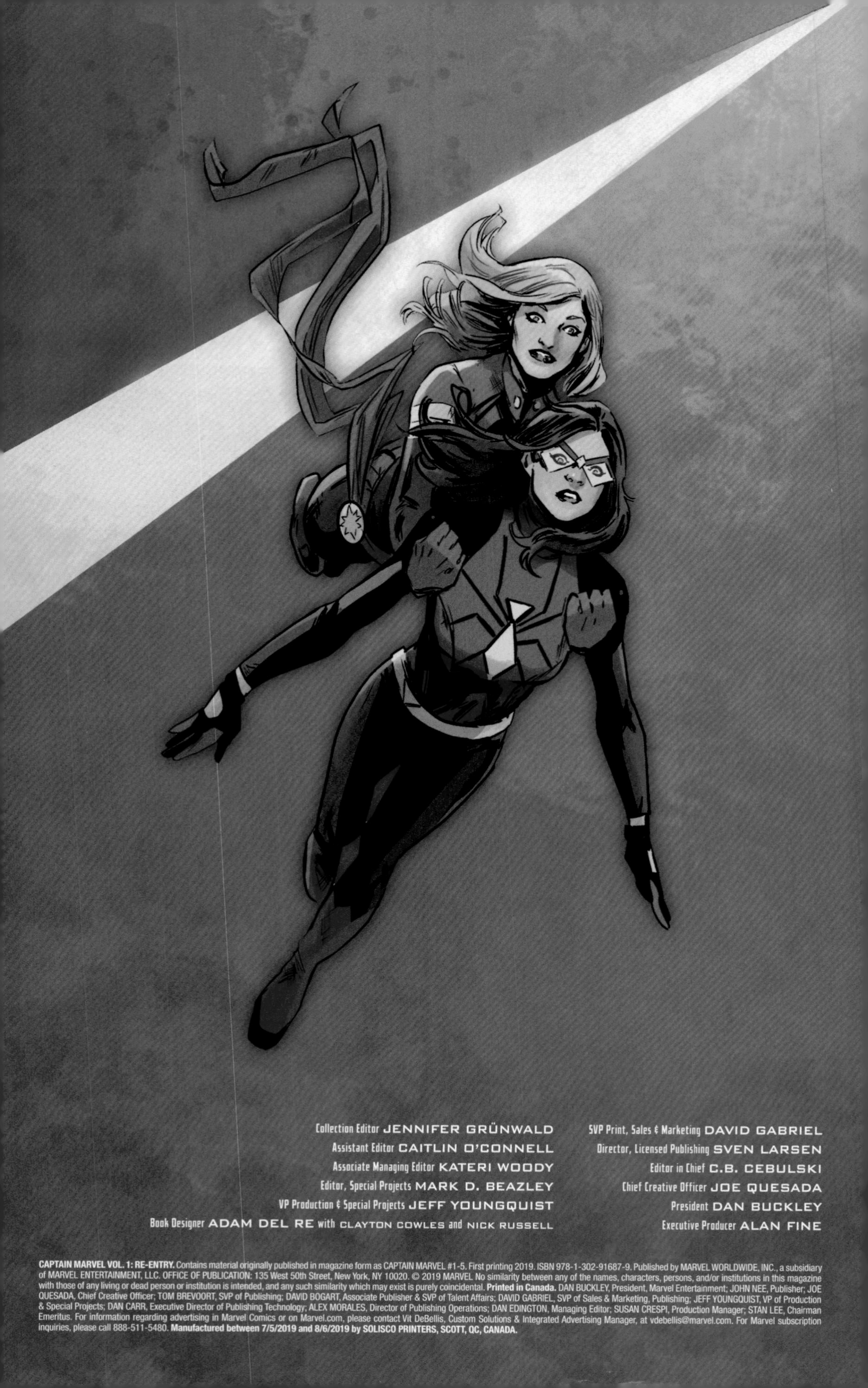

Collection Editor JENNIFER GRÜNWALD
Assistant Editor CAITLIN O'CONNELL
Associate Managing Editor KATERI WOODY
Editor, Special Projects MARK D. BEAZLEY
VP Production & Special Projects JEFF YOUNGQUIST
Book Designer ADAM DEL RE with CLAYTON COWLES and NICK RUSSELL

SVP Print, Sales & Marketing DAVID GABRIEL
Director, Licensed Publishing SVEN LARSEN
Editor in Chief C.B. CEBULSKI
Chief Creative Officer JOE QUESADA
President DAN BUCKLEY
Executive Producer ALAN FINE

CAPTAIN MARVEL VOL. 1: RE-ENTRY. Contains material originally published in magazine form as CAPTAIN MARVEL #1-5. First printing 2019. ISBN 978-1-302-91687-9. Published by MARVEL WORLDWIDE, INC., a subsidiary of MARVEL ENTERTAINMENT, LLC. OFFICE OF PUBLICATION: 135 West 50th Street, New York, NY 10020. © 2019 MARVEL No similarity between any of the names, characters, persons, and/or institutions in this magazine with those of any living or dead person or institution is intended, and any such similarity which may exist is purely coincidental. **Printed in Canada.** DAN BUCKLEY, President, Marvel Entertainment; JOHN NEE, Publisher; JOE QUESADA, Chief Creative Officer; TOM BREVOORT, SVP of Publishing; DAVID BOGART, Associate Publisher & SVP of Talent Affairs; DAVID GABRIEL, SVP of Sales & Marketing, Publishing; JEFF YOUNGQUIST, VP of Production & Special Projects; DAN CARR, Executive Director of Publishing Technology; ALEX MORALES, Director of Publishing Operations; DAN EDINGTON, Managing Editor; SUSAN CRESPI, Production Manager; STAN LEE, Chairman Emeritus. For information regarding advertising in Marvel Comics or on Marvel.com, please contact Vit DeBellis, Custom Solutions & Integrated Advertising Manager, at vdebellis@marvel.com. For Marvel subscription inquiries, please call 888-511-5480. **Manufactured between 7/5/2019 and 8/6/2019 by SOLISCO PRINTERS, SCOTT, QC, CANADA.**

Born to a Kree mother and human father, former U.S. Air Force pilot **CAROL DANVERS** became a super hero when a Kree device activated her latent powers. Now, she's an Avenger and Earth's Mightiest Hero.

CAPTAIN MARVEL

RE-ENTRY

The past year has been difficult for Carol. Her brother suffered a life-threatening injury, and Carol stepped down from the Avengers and Earth's Space Defense Program, Alpha Flight, to care for him. Then a Kree assassin attacked her family home and killed her mother, who had been hiding her identity as a Kree warrior from Carol all this time.

Now, with her brother recovered and a better understanding of her own history, it's time for Captain Marvel to take flight once again.

KELLY THOMPSON
Writer

CARMEN CARNERO
Artist

TAMRA BONVILLAIN
Color Artist

VC's CLAYTON COWLES
Letterer

AMANDA CONNER & PAUL MOUNTS
Cover Art

SARAH BRUNSTAD
Editor

WIL MOSS
Consulting Editor

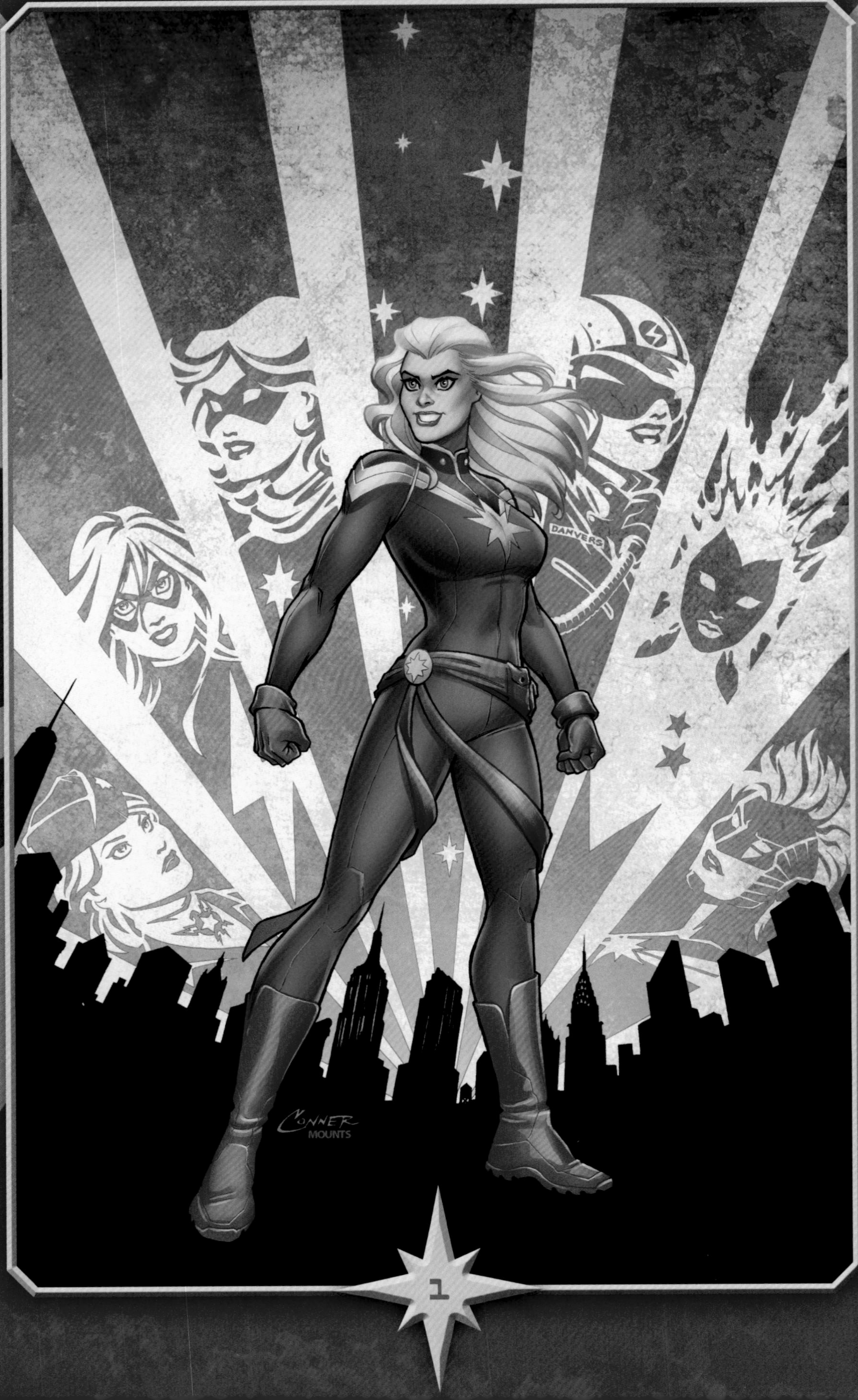
DANVERS
CONNER
MOUNTS
1

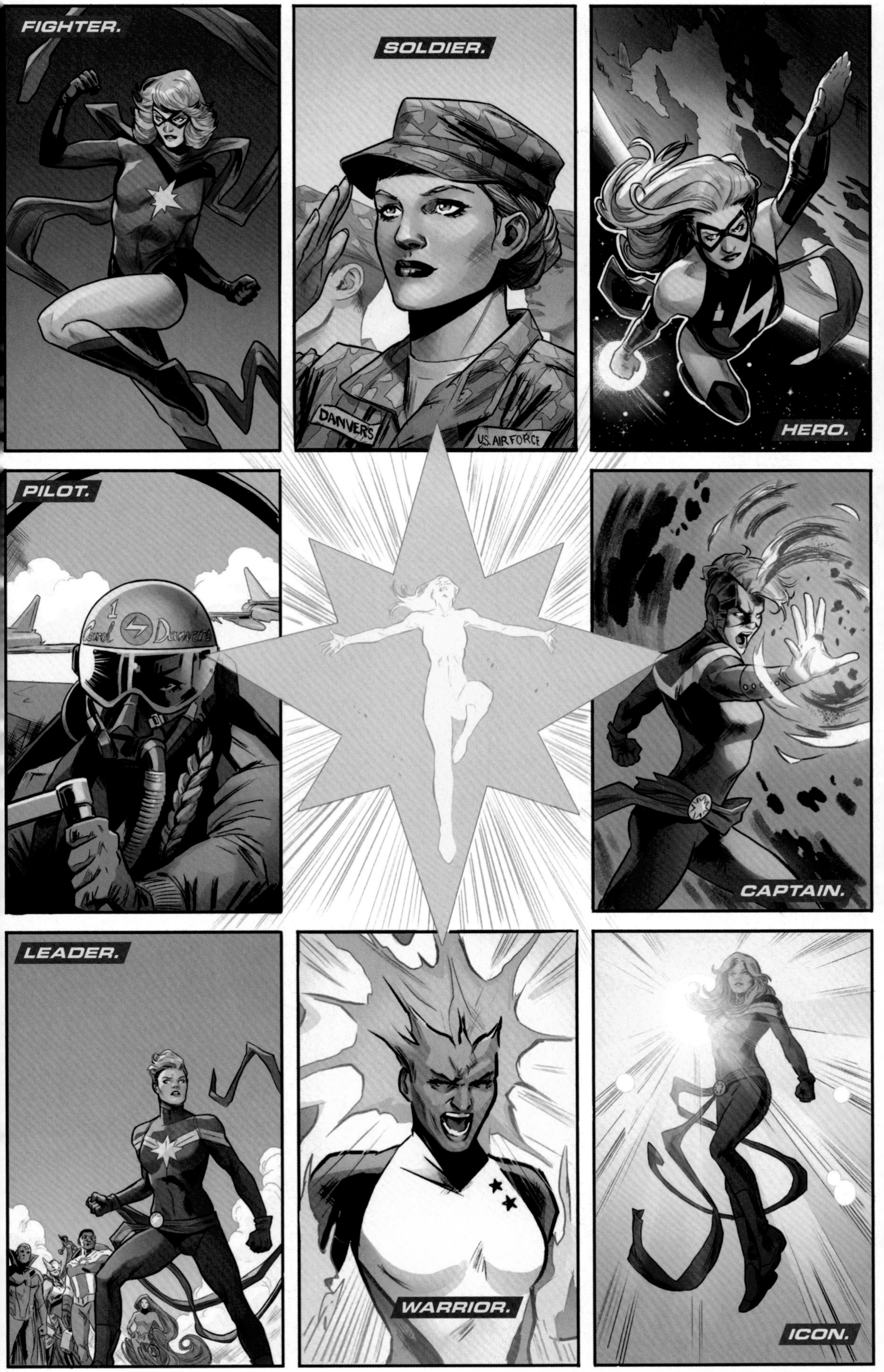
FIGHTER.
SOLDIER.
DANVERS
U.S. AIR FORCE
HERO.
PILOT.
1
Carol Danvers
CAPTAIN.
LEADER.
WARRIOR.
ICON.

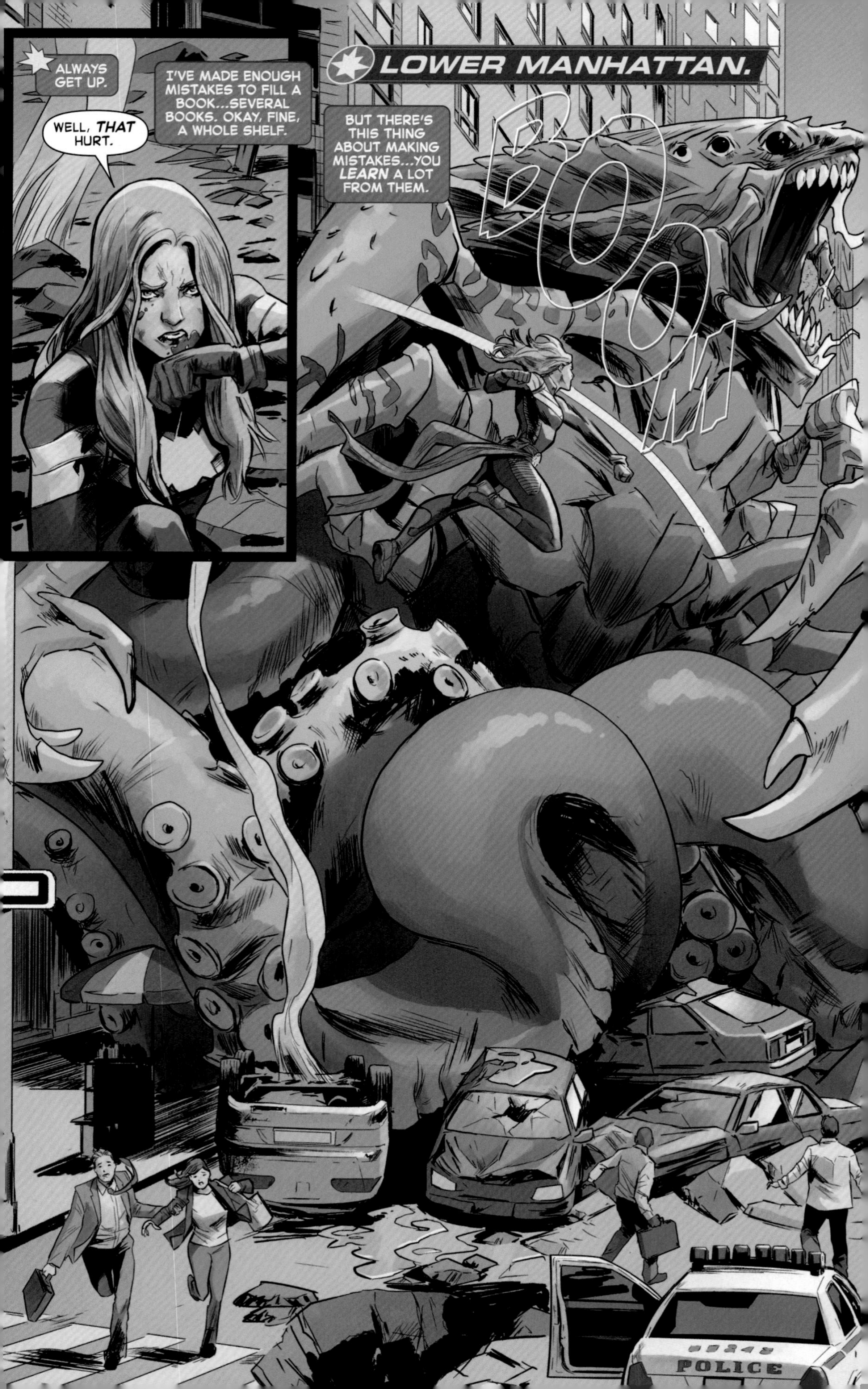
ALWAYS GET UP.
WELL, THAT HURT.
I'VE MADE ENOUGH MISTAKES TO FILL A BOOK...SEVERAL BOOKS. OKAY, FINE, A WHOLE SHELF.
LOWER MANHATTAN.
BUT THERE'S THIS THING ABOUT MAKING MISTAKES...YOU LEARN A LOT FROM THEM.
BOOM
POLICE

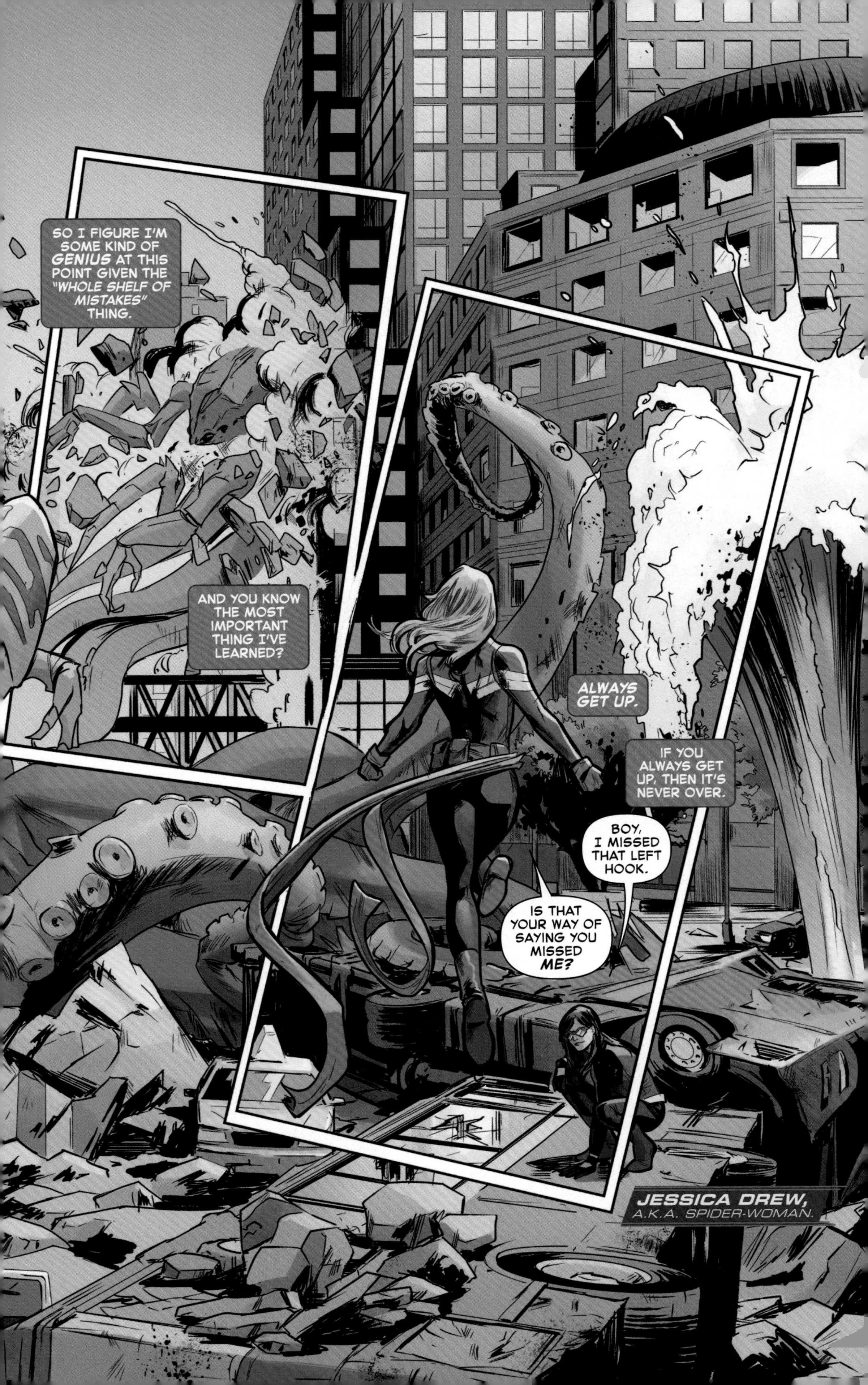
SO I FIGURE I'M SOME KIND OF GENIUS AT THIS POINT GIVEN THE "WHOLE SHELF OF MISTAKES" THING.
AND YOU KNOW THE MOST IMPORTANT THING I'VE LEARNED?
ALWAYS GET UP.
IF YOU ALWAYS GET UP, THEN IT'S NEVER OVER.
BOY, I MISSED THAT LEFT HOOK.
IS THAT YOUR WAY OF SAYING YOU MISSED ME?
JESSICA DREW,
A.K.A. SPIDER-WOMAN.

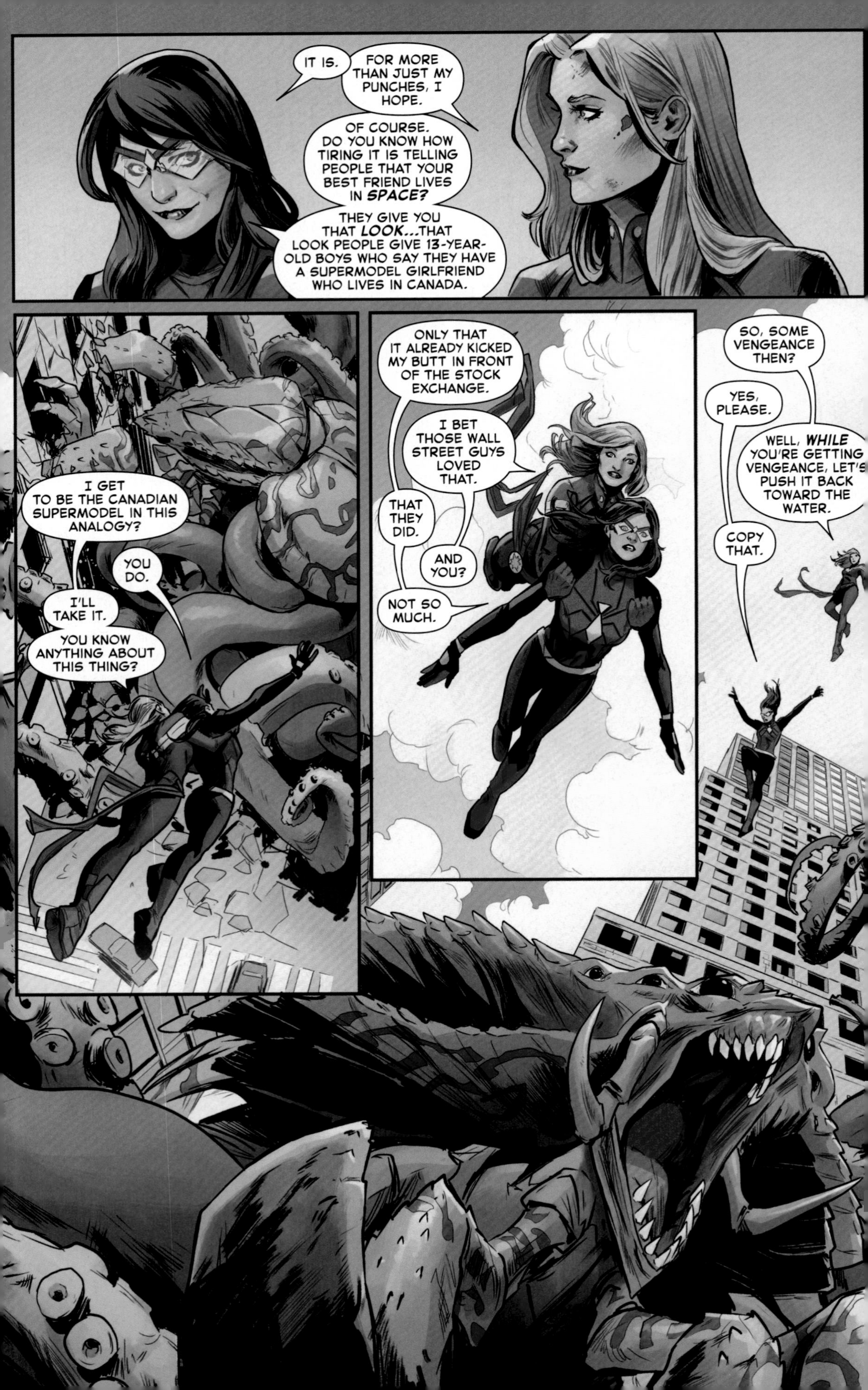
IT IS.
FOR MORE THAN JUST MY PUNCHES, I HOPE.
OF COURSE. DO YOU KNOW HOW TIRING IT IS TELLING PEOPLE THAT YOUR BEST FRIEND LIVES IN SPACE?
THEY GIVE YOU THAT LOOK...THAT LOOK PEOPLE GIVE 13-YEAR-OLD BOYS WHO SAY THEY HAVE A SUPERMODEL GIRLFRIEND WHO LIVES IN CANADA.
I GET TO BE THE CANADIAN SUPERMODEL IN THIS ANALOGY?
YOU DO.
I'LL TAKE IT.
YOU KNOW ANYTHING ABOUT THIS THING?
ONLY THAT IT ALREADY KICKED MY BUTT IN FRONT OF THE STOCK EXCHANGE.
I BET THOSE WALL STREET GUYS LOVED THAT.
THAT THEY DID.
AND YOU?
NOT SO MUCH.
SO, SOME VENGEANCE THEN?
YES, PLEASE.
WELL, WHILE YOU'RE GETTING VENGEANCE, LET'S PUSH IT BACK TOWARD THE WATER.
COPY THAT.

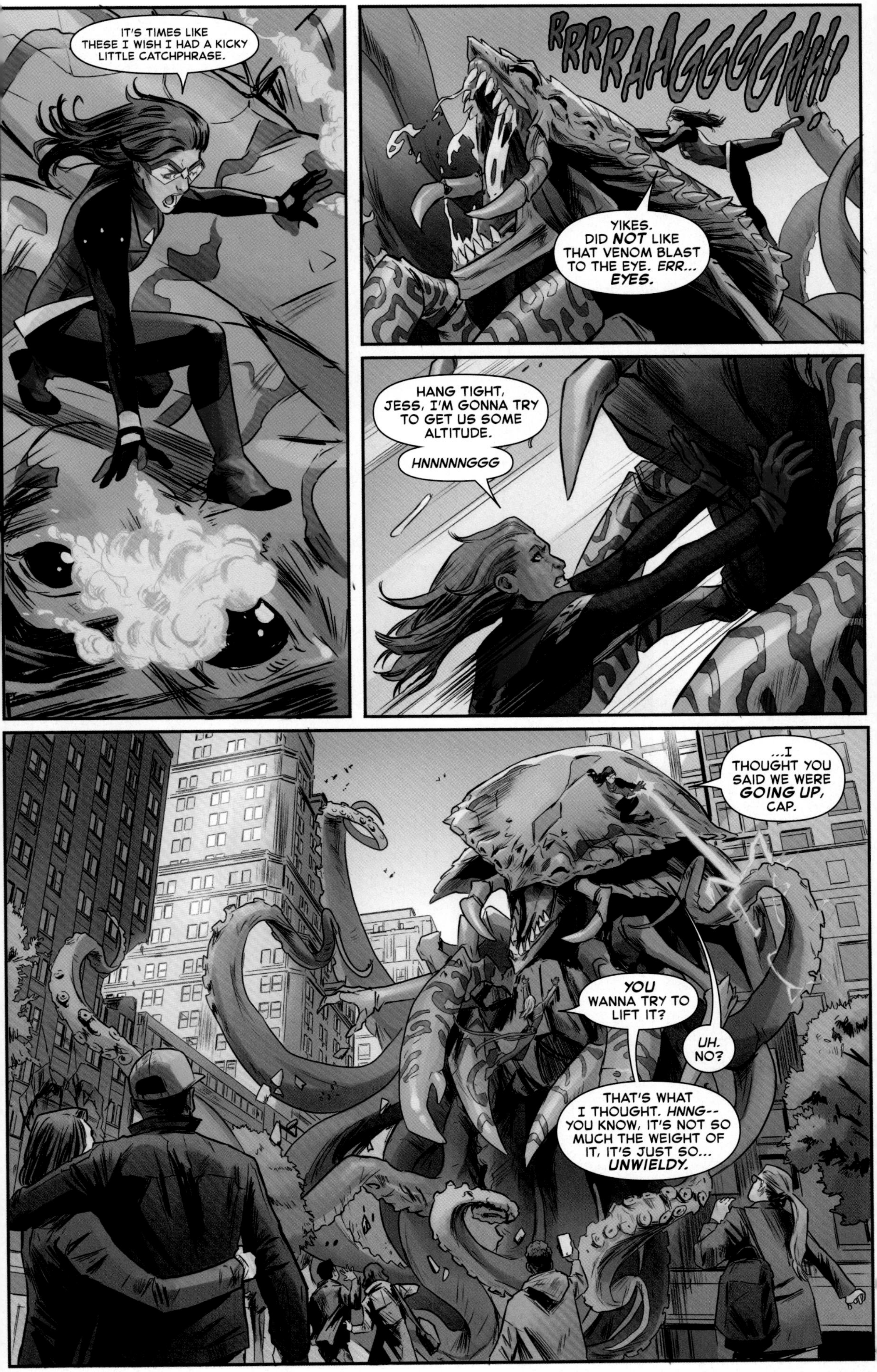
IT'S TIMES LIKE THESE I WISH I HAD A KICKY LITTLE CATCHPHRASE.
RRRRAAGGGGHH
YIKES. DID NOT LIKE THAT VENOM BLAST TO THE EYE. ERR... EYES.
HANG TIGHT, JESS, I'M GONNA TRY TO GET US SOME ALTITUDE.
HNNNNNGGG
...I THOUGHT YOU SAID WE WERE GOING UP, CAP.
YOU WANNA TRY TO LIFT IT?
UH. NO?
THAT'S WHAT I THOUGHT. HNNG-- YOU KNOW, IT'S NOT SO MUCH THE WEIGHT OF IT, IT'S JUST SO... UNWIELDY.

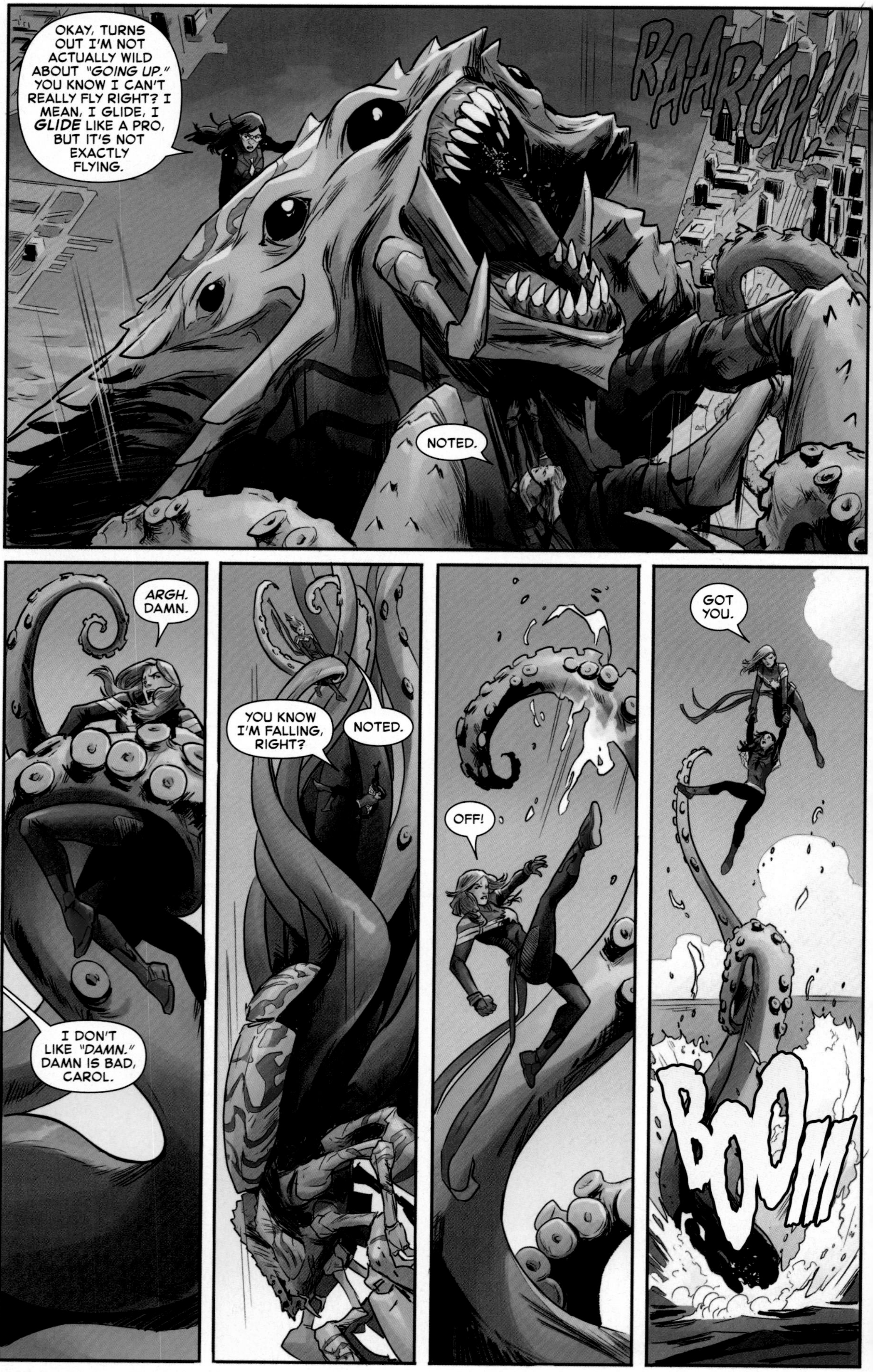
OKAY, TURNS OUT I'M NOT ACTUALLY WILD ABOUT "GOING UP." YOU KNOW I CAN'T REALLY FLY RIGHT? I MEAN, I GLIDE, I GLIDE LIKE A PRO, BUT IT'S NOT EXACTLY FLYING.
RAARGH!!
NOTED.
ARGH. DAMN.
I DON'T LIKE "DAMN." DAMN IS BAD, CAROL.
YOU KNOW I'M FALLING, RIGHT?
NOTED.
OFF!
GOT YOU.
BOOM

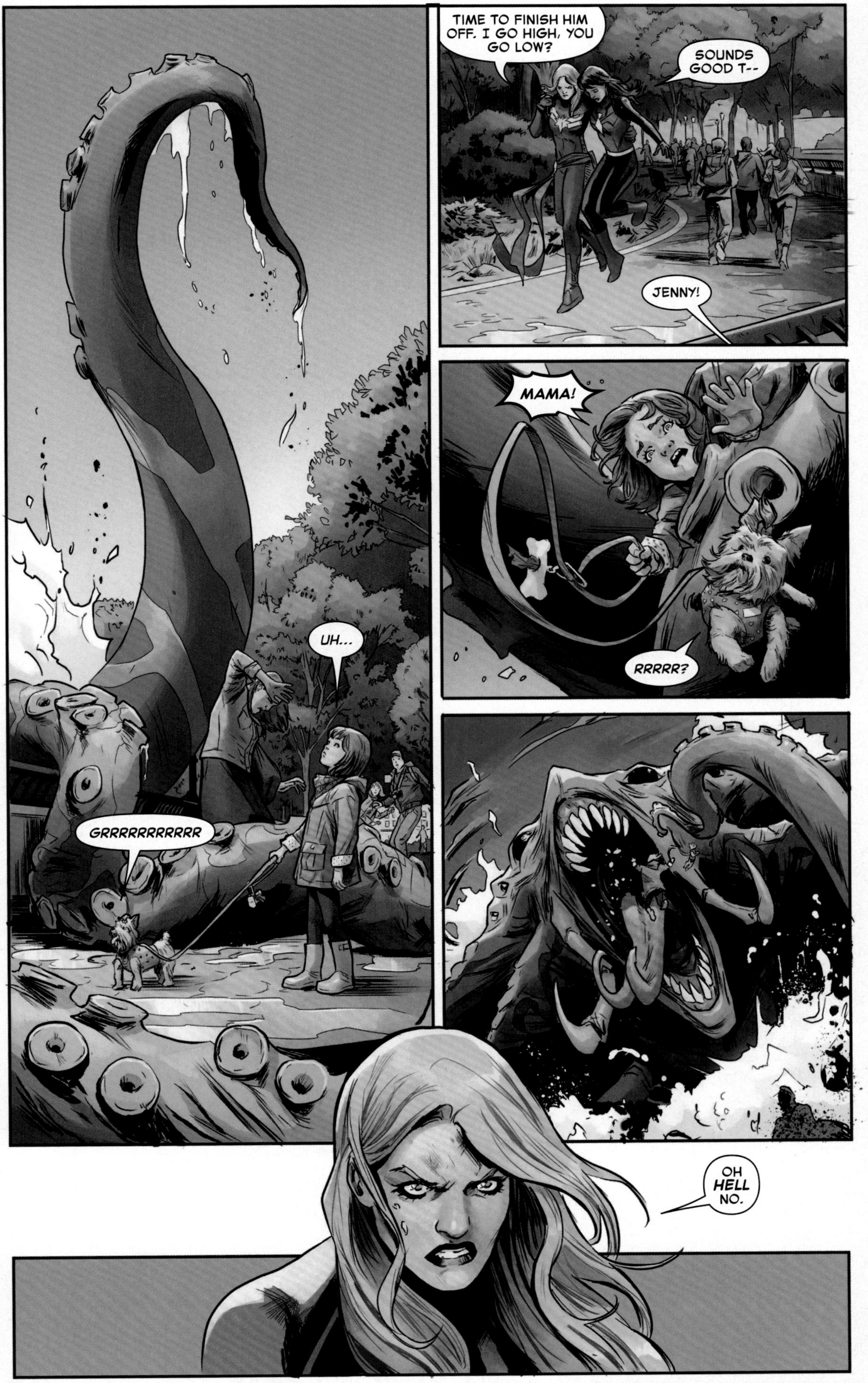
UH...
GRRRRRRRRRRR
TIME TO FINISH HIM OFF. I GO HIGH, YOU GO LOW?
SOUNDS GOOD T--
JENNY!
MAMA!
RRRRR?
OH HELL NO.

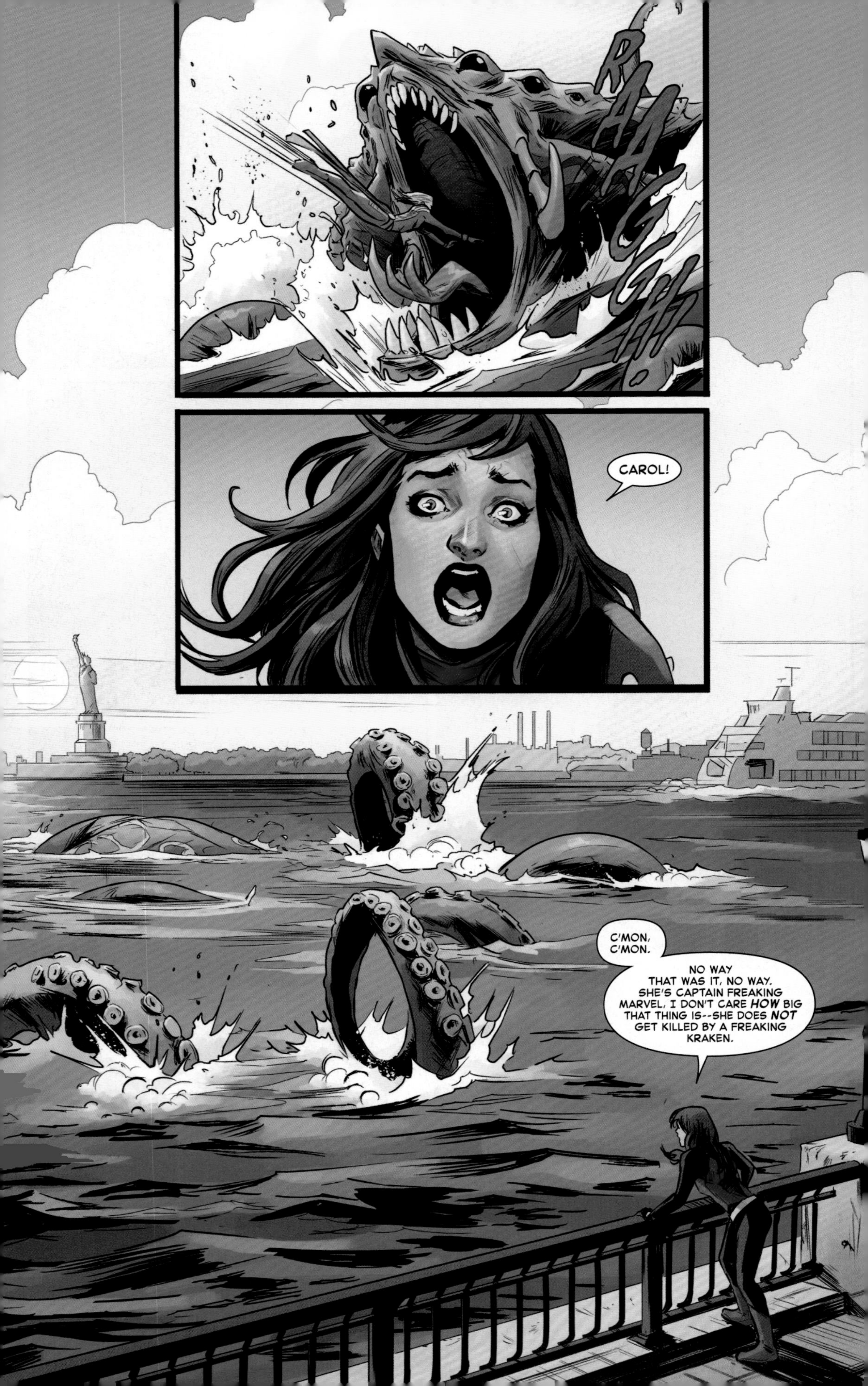
RAAAGH!
CAROL!
C'MON, C'MON.
NO WAY THAT WAS IT, NO WAY. SHE'S CAPTAIN FREAKING MARVEL, I DON'T CARE **HOW** BIG THAT THING IS--SHE DOES **NOT** GET KILLED BY A FREAKING KRAKEN.

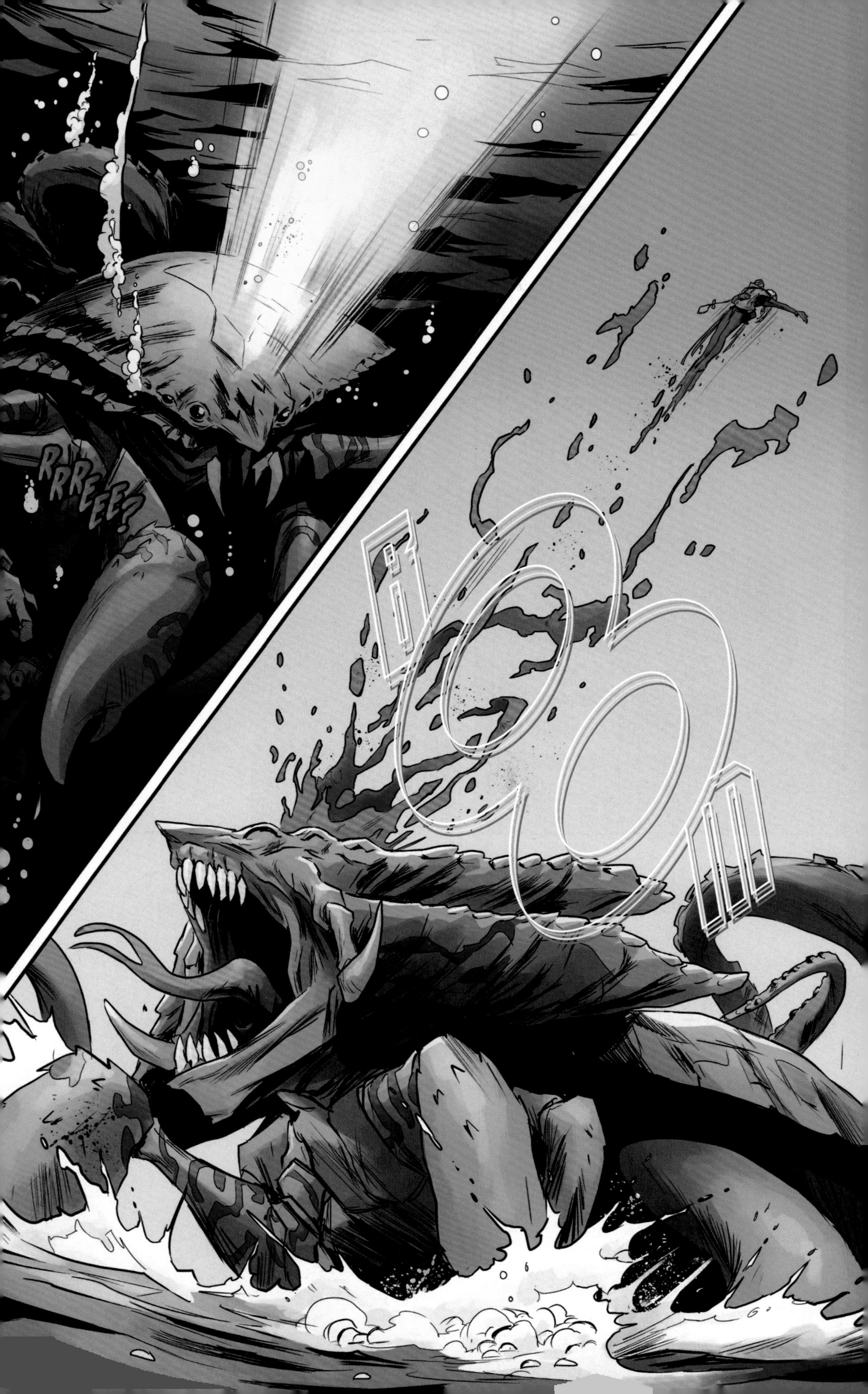
RRREEE?
¡OO!!

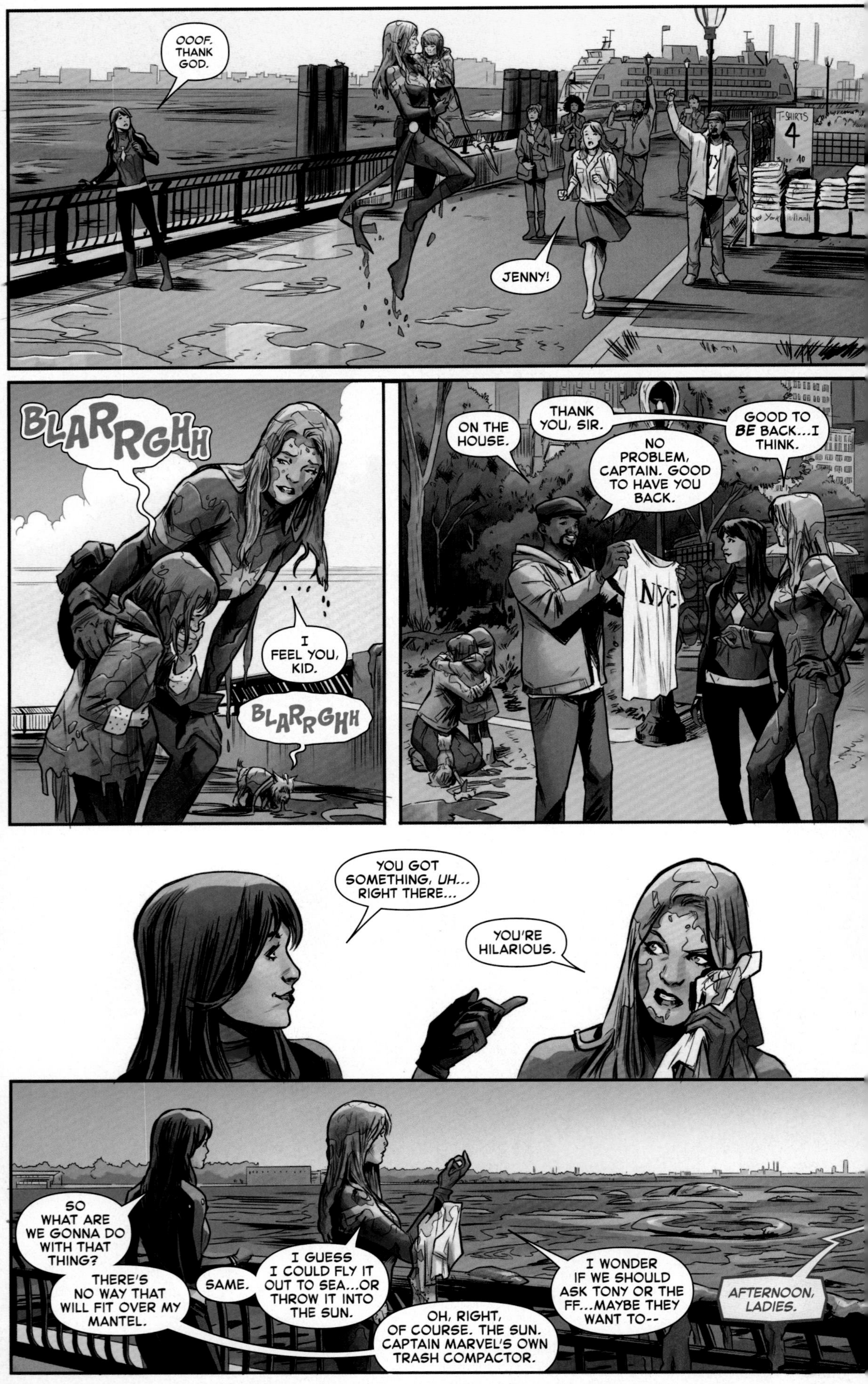
OOOF. THANK GOD.
JENNY!
T-SHIRTS 4 for 10
BLARRGHH
I FEEL YOU, KID.
BLARRGHH
ON THE HOUSE.
THANK YOU, SIR.
NO PROBLEM, CAPTAIN. GOOD TO HAVE YOU BACK.
GOOD TO BE BACK...I THINK.
NYC
YOU GOT SOMETHING, UH... RIGHT THERE...
YOU'RE HILARIOUS.
SO WHAT ARE WE GONNA DO WITH THAT THING?
THERE'S NO WAY THAT WILL FIT OVER MY MANTEL.
SAME.
I GUESS I COULD FLY IT OUT TO SEA...OR THROW IT INTO THE SUN.
OH, RIGHT, OF COURSE. THE SUN. CAPTAIN MARVEL'S OWN TRASH COMPACTOR.
I WONDER IF WE SHOULD ASK TONY OR THE FF...MAYBE THEY WANT TO--
AFTERNOON, LADIES.

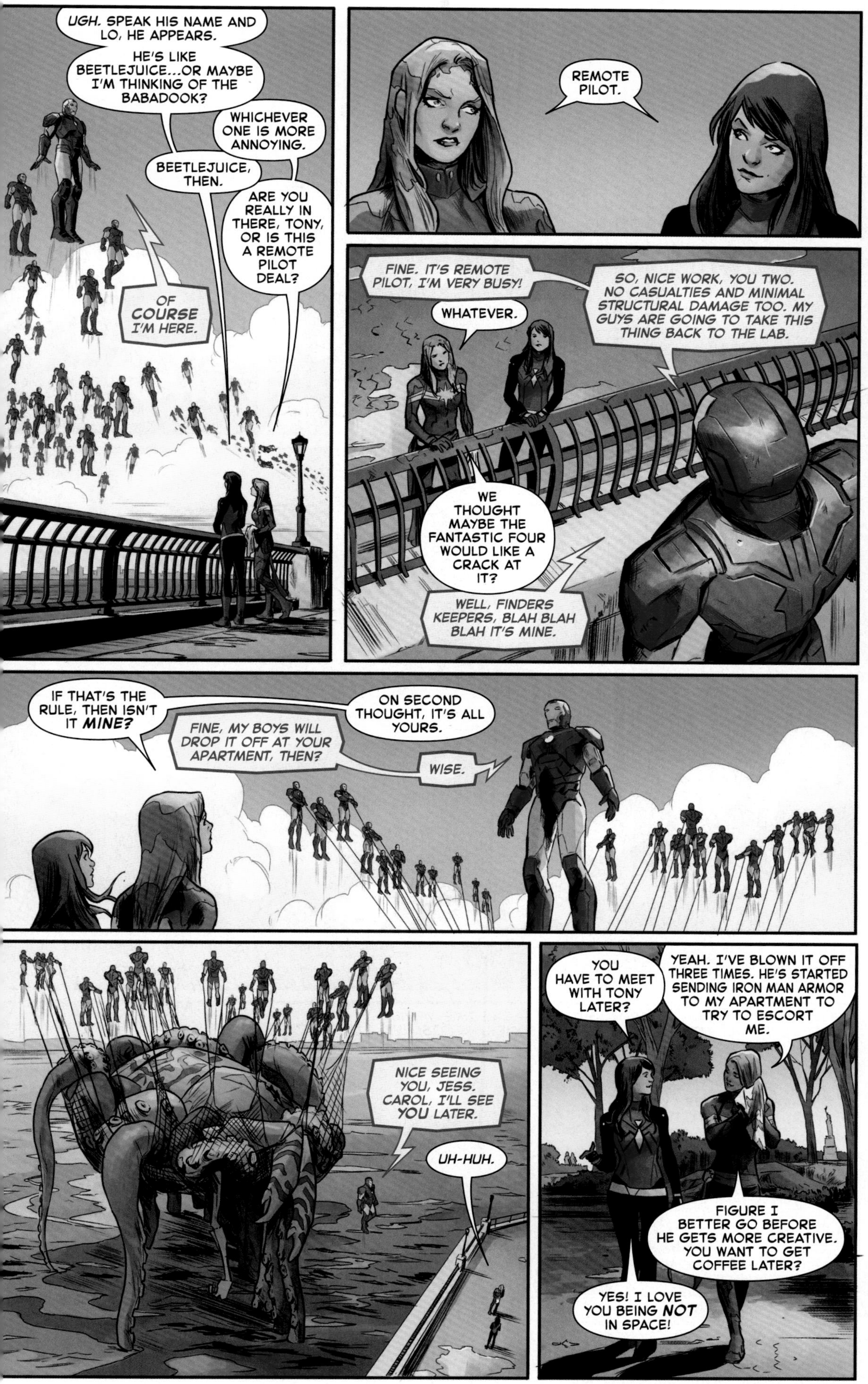
UGH. SPEAK HIS NAME AND LO, HE APPEARS.
HE'S LIKE BEETLEJUICE...OR MAYBE I'M THINKING OF THE BABADOOK?
WHICHEVER ONE IS MORE ANNOYING.
BEETLEJUICE, THEN.
ARE YOU REALLY IN THERE, TONY, OR IS THIS A REMOTE PILOT DEAL?
OF COURSE I'M HERE.
REMOTE PILOT.
FINE. IT'S REMOTE PILOT, I'M VERY BUSY!
WHATEVER.
SO, NICE WORK, YOU TWO. NO CASUALTIES AND MINIMAL STRUCTURAL DAMAGE TOO. MY GUYS ARE GOING TO TAKE THIS THING BACK TO THE LAB.
WE THOUGHT MAYBE THE FANTASTIC FOUR WOULD LIKE A CRACK AT IT?
WELL, FINDERS KEEPERS, BLAH BLAH BLAH IT'S MINE.
IF THAT'S THE RULE, THEN ISN'T IT MINE?
ON SECOND THOUGHT, IT'S ALL YOURS.
FINE, MY BOYS WILL DROP IT OFF AT YOUR APARTMENT, THEN?
WISE.
NICE SEEING YOU, JESS. CAROL, I'LL SEE YOU LATER.
UH-HUH.
YOU HAVE TO MEET WITH TONY LATER?
YEAH. I'VE BLOWN IT OFF THREE TIMES. HE'S STARTED SENDING IRON MAN ARMOR TO MY APARTMENT TO TRY TO ESCORT ME.
FIGURE I BETTER GO BEFORE HE GETS MORE CREATIVE. YOU WANT TO GET COFFEE LATER?
YES! I LOVE YOU BEING NOT IN SPACE!

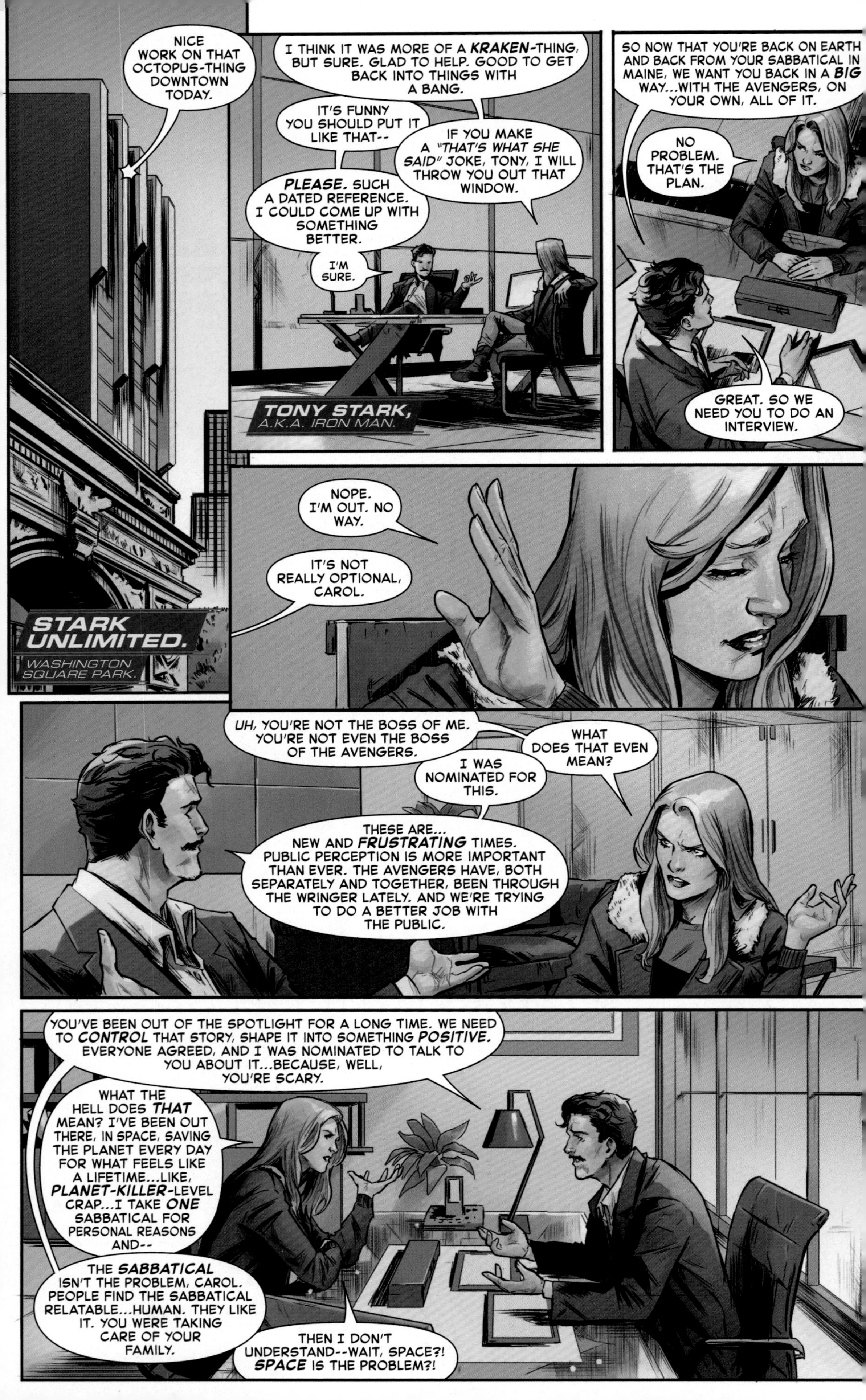

NICE WORK ON THAT OCTOPUS-THING DOWNTOWN TODAY.
STARK UNLIMITED.
WASHINGTON SQUARE PARK.
I THINK IT WAS MORE OF A KRAKEN-THING, BUT SURE. GLAD TO HELP. GOOD TO GET BACK INTO THINGS WITH A BANG.
IT'S FUNNY YOU SHOULD PUT IT LIKE THAT--
IF YOU MAKE A "THAT'S WHAT SHE SAID" JOKE, TONY, I WILL THROW YOU OUT THAT WINDOW.
PLEASE. SUCH A DATED REFERENCE. I COULD COME UP WITH SOMETHING BETTER.
I'M SURE.
TONY STARK,
A.K.A. IRON MAN.
SO NOW THAT YOU'RE BACK ON EARTH AND BACK FROM YOUR SABBATICAL IN MAINE, WE WANT YOU BACK IN A BIG WAY...WITH THE AVENGERS, ON YOUR OWN, ALL OF IT.
NO PROBLEM. THAT'S THE PLAN.
GREAT. SO WE NEED YOU TO DO AN INTERVIEW.
NOPE. I'M OUT. NO WAY.
IT'S NOT REALLY OPTIONAL, CAROL.
UH, YOU'RE NOT THE BOSS OF ME. YOU'RE NOT EVEN THE BOSS OF THE AVENGERS.
WHAT DOES THAT EVEN MEAN?
I WAS NOMINATED FOR THIS.
THESE ARE... NEW AND FRUSTRATING TIMES. PUBLIC PERCEPTION IS MORE IMPORTANT THAN EVER. THE AVENGERS HAVE, BOTH SEPARATELY AND TOGETHER, BEEN THROUGH THE WRINGER LATELY. AND WE'RE TRYING TO DO A BETTER JOB WITH THE PUBLIC.
YOU'VE BEEN OUT OF THE SPOTLIGHT FOR A LONG TIME. WE NEED TO CONTROL THAT STORY, SHAPE IT INTO SOMETHING POSITIVE. EVERYONE AGREED, AND I WAS NOMINATED TO TALK TO YOU ABOUT IT...BECAUSE, WELL, YOU'RE SCARY.
WHAT THE HELL DOES THAT MEAN? I'VE BEEN OUT THERE, IN SPACE, SAVING THE PLANET EVERY DAY FOR WHAT FEELS LIKE A LIFETIME...LIKE, PLANET-KILLER-LEVEL CRAP...I TAKE ONE SABBATICAL FOR PERSONAL REASONS AND--
THE SABBATICAL ISN'T THE PROBLEM, CAROL. PEOPLE FIND THE SABBATICAL RELATABLE...HUMAN. THEY LIKE IT. YOU WERE TAKING CARE OF YOUR FAMILY.
THEN I DON'T UNDERSTAND--WAIT, SPACE?! SPACE IS THE PROBLEM?!

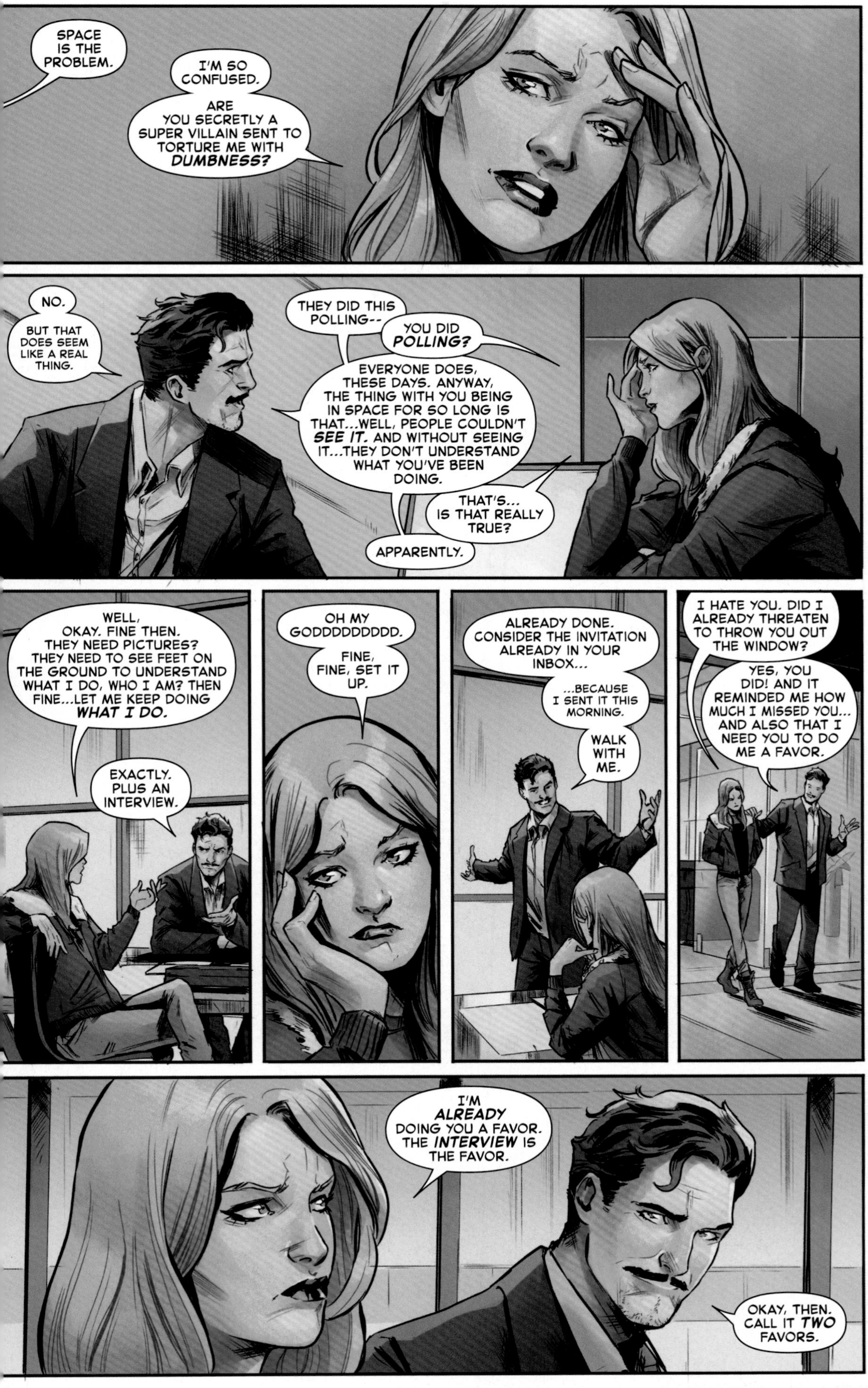
SPACE IS THE PROBLEM.
I'M SO CONFUSED.
ARE YOU SECRETLY A SUPER VILLAIN SENT TO TORTURE ME WITH DUMBNESS?
NO.
BUT THAT DOES SEEM LIKE A REAL THING.
THEY DID THIS POLLING--
YOU DID POLLING?
EVERYONE DOES, THESE DAYS. ANYWAY, THE THING WITH YOU BEING IN SPACE FOR SO LONG IS THAT...WELL, PEOPLE COULDN'T SEE IT. AND WITHOUT SEEING IT...THEY DON'T UNDERSTAND WHAT YOU'VE BEEN DOING.
THAT'S... IS THAT REALLY TRUE?
APPARENTLY.
WELL, OKAY. FINE THEN. THEY NEED PICTURES? THEY NEED TO SEE FEET ON THE GROUND TO UNDERSTAND WHAT I DO, WHO I AM? THEN FINE...LET ME KEEP DOING WHAT I DO.
EXACTLY. PLUS AN INTERVIEW.
OH MY GODDDDDDDDD.
FINE, FINE, SET IT UP.
ALREADY DONE. CONSIDER THE INVITATION ALREADY IN YOUR INBOX...
...BECAUSE I SENT IT THIS MORNING.
WALK WITH ME.
I HATE YOU. DID I ALREADY THREATEN TO THROW YOU OUT THE WINDOW?
YES, YOU DID! AND IT REMINDED ME HOW MUCH I MISSED YOU... AND ALSO THAT I NEED YOU TO DO ME A FAVOR.
I'M ALREADY DOING YOU A FAVOR. THE INTERVIEW IS THE FAVOR.
OKAY, THEN. CALL IT TWO FAVORS.

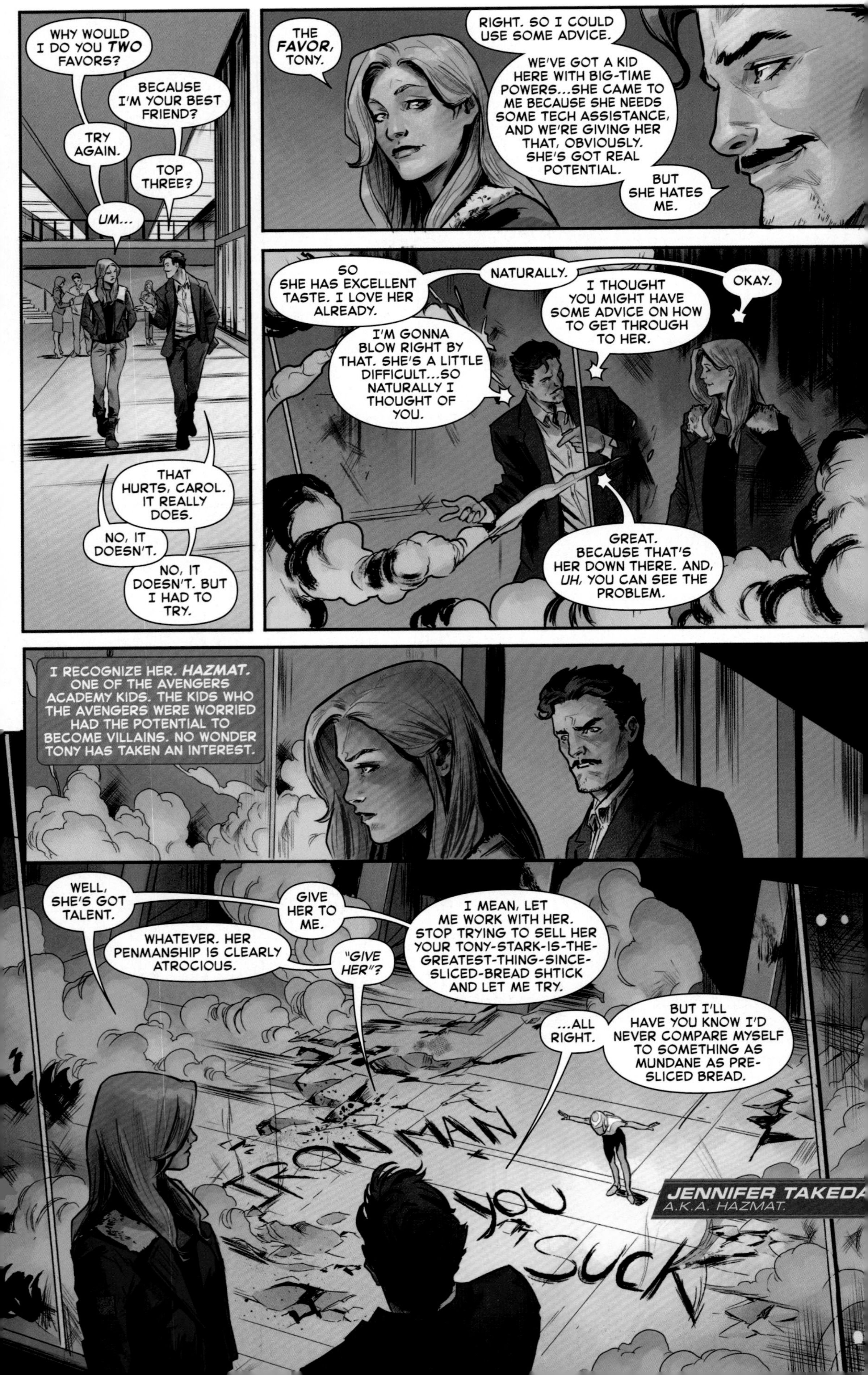
WHY WOULD I DO YOU *TWO* FAVORS?
BECAUSE I'M YOUR BEST FRIEND?
TRY AGAIN.
TOP THREE?
UM...
THAT HURTS, CAROL. IT REALLY DOES.
NO, IT DOESN'T.
NO, IT DOESN'T. BUT I HAD TO TRY.
THE *FAVOR,* TONY.
RIGHT. SO I COULD USE SOME ADVICE.
WE'VE GOT A KID HERE WITH BIG-TIME POWERS...SHE CAME TO ME BECAUSE SHE NEEDS SOME TECH ASSISTANCE, AND WE'RE GIVING HER THAT, OBVIOUSLY. SHE'S GOT REAL POTENTIAL.
BUT SHE HATES ME.
SO SHE HAS EXCELLENT TASTE. I LOVE HER ALREADY.
NATURALLY.
I'M GONNA BLOW RIGHT BY THAT. SHE'S A LITTLE DIFFICULT...SO NATURALLY I THOUGHT OF YOU.
I THOUGHT YOU MIGHT HAVE SOME ADVICE ON HOW TO GET THROUGH TO HER.
OKAY.
GREAT. BECAUSE THAT'S HER DOWN THERE. AND, *UH,* YOU CAN SEE THE PROBLEM.
I RECOGNIZE HER. *HAZMAT.* ONE OF THE AVENGERS ACADEMY KIDS. THE KIDS WHO THE AVENGERS WERE WORRIED HAD THE POTENTIAL TO BECOME VILLAINS. NO WONDER TONY HAS TAKEN AN INTEREST.
WELL, SHE'S GOT TALENT.
WHATEVER. HER PENMANSHIP IS CLEARLY ATROCIOUS.
GIVE HER TO ME.
"GIVE HER"?
I MEAN, LET ME WORK WITH HER. STOP TRYING TO SELL HER YOUR TONY-STARK-IS-THE-GREATEST-THING-SINCE-SLICED-BREAD SHTICK AND LET ME TRY.
...ALL RIGHT.
BUT I'LL HAVE YOU KNOW I'D NEVER COMPARE MYSELF TO SOMETHING AS MUNDANE AS PRE-SLICED BREAD.
IRON MAN YOU SUCK
JENNIFER TAKEDA
A.K.A. HAZMAT.

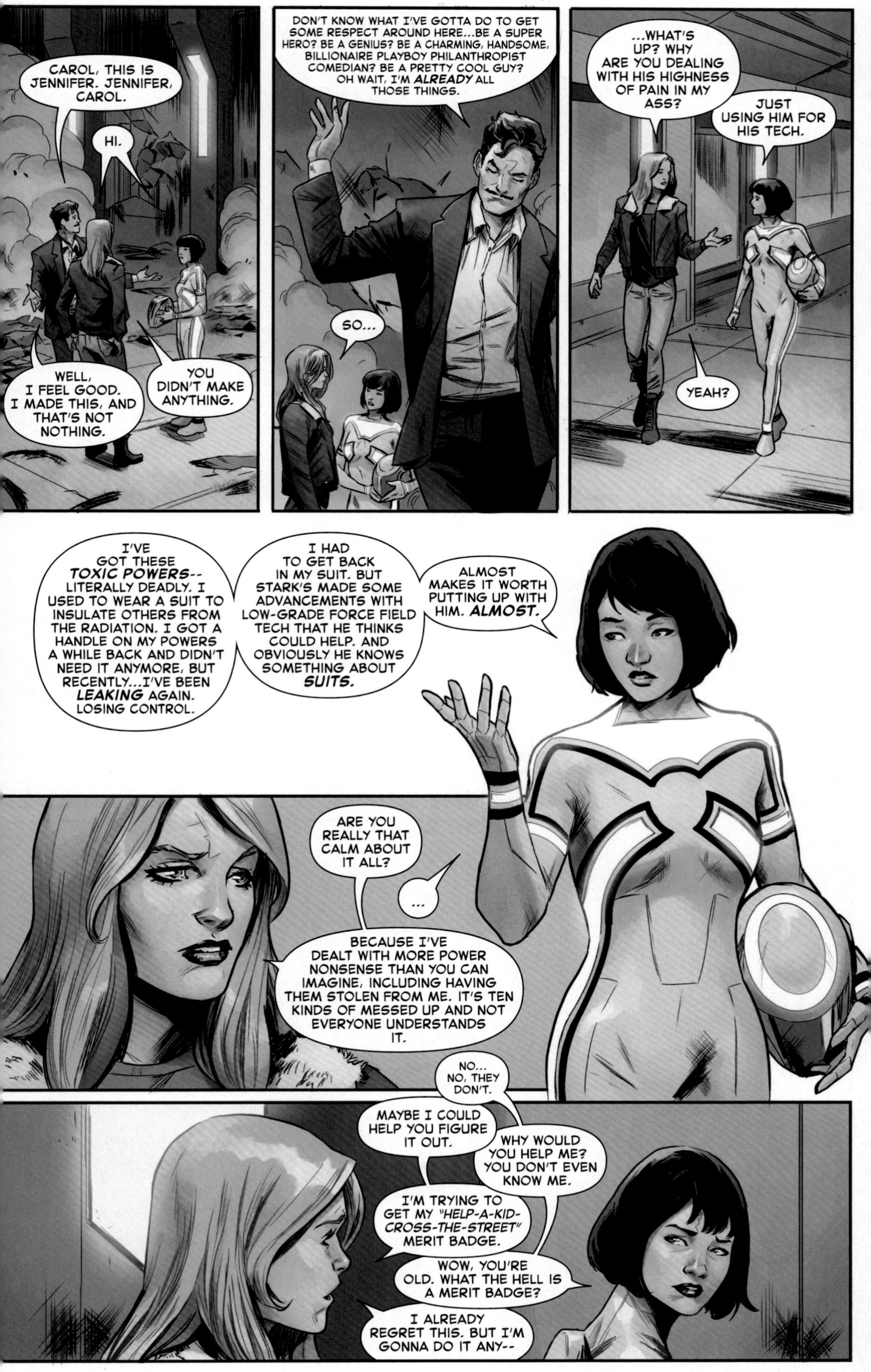
CAROL, THIS IS JENNIFER. JENNIFER, CAROL.
HI.
WELL, I FEEL GOOD. I MADE THIS, AND THAT'S NOT NOTHING.
YOU DIDN'T MAKE ANYTHING.
DON'T KNOW WHAT I'VE GOTTA DO TO GET SOME RESPECT AROUND HERE...BE A SUPER HERO? BE A GENIUS? BE A CHARMING, HANDSOME, BILLIONAIRE PLAYBOY PHILANTHROPIST COMEDIAN? BE A PRETTY COOL GUY? OH WAIT, I'M *ALREADY* ALL THOSE THINGS.
SO...
...WHAT'S UP? WHY ARE YOU DEALING WITH HIS HIGHNESS OF PAIN IN MY ASS?
JUST USING HIM FOR HIS TECH.
YEAH?
I'VE GOT THESE ***TOXIC POWERS***--LITERALLY DEADLY. I USED TO WEAR A SUIT TO INSULATE OTHERS FROM THE RADIATION. I GOT A HANDLE ON MY POWERS A WHILE BACK AND DIDN'T NEED IT ANYMORE, BUT RECENTLY...I'VE BEEN ***LEAKING*** AGAIN. LOSING CONTROL.
I HAD TO GET BACK IN MY SUIT. BUT STARK'S MADE SOME ADVANCEMENTS WITH LOW-GRADE FORCE FIELD TECH THAT HE THINKS COULD HELP. AND OBVIOUSLY HE KNOWS SOMETHING ABOUT ***SUITS.***
ALMOST MAKES IT WORTH PUTTING UP WITH HIM. ***ALMOST.***
ARE YOU REALLY THAT CALM ABOUT IT ALL?
...
BECAUSE I'VE DEALT WITH MORE POWER NONSENSE THAN YOU CAN IMAGINE, INCLUDING HAVING THEM STOLEN FROM ME. IT'S TEN KINDS OF MESSED UP AND NOT EVERYONE UNDERSTANDS IT.
NO... NO, THEY DON'T.
MAYBE I COULD HELP YOU FIGURE IT OUT.
WHY WOULD YOU HELP ME? YOU DON'T EVEN KNOW ME.
I'M TRYING TO GET MY *"HELP-A-KID-CROSS-THE-STREET"* MERIT BADGE.
WOW, YOU'RE OLD. WHAT THE HELL IS A MERIT BADGE?
I ALREADY REGRET THIS. BUT I'M GONNA DO IT ANY--

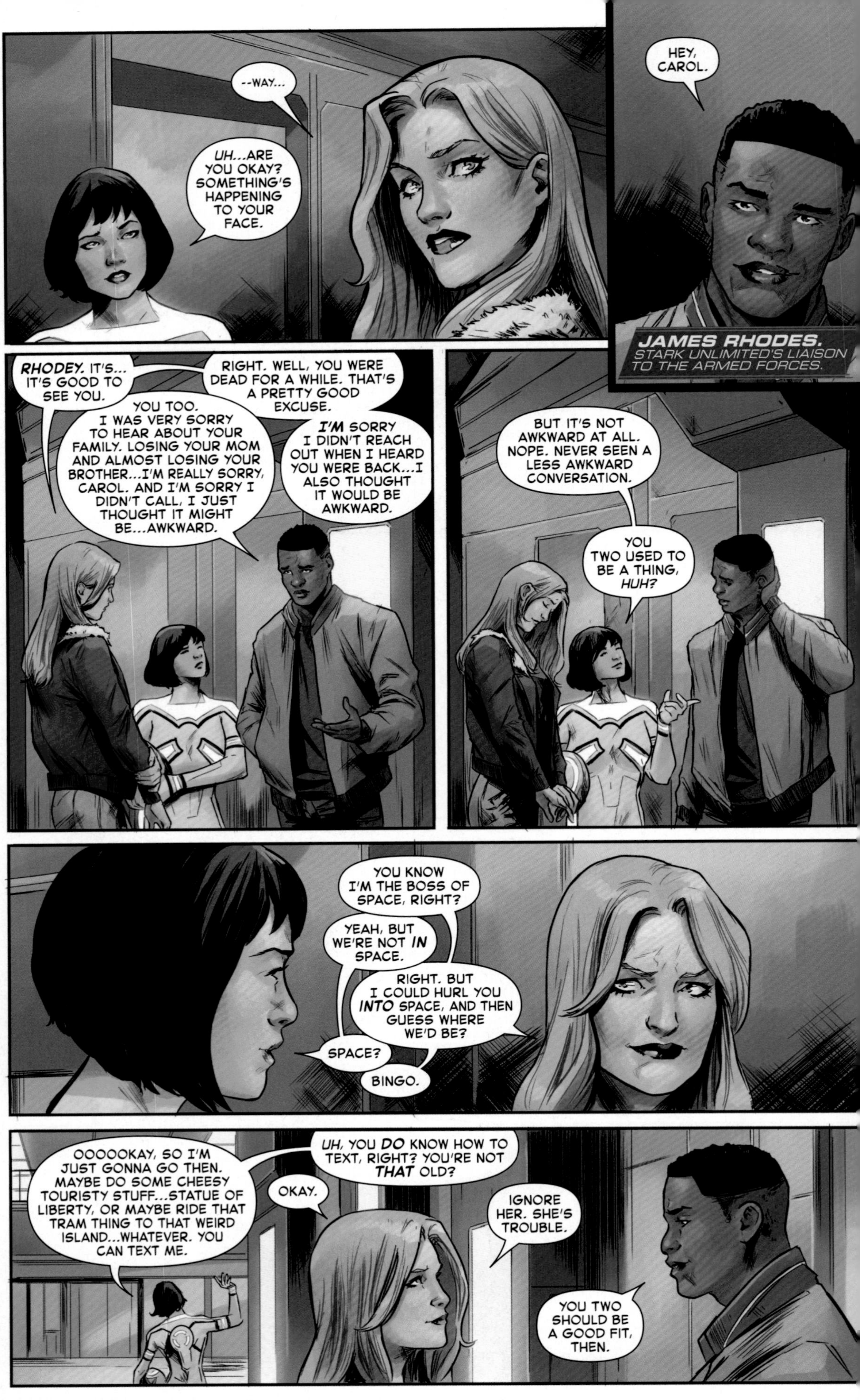
--WAY...
UH...ARE YOU OKAY? SOMETHING'S HAPPENING TO YOUR FACE.
HEY, CAROL.
JAMES RHODES. STARK UNLIMITED'S LIAISON TO THE ARMED FORCES.
RHODEY. IT'S... IT'S GOOD TO SEE YOU.
RIGHT. WELL, YOU WERE DEAD FOR A WHILE. THAT'S A PRETTY GOOD EXCUSE.
YOU TOO. I WAS VERY SORRY TO HEAR ABOUT YOUR FAMILY. LOSING YOUR MOM AND ALMOST LOSING YOUR BROTHER...I'M REALLY SORRY, CAROL. AND I'M SORRY I DIDN'T CALL, I JUST THOUGHT IT MIGHT BE...AWKWARD.
I'M SORRY I DIDN'T REACH OUT WHEN I HEARD YOU WERE BACK...I ALSO THOUGHT IT WOULD BE AWKWARD.
BUT IT'S NOT AWKWARD AT ALL. NOPE. NEVER SEEN A LESS AWKWARD CONVERSATION.
YOU TWO USED TO BE A THING, HUH?
YOU KNOW I'M THE BOSS OF SPACE, RIGHT?
YEAH, BUT WE'RE NOT IN SPACE.
RIGHT. BUT I COULD HURL YOU INTO SPACE, AND THEN GUESS WHERE WE'D BE?
SPACE?
BINGO.
OOOOOKAY, SO I'M JUST GONNA GO THEN. MAYBE DO SOME CHEESY TOURISTY STUFF...STATUE OF LIBERTY, OR MAYBE RIDE THAT TRAM THING TO THAT WEIRD ISLAND...WHATEVER. YOU CAN TEXT ME.
UH, YOU DO KNOW HOW TO TEXT, RIGHT? YOU'RE NOT THAT OLD?
OKAY.
IGNORE HER. SHE'S TROUBLE.
YOU TWO SHOULD BE A GOOD FIT, THEN.

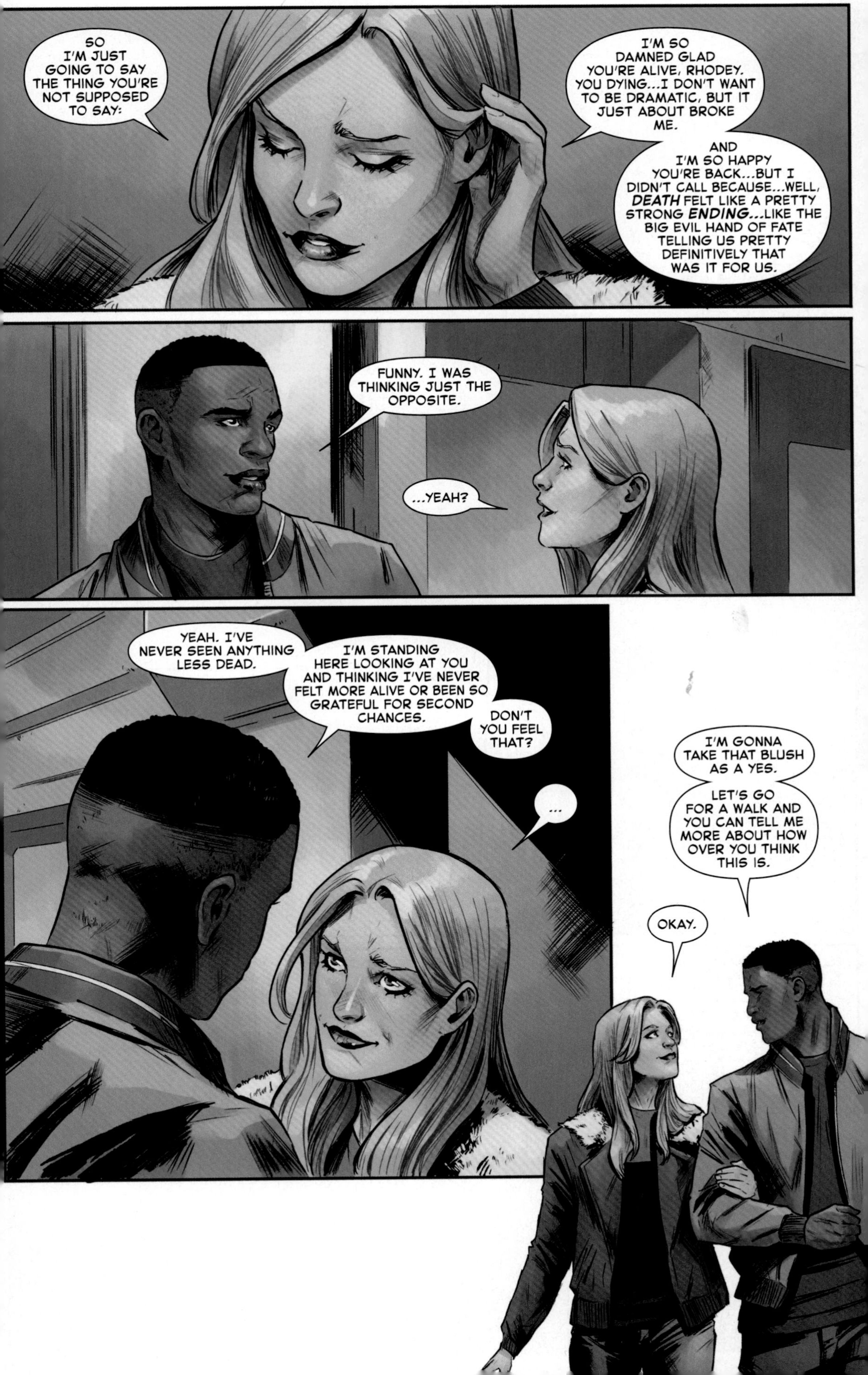
SO I'M JUST GOING TO SAY THE THING YOU'RE NOT SUPPOSED TO SAY:
I'M SO DAMNED GLAD YOU'RE ALIVE, RHODEY. YOU DYING...I DON'T WANT TO BE DRAMATIC, BUT IT JUST ABOUT BROKE ME.
AND I'M SO HAPPY YOU'RE BACK...BUT I DIDN'T CALL BECAUSE...WELL, *DEATH* FELT LIKE A PRETTY STRONG *ENDING...*LIKE THE BIG EVIL HAND OF FATE TELLING US PRETTY DEFINITIVELY THAT WAS IT FOR US.
FUNNY. I WAS THINKING JUST THE OPPOSITE.
...YEAH?
YEAH. I'VE NEVER SEEN ANYTHING LESS DEAD.
I'M STANDING HERE LOOKING AT YOU AND THINKING I'VE NEVER FELT MORE ALIVE OR BEEN SO GRATEFUL FOR SECOND CHANCES.
DON'T YOU FEEL THAT?
...
I'M GONNA TAKE THAT BLUSH AS A YES.
LET'S GO FOR A WALK AND YOU CAN TELL ME MORE ABOUT HOW OVER YOU THINK THIS IS.
OKAY.

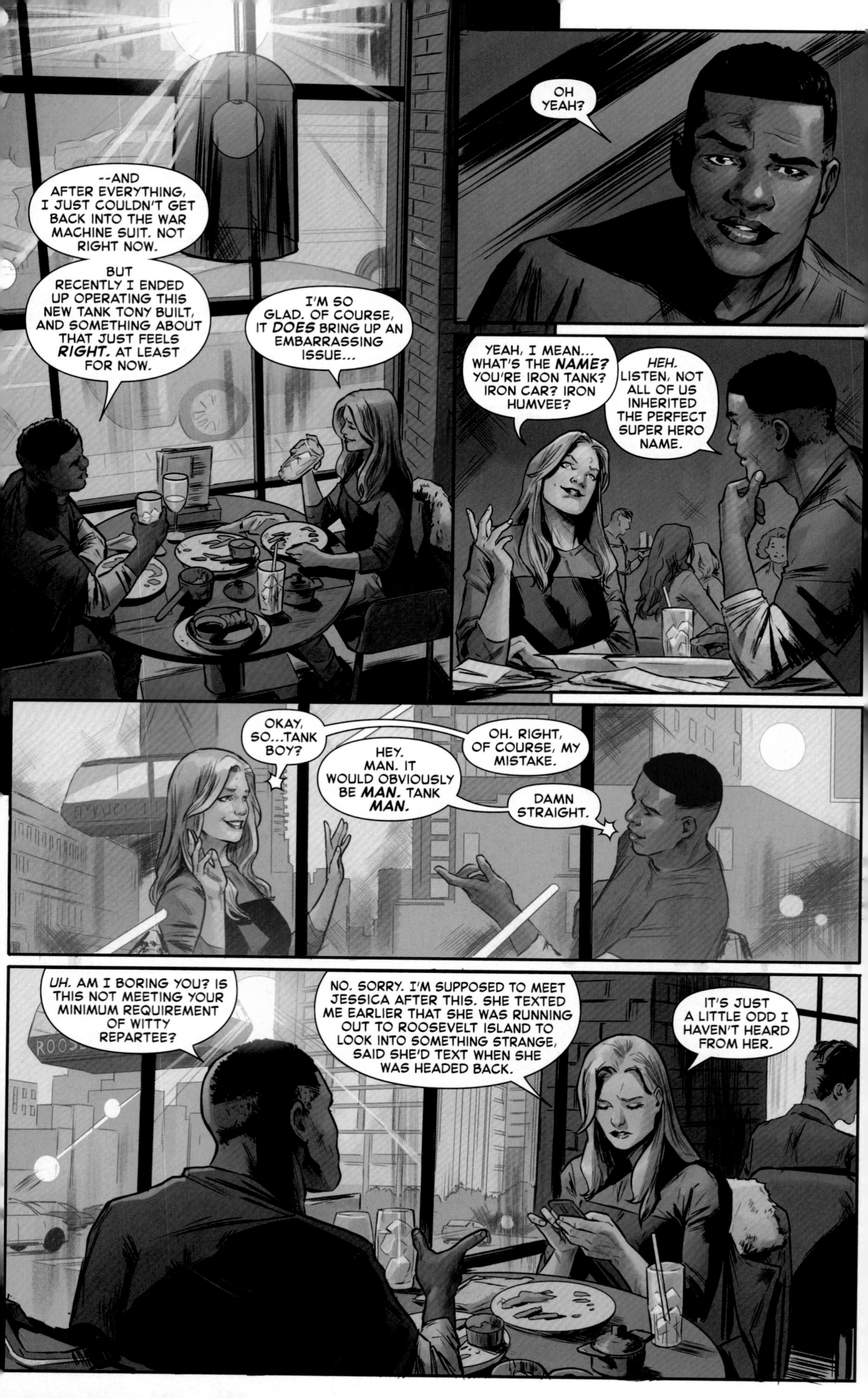
--AND AFTER EVERYTHING, I JUST COULDN'T GET BACK INTO THE WAR MACHINE SUIT. NOT RIGHT NOW.
BUT RECENTLY I ENDED UP OPERATING THIS NEW TANK TONY BUILT, AND SOMETHING ABOUT THAT JUST FEELS *RIGHT.* AT LEAST FOR NOW.
I'M SO GLAD. OF COURSE, IT *DOES* BRING UP AN EMBARRASSING ISSUE...
OH YEAH?
YEAH, I MEAN... WHAT'S THE *NAME?* YOU'RE IRON TANK? IRON CAR? IRON HUMVEE?
HEH. LISTEN, NOT ALL OF US INHERITED THE PERFECT SUPER HERO NAME.
OKAY, SO...TANK BOY?
HEY. MAN. IT WOULD OBVIOUSLY BE *MAN.* TANK *MAN.*
OH. RIGHT, OF COURSE, MY MISTAKE.
DAMN STRAIGHT.
UH. AM I BORING YOU? IS THIS NOT MEETING YOUR MINIMUM REQUIREMENT OF WITTY REPARTEE?
NO. SORRY. I'M SUPPOSED TO MEET JESSICA AFTER THIS. SHE TEXTED ME EARLIER THAT SHE WAS RUNNING OUT TO ROOSEVELT ISLAND TO LOOK INTO SOMETHING STRANGE, SAID SHE'D TEXT WHEN SHE WAS HEADED BACK.
IT'S JUST A LITTLE ODD I HAVEN'T HEARD FROM HER.

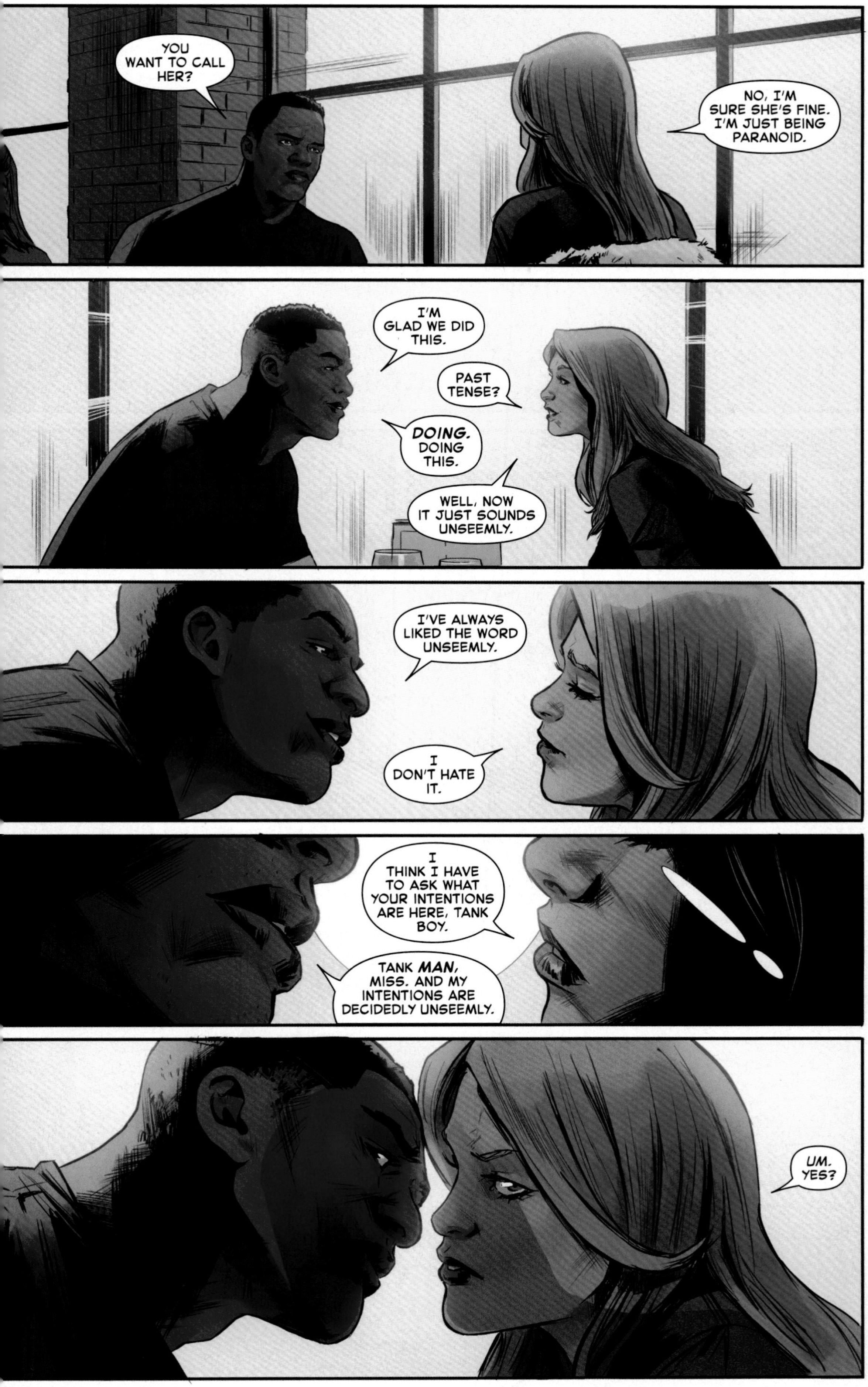
YOU WANT TO CALL HER?
NO, I'M SURE SHE'S FINE. I'M JUST BEING PARANOID.
I'M GLAD WE DID THIS.
PAST TENSE?
DOING. DOING THIS.
WELL, NOW IT JUST SOUNDS UNSEEMLY.
I'VE ALWAYS LIKED THE WORD UNSEEMLY.
I DON'T HATE IT.
I THINK I HAVE TO ASK WHAT YOUR INTENTIONS ARE HERE, TANK BOY.
TANK *MAN,* MISS. AND MY INTENTIONS ARE DECIDEDLY UNSEEMLY.
UM. YES?

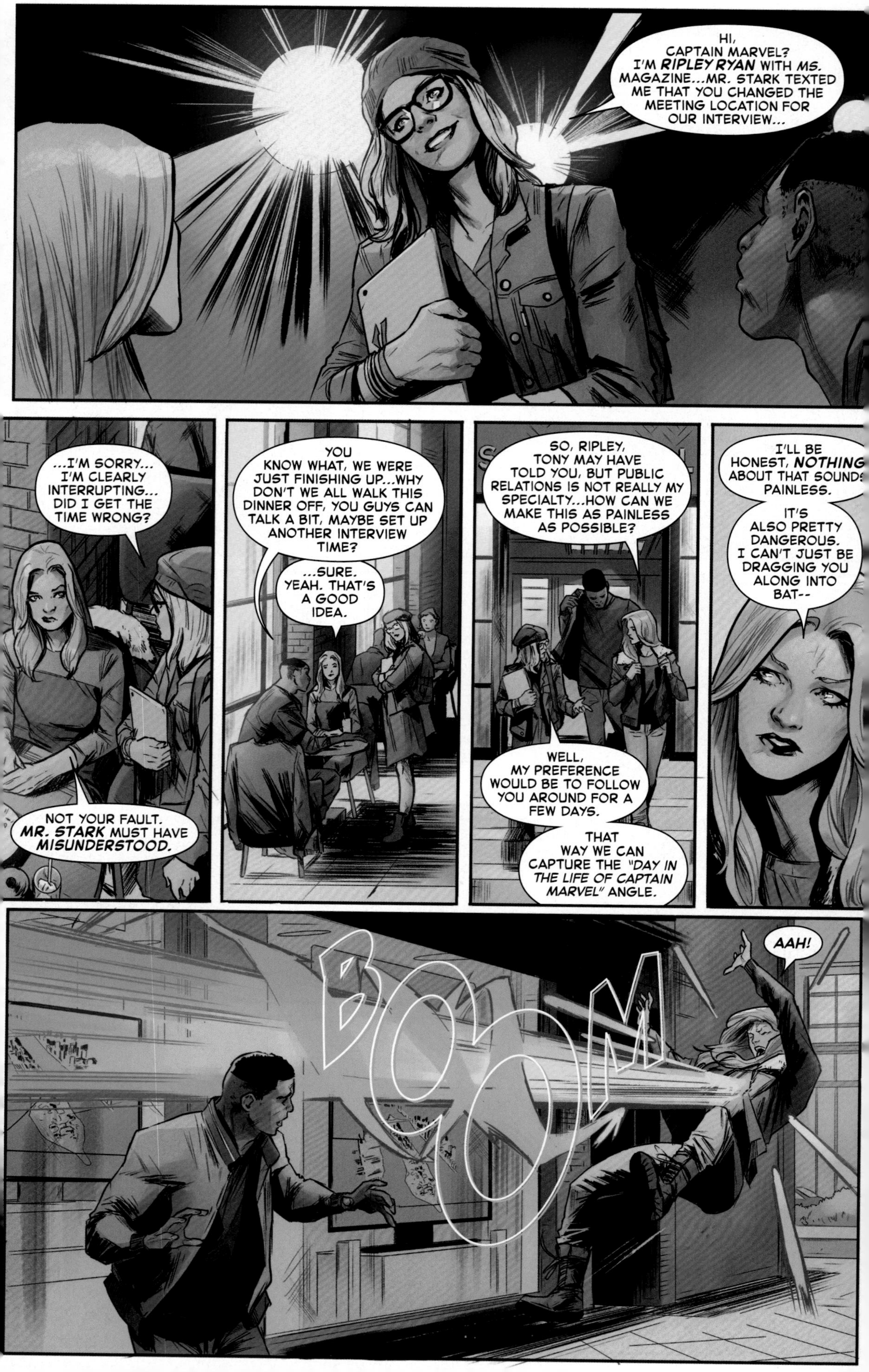
HI, CAPTAIN MARVEL? I'M RIPLEY RYAN WITH MS. MAGAZINE...MR. STARK TEXTED ME THAT YOU CHANGED THE MEETING LOCATION FOR OUR INTERVIEW...
...I'M SORRY... I'M CLEARLY INTERRUPTING... DID I GET THE TIME WRONG?
NOT YOUR FAULT. MR. STARK MUST HAVE MISUNDERSTOOD.
YOU KNOW WHAT, WE WERE JUST FINISHING UP...WHY DON'T WE ALL WALK THIS DINNER OFF, YOU GUYS CAN TALK A BIT, MAYBE SET UP ANOTHER INTERVIEW TIME?
...SURE. YEAH. THAT'S A GOOD IDEA.
SO, RIPLEY, TONY MAY HAVE TOLD YOU, BUT PUBLIC RELATIONS IS NOT REALLY MY SPECIALTY...HOW CAN WE MAKE THIS AS PAINLESS AS POSSIBLE?
WELL, MY PREFERENCE WOULD BE TO FOLLOW YOU AROUND FOR A FEW DAYS.
THAT WAY WE CAN CAPTURE THE "DAY IN THE LIFE OF CAPTAIN MARVEL" ANGLE.
I'LL BE HONEST, NOTHING ABOUT THAT SOUNDS PAINLESS.
IT'S ALSO PRETTY DANGEROUS. I CAN'T JUST BE DRAGGING YOU ALONG INTO BAT--
BOOOM
AAH!

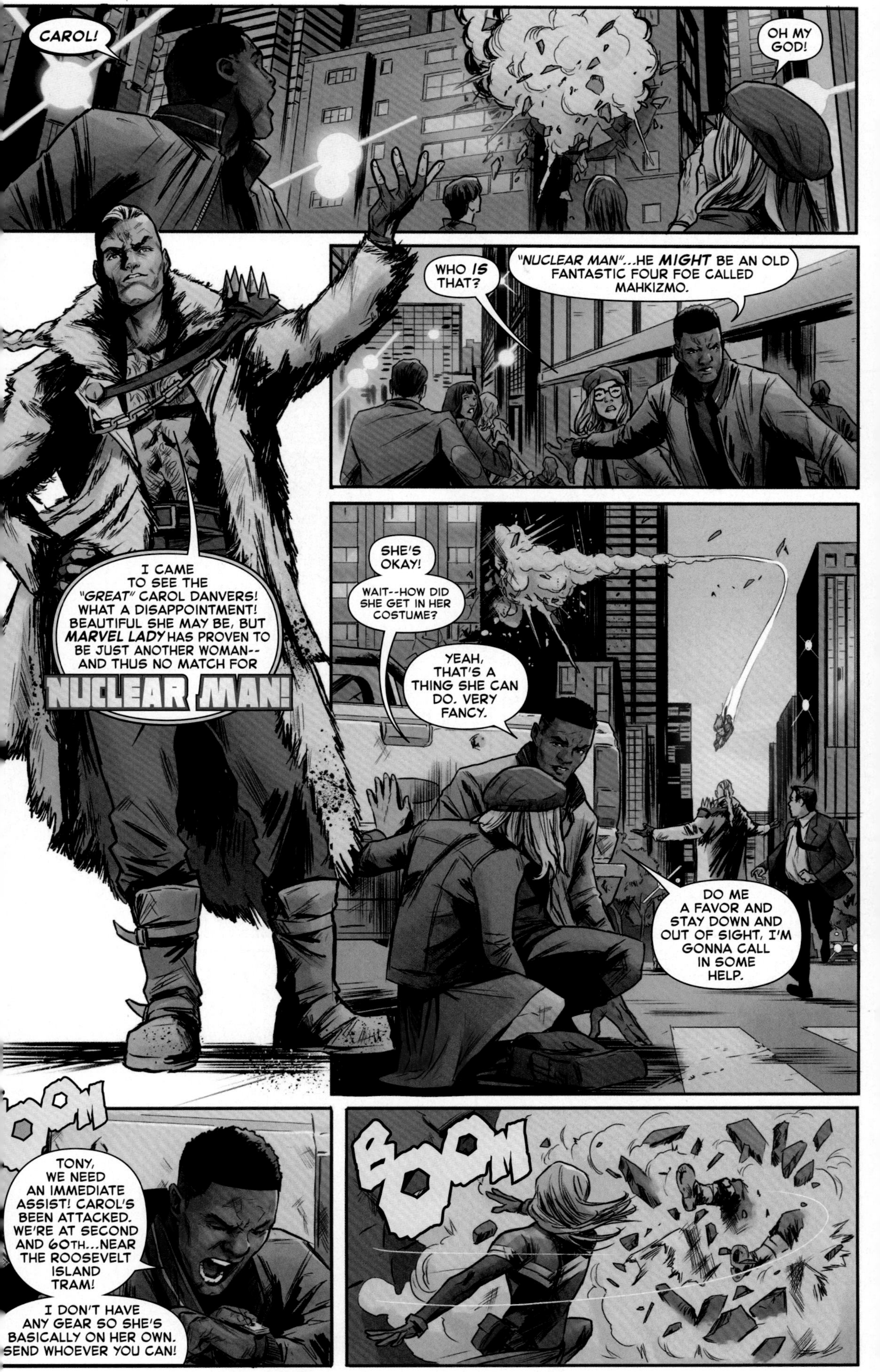
CAROL!
OH MY GOD!
I CAME TO SEE THE "GREAT" CAROL DANVERS! WHAT A DISAPPOINTMENT! BEAUTIFUL SHE MAY BE, BUT MARVEL LADY HAS PROVEN TO BE JUST ANOTHER WOMAN-- AND THUS NO MATCH FOR
NUCLEAR MAN!
WHO IS THAT?
"NUCLEAR MAN"...HE MIGHT BE AN OLD FANTASTIC FOUR FOE CALLED MAHKIZMO.
SHE'S OKAY!
WAIT--HOW DID SHE GET IN HER COSTUME?
YEAH, THAT'S A THING SHE CAN DO. VERY FANCY.
DO ME A FAVOR AND STAY DOWN AND OUT OF SIGHT, I'M GONNA CALL IN SOME HELP.
BOOM
TONY, WE NEED AN IMMEDIATE ASSIST! CAROL'S BEEN ATTACKED. WE'RE AT SECOND AND 60TH...NEAR THE ROOSEVELT ISLAND TRAM!
I DON'T HAVE ANY GEAR SO SHE'S BASICALLY ON HER OWN. SEND WHOEVER YOU CAN!
BOOM

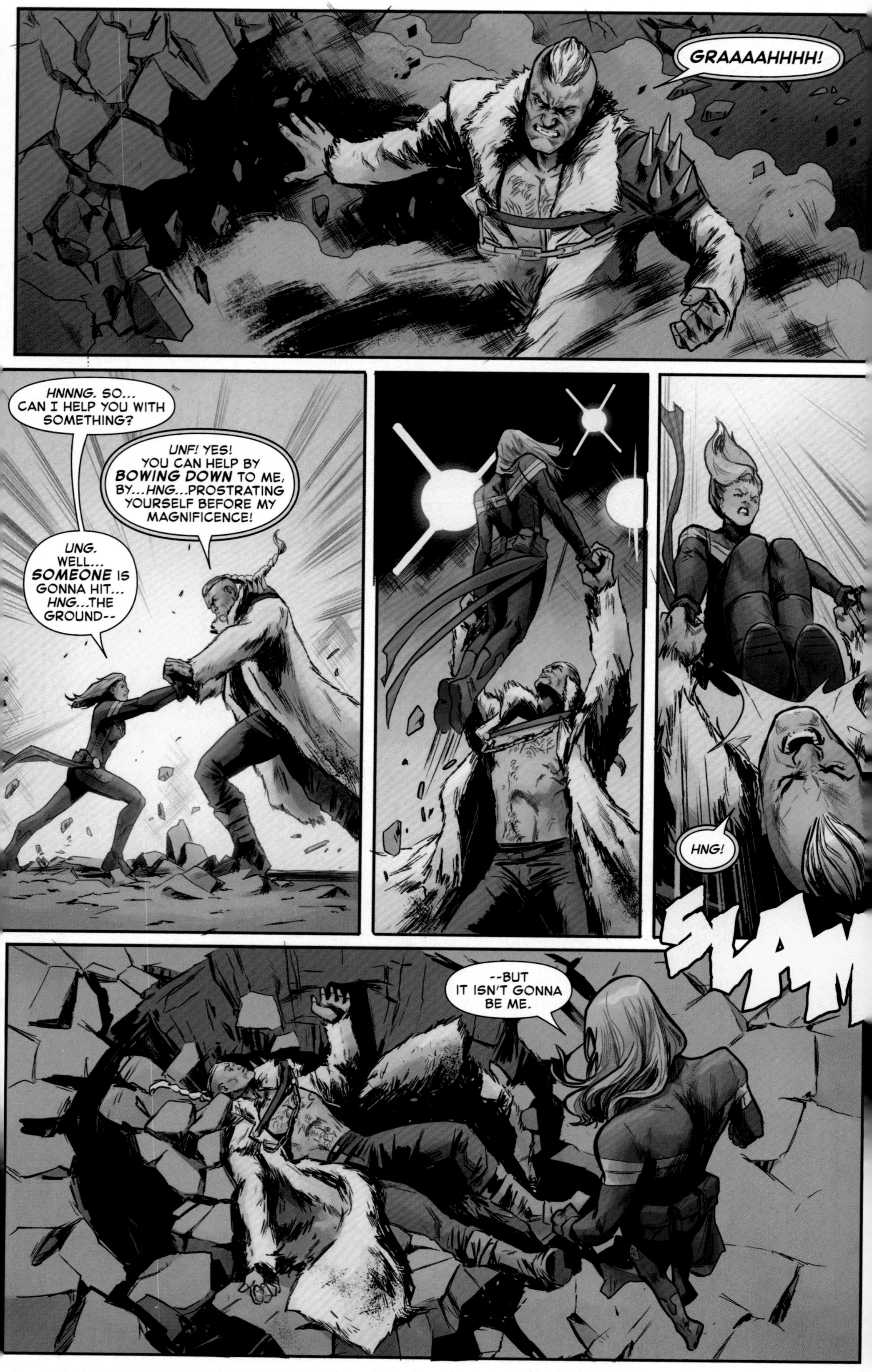
GRAAAAHHHH!
HNNNG. SO... CAN I HELP YOU WITH SOMETHING?
UNF! YES! YOU CAN HELP BY BOWING DOWN TO ME, BY...HNG...PROSTRATING YOURSELF BEFORE MY MAGNIFICENCE!
UNG. WELL... SOMEONE IS GONNA HIT... HNG...THE GROUND--
HNG!
SLAM
--BUT IT ISN'T GONNA BE ME.

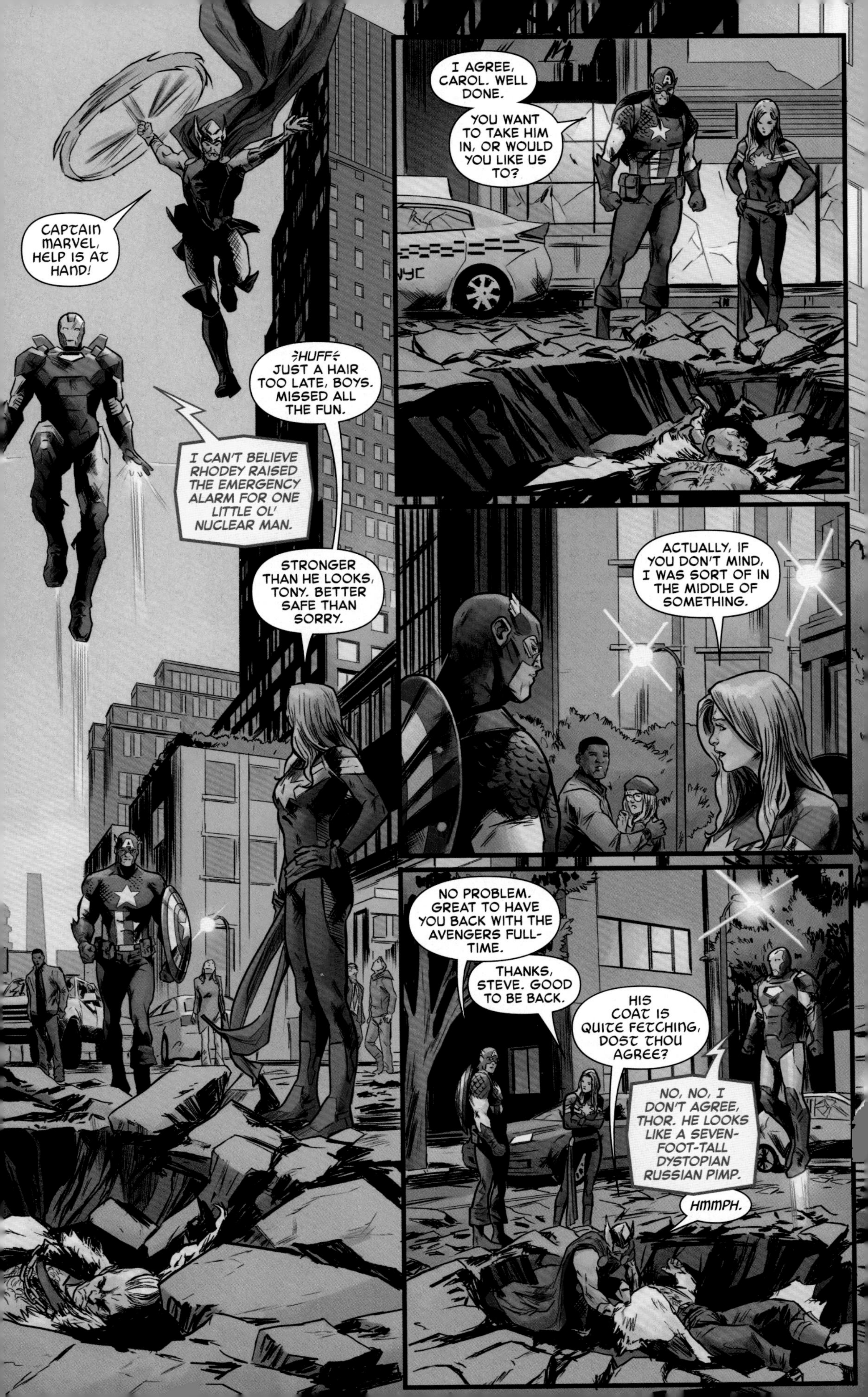
CAPTAIN MARVEL, HELP IS AT HAND!
I CAN'T BELIEVE RHODEY RAISED THE EMERGENCY ALARM FOR ONE LITTLE OL' NUCLEAR MAN.
≠HUFF≠ JUST A HAIR TOO LATE, BOYS. MISSED ALL THE FUN.
STRONGER THAN HE LOOKS, TONY. BETTER SAFE THAN SORRY.
I AGREE, CAROL. WELL DONE.
YOU WANT TO TAKE HIM IN, OR WOULD YOU LIKE US TO?
ACTUALLY, IF YOU DON'T MIND, I WAS SORT OF IN THE MIDDLE OF SOMETHING.
NO PROBLEM. GREAT TO HAVE YOU BACK WITH THE AVENGERS FULL-TIME.
THANKS, STEVE. GOOD TO BE BACK.
HIS COAT IS QUITE FETCHING, DOST THOU AGREE?
NO, NO, I DON'T AGREE, THOR. HE LOOKS LIKE A SEVEN-FOOT-TALL DYSTOPIAN RUSSIAN PIMP.
HMMPH.

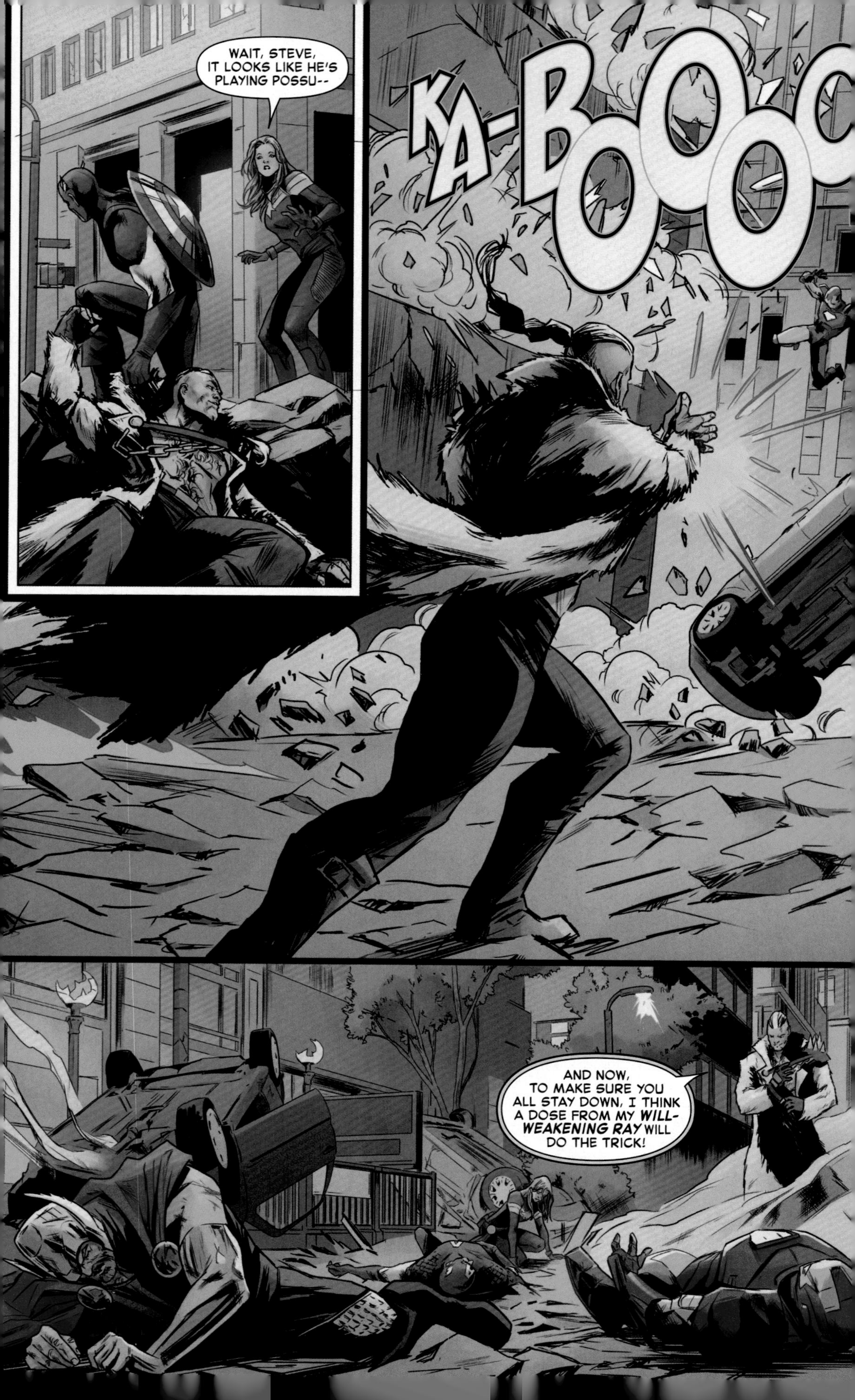
WAIT, STEVE, IT LOOKS LIKE HE'S PLAYING POSSU--
KA-BOOOOC
AND NOW, TO MAKE SURE YOU ALL STAY DOWN, I THINK A DOSE FROM MY WILL-WEAKENING RAY WILL DO THE TRICK!

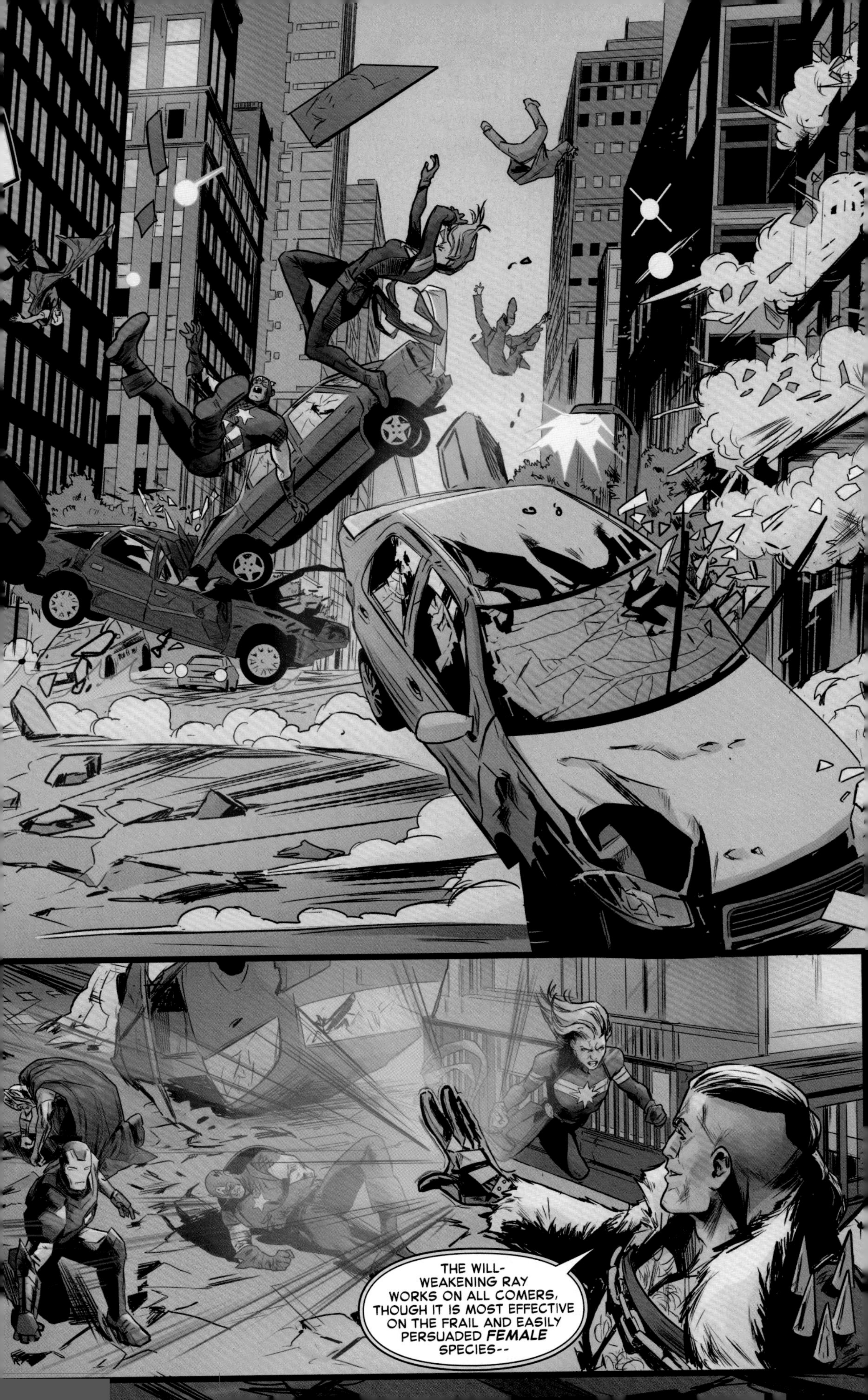
THE WILL-WEAKENING RAY WORKS ON ALL COMERS, THOUGH IT IS MOST EFFECTIVE ON THE FRAIL AND EASILY PERSUADED *FEMALE* SPECIES--

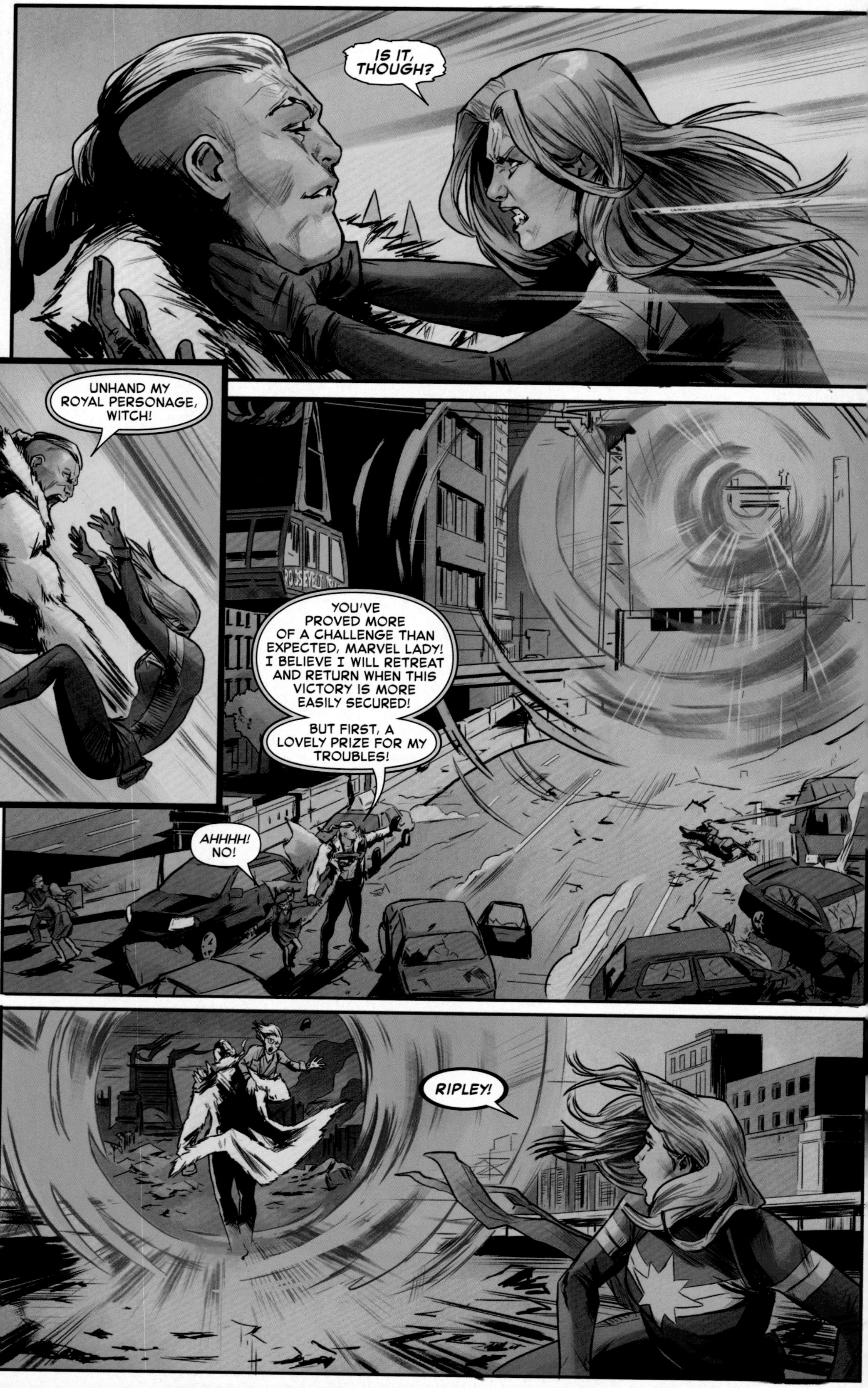
IS IT, THOUGH?
UNHAND MY ROYAL PERSONAGE, WITCH!
YOU'VE PROVED MORE OF A CHALLENGE THAN EXPECTED, MARVEL LADY! I BELIEVE I WILL RETREAT AND RETURN WHEN THIS VICTORY IS MORE EASILY SECURED!
BUT FIRST, A LOVELY PRIZE FOR MY TROUBLES!
AHHHH! NO!
RIPLEY!

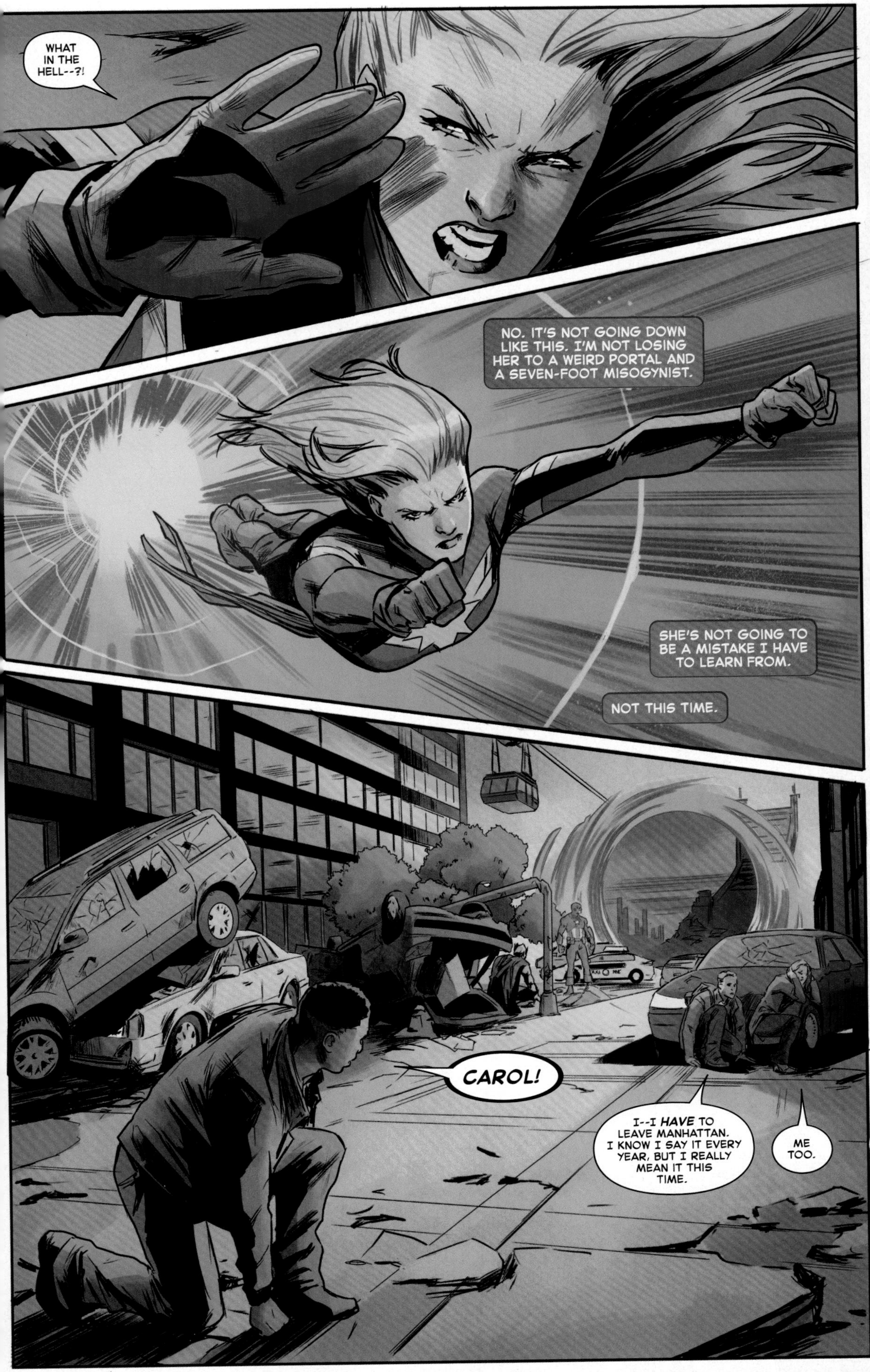
WHAT IN THE HELL--?!
NO. IT'S NOT GOING DOWN LIKE THIS. I'M NOT LOSING HER TO A WEIRD PORTAL AND A SEVEN-FOOT MISOGYNIST.
SHE'S NOT GOING TO BE A MISTAKE I HAVE TO LEARN FROM.
NOT THIS TIME.
CAROL!
I--I *HAVE* TO LEAVE MANHATTAN. I KNOW I SAY IT EVERY YEAR, BUT I REALLY MEAN IT THIS TIME.
ME TOO.

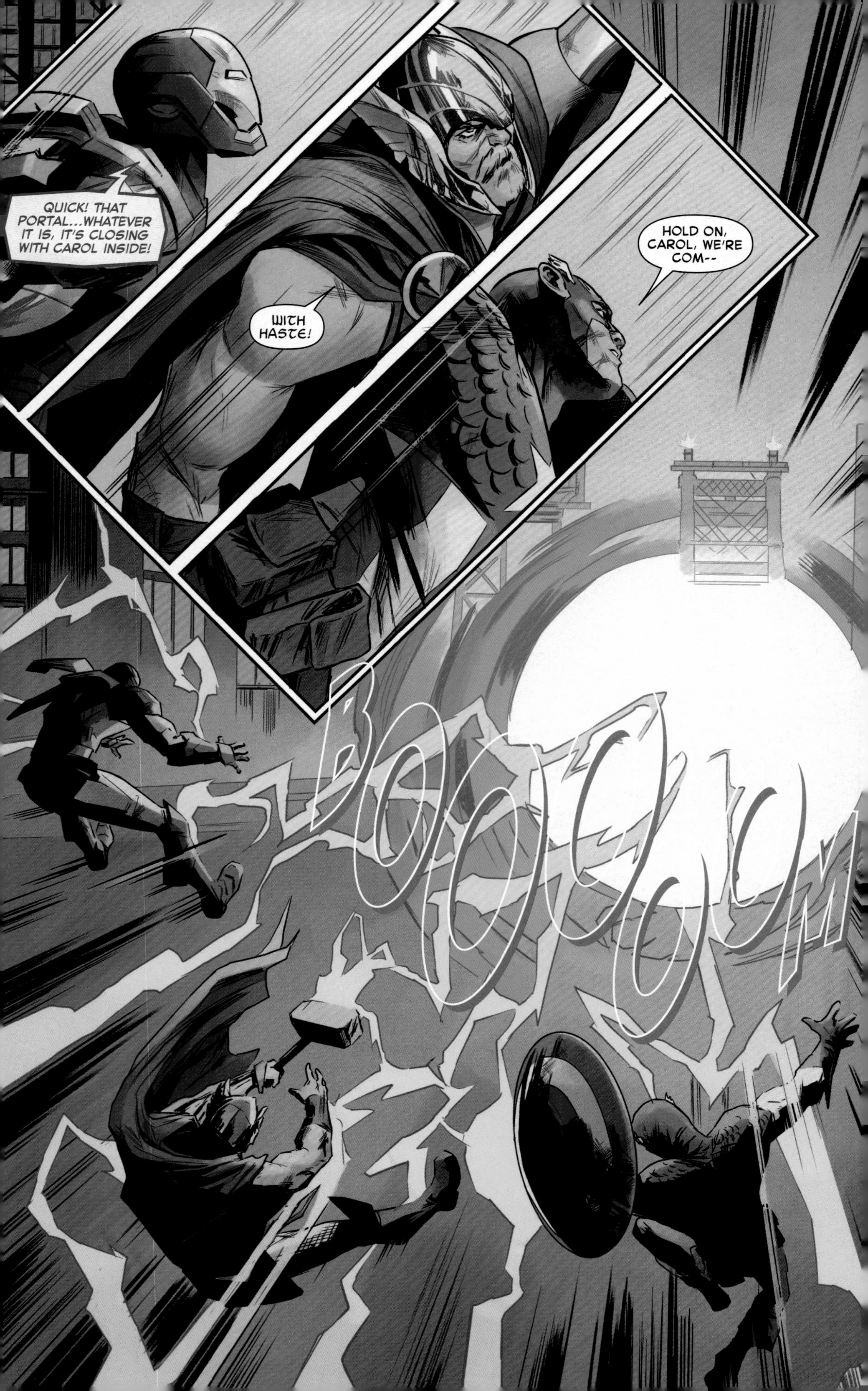
QUICK! THAT PORTAL...WHATEVER IT IS, IT'S CLOSING WITH CAROL INSIDE!
WITH HASTE!
HOLD ON, CAROL, WE'RE COM--
BOOOOOOOM

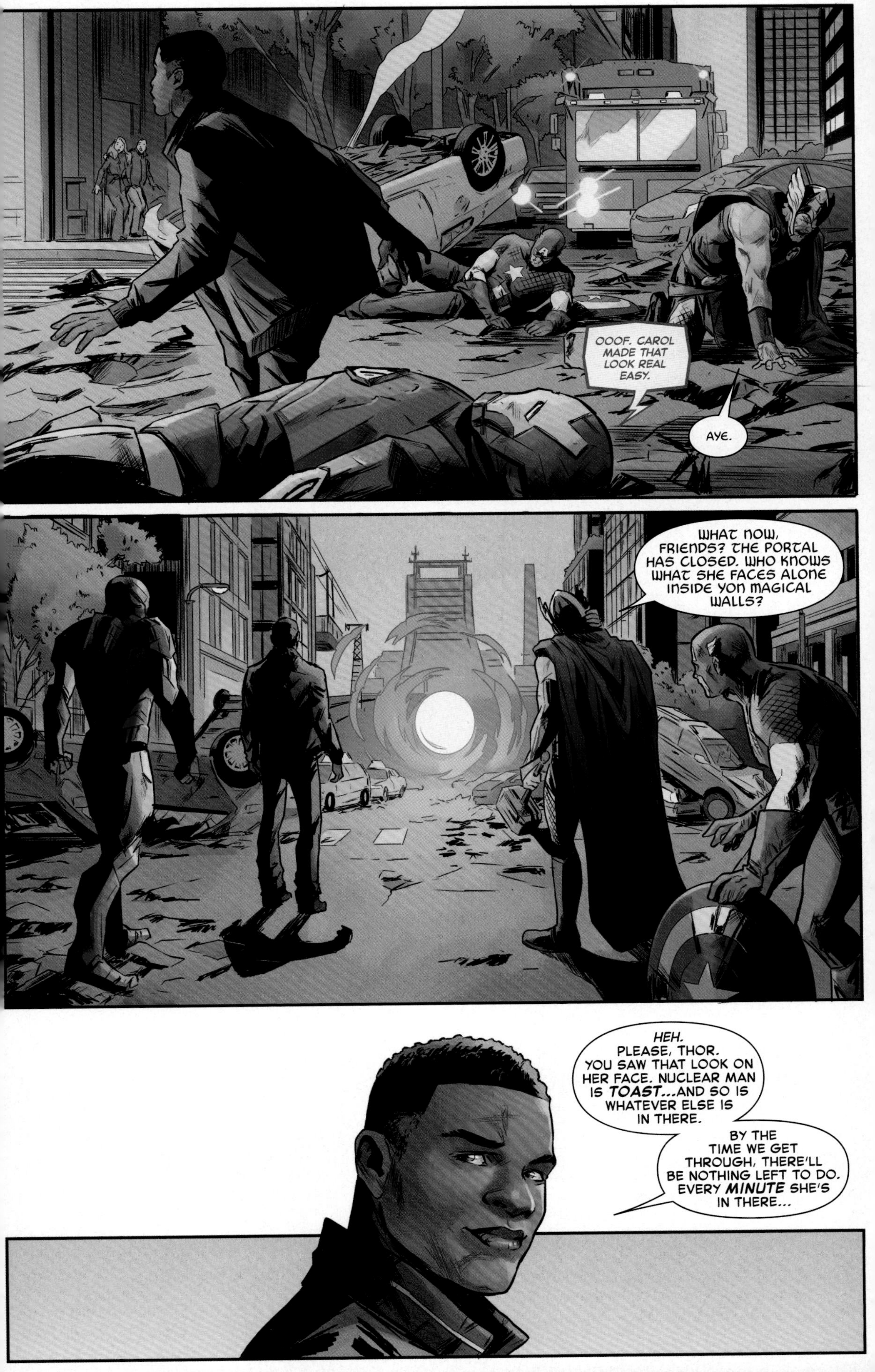
OOOF. CAROL MADE THAT LOOK REAL EASY.
AYE.
WHAT NOW, FRIENDS? THE PORTAL HAS CLOSED. WHO KNOWS WHAT SHE FACES ALONE INSIDE YON MAGICAL WALLS?
HEH. PLEASE, THOR. YOU SAW THAT LOOK ON HER FACE. NUCLEAR MAN IS TOAST...AND SO IS WHATEVER ELSE IS IN THERE.
BY THE TIME WE GET THROUGH, THERE'LL BE NOTHING LEFT TO DO. EVERY MINUTE SHE'S IN THERE...

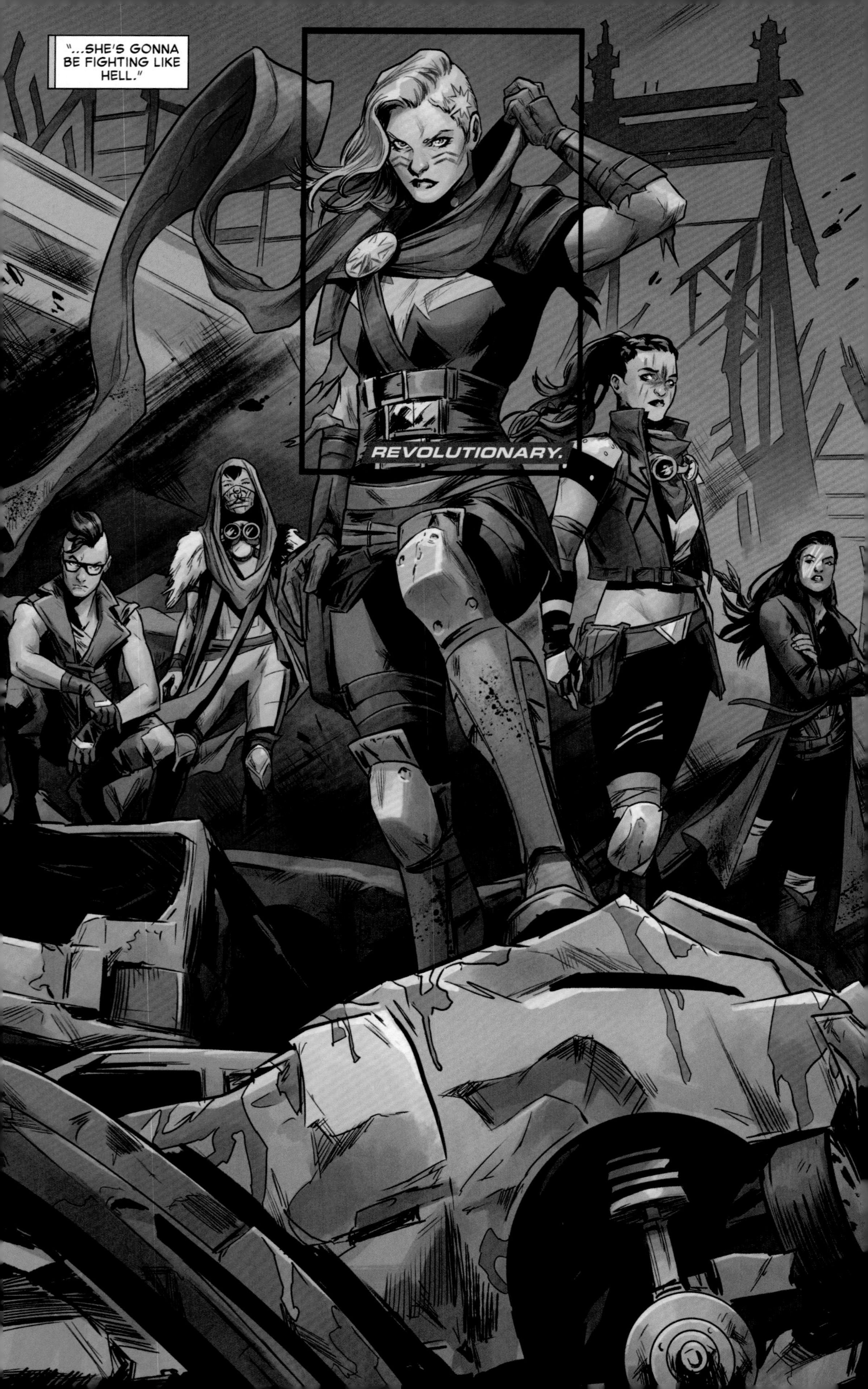
"...SHE'S GONNA BE FIGHTING LIKE HELL."
REVOLUTIONARY.

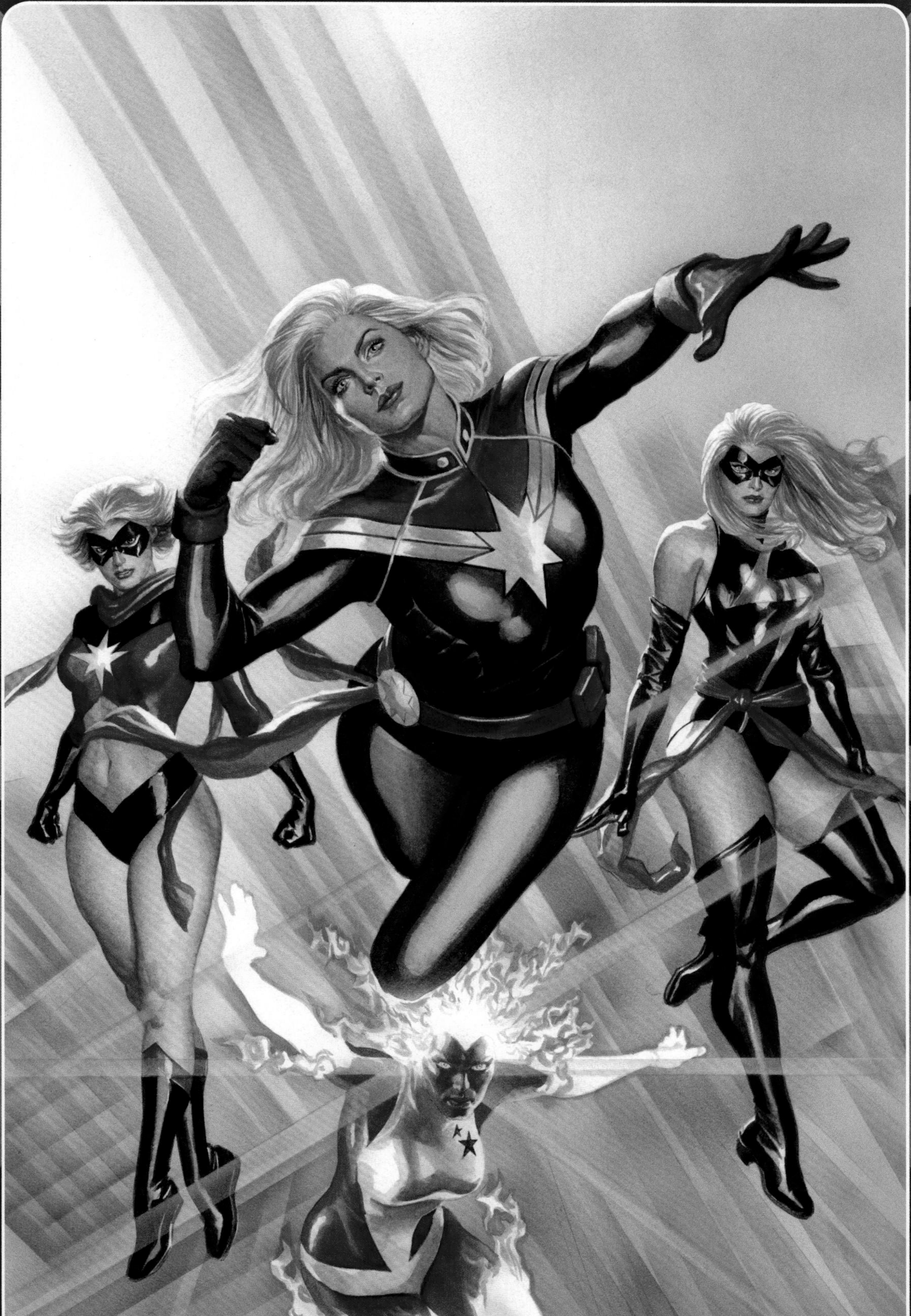

ALEX ROSS
1 VARIANT

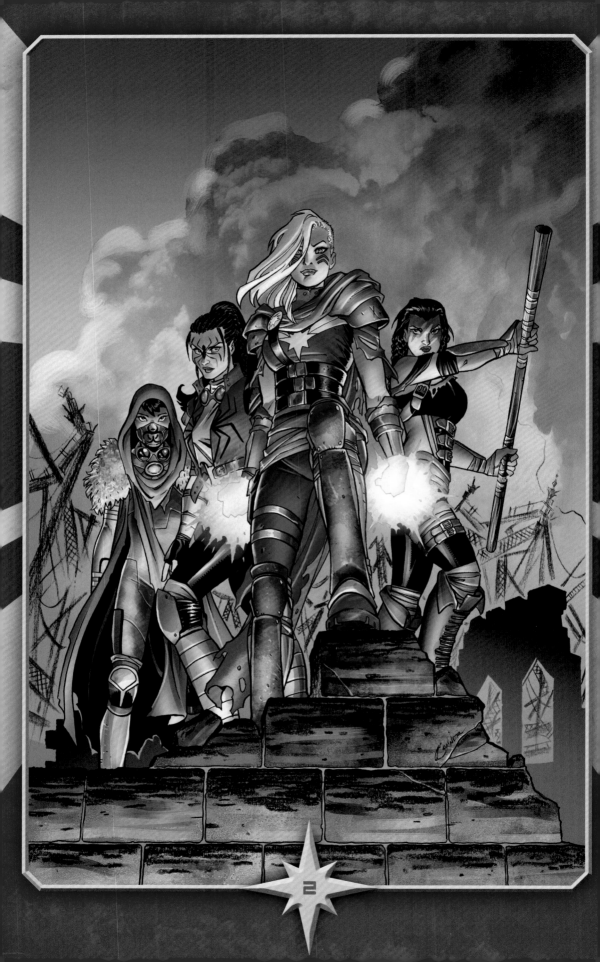

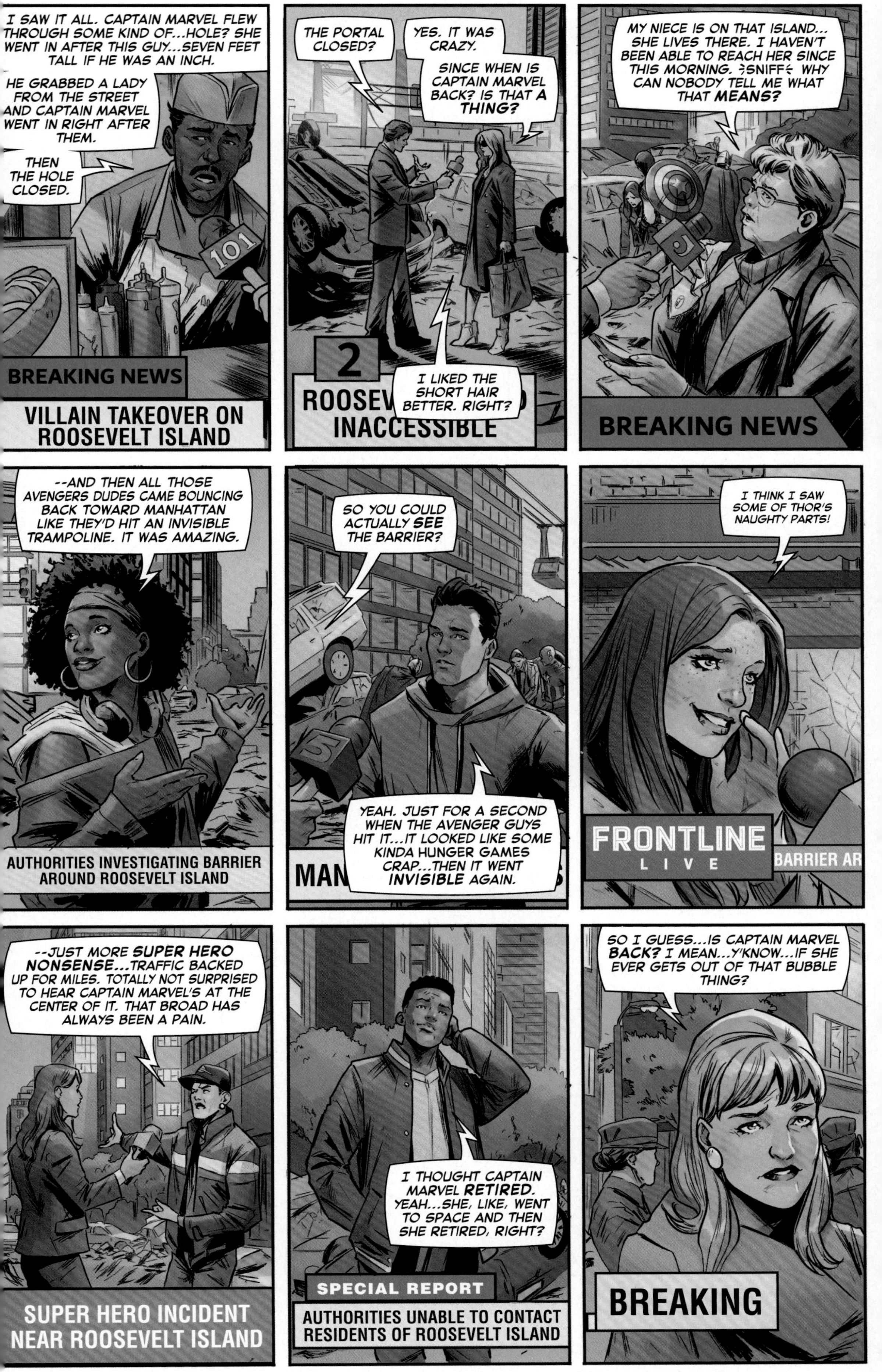
I SAW IT ALL. CAPTAIN MARVEL FLEW THROUGH SOME KIND OF...HOLE? SHE WENT IN AFTER THIS GUY...SEVEN FEET TALL IF HE WAS AN INCH.
HE GRABBED A LADY FROM THE STREET AND CAPTAIN MARVEL WENT IN RIGHT AFTER THEM.
THEN THE HOLE CLOSED.
101
BREAKING NEWS
VILLAIN TAKEOVER ON ROOSEVELT ISLAND
THE PORTAL CLOSED?
YES. IT WAS CRAZY.
SINCE WHEN IS CAPTAIN MARVEL BACK? IS THAT A THING?
I LIKED THE SHORT HAIR BETTER. RIGHT?
2
ROOSEV D
INACCESSIBLE
MY NIECE IS ON THAT ISLAND... SHE LIVES THERE. I HAVEN'T BEEN ABLE TO REACH HER SINCE THIS MORNING. *SNIFF* WHY CAN NOBODY TELL ME WHAT THAT MEANS?
BREAKING NEWS
--AND THEN ALL THOSE AVENGERS DUDES CAME BOUNCING BACK TOWARD MANHATTAN LIKE THEY'D HIT AN INVISIBLE TRAMPOLINE. IT WAS AMAZING.
AUTHORITIES INVESTIGATING BARRIER AROUND ROOSEVELT ISLAND
SO YOU COULD ACTUALLY SEE THE BARRIER?
YEAH. JUST FOR A SECOND WHEN THE AVENGER GUYS HIT IT...IT LOOKED LIKE SOME KINDA HUNGER GAMES CRAP...THEN IT WENT INVISIBLE AGAIN.
MAN S
I THINK I SAW SOME OF THOR'S NAUGHTY PARTS!
FRONTLINE LIVE
BARRIER AR
--JUST MORE SUPER HERO NONSENSE...TRAFFIC BACKED UP FOR MILES. TOTALLY NOT SURPRISED TO HEAR CAPTAIN MARVEL'S AT THE CENTER OF IT. THAT BROAD HAS ALWAYS BEEN A PAIN.
SUPER HERO INCIDENT NEAR ROOSEVELT ISLAND
I THOUGHT CAPTAIN MARVEL RETIRED. YEAH...SHE, LIKE, WENT TO SPACE AND THEN SHE RETIRED, RIGHT?
SPECIAL REPORT
AUTHORITIES UNABLE TO CONTACT RESIDENTS OF ROOSEVELT ISLAND
SO I GUESS...IS CAPTAIN MARVEL BACK? I MEAN...Y'KNOW...IF SHE EVER GETS OUT OF THAT BUBBLE THING?
BREAKING

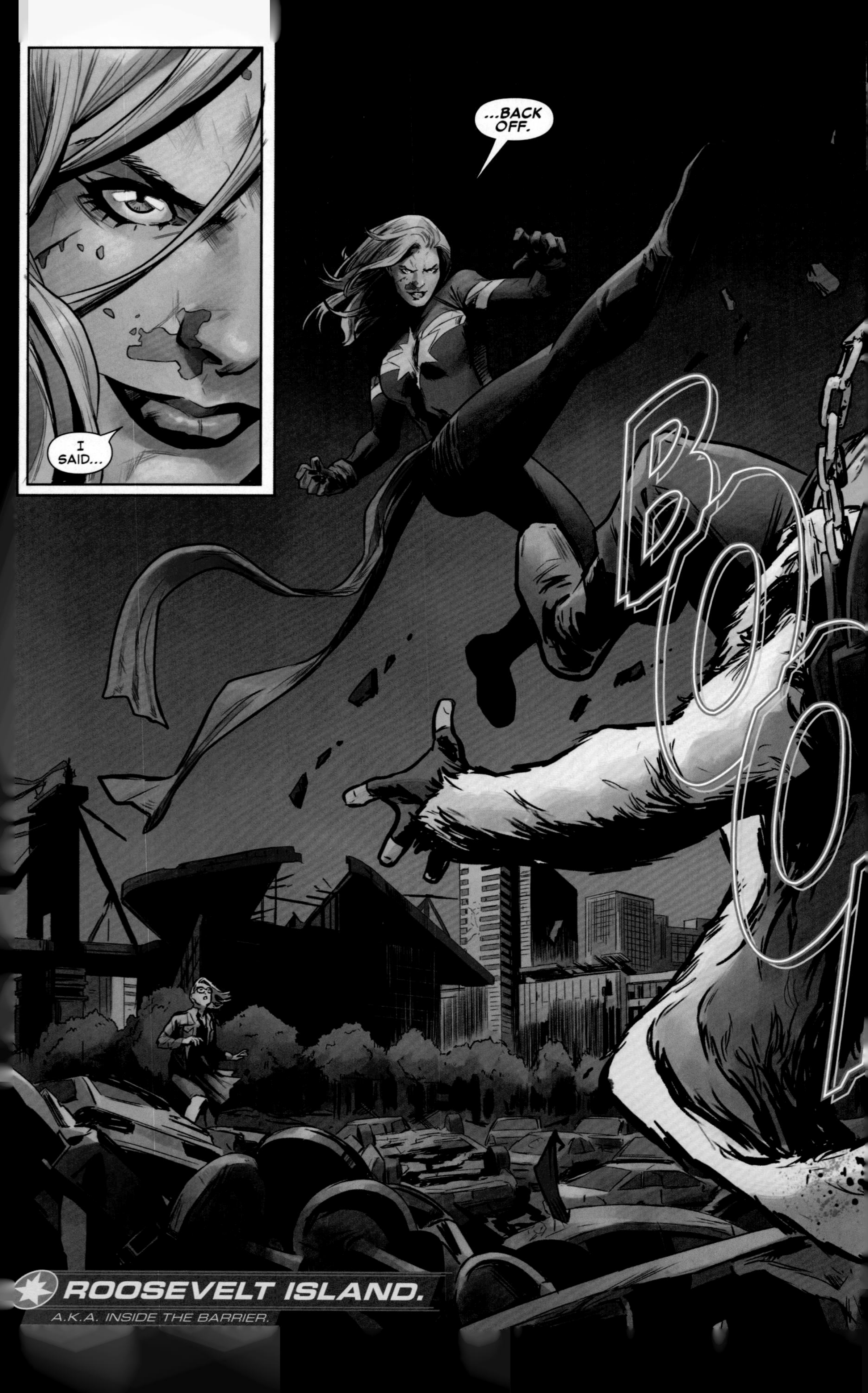
I SAID...
...BACK OFF.
BOOOM
ROOSEVELT ISLAND.
A.K.A. INSIDE THE BARRIER.

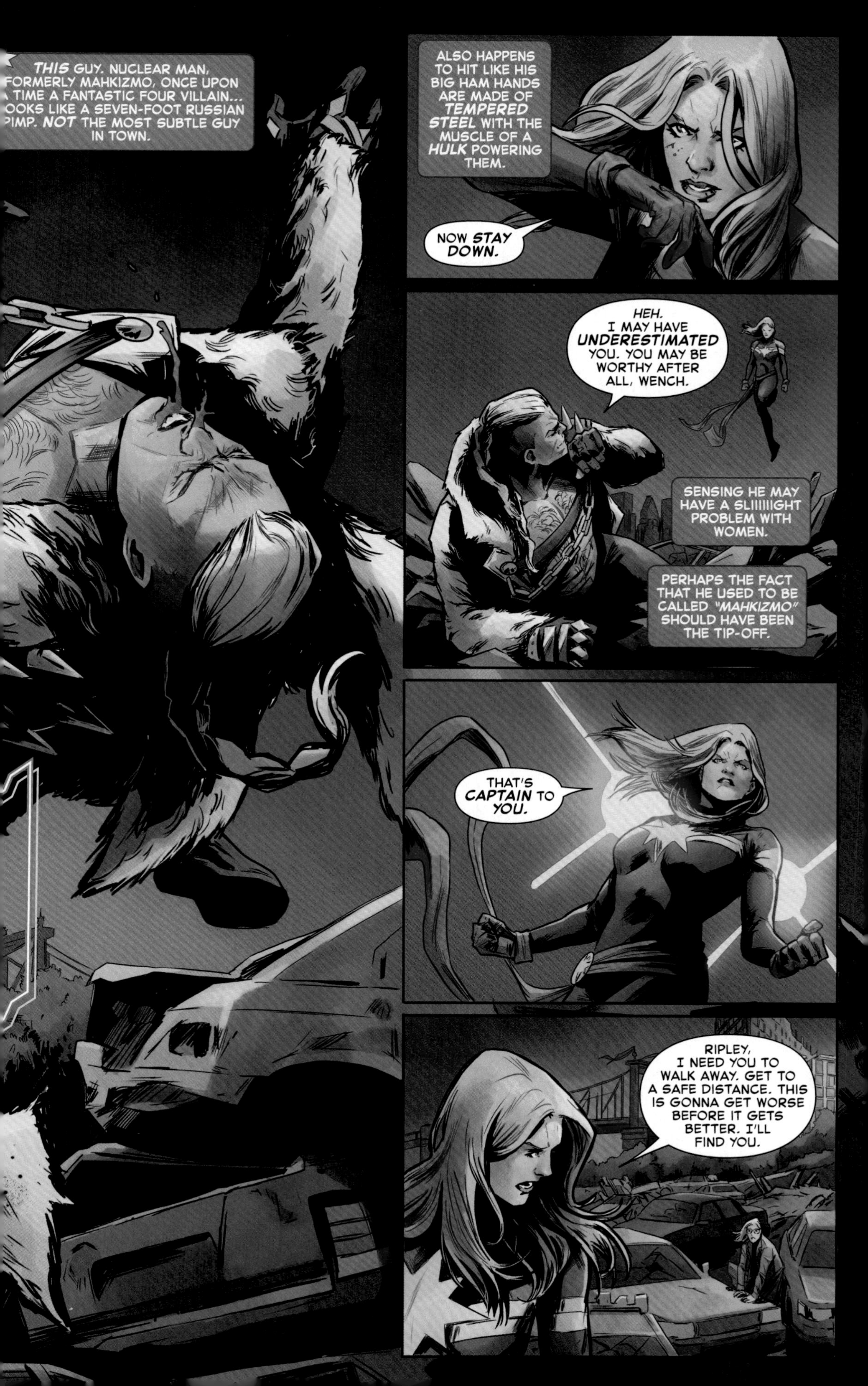
THIS GUY. NUCLEAR MAN, FORMERLY MAHKIZMO, ONCE UPON A TIME A FANTASTIC FOUR VILLAIN... LOOKS LIKE A SEVEN-FOOT RUSSIAN PIMP. NOT THE MOST SUBTLE GUY IN TOWN.
ALSO HAPPENS TO HIT LIKE HIS BIG HAM HANDS ARE MADE OF TEMPERED STEEL WITH THE MUSCLE OF A HULK POWERING THEM.
NOW STAY DOWN.
HEH. I MAY HAVE UNDERESTIMATED YOU. YOU MAY BE WORTHY AFTER ALL, WENCH.
SENSING HE MAY HAVE A SLIIIIIIGHT PROBLEM WITH WOMEN.
PERHAPS THE FACT THAT HE USED TO BE CALLED "MAHKIZMO" SHOULD HAVE BEEN THE TIP-OFF.
THAT'S CAPTAIN TO YOU.
RIPLEY, I NEED YOU TO WALK AWAY. GET TO A SAFE DISTANCE. THIS IS GONNA GET WORSE BEFORE IT GETS BETTER. I'LL FIND YOU.

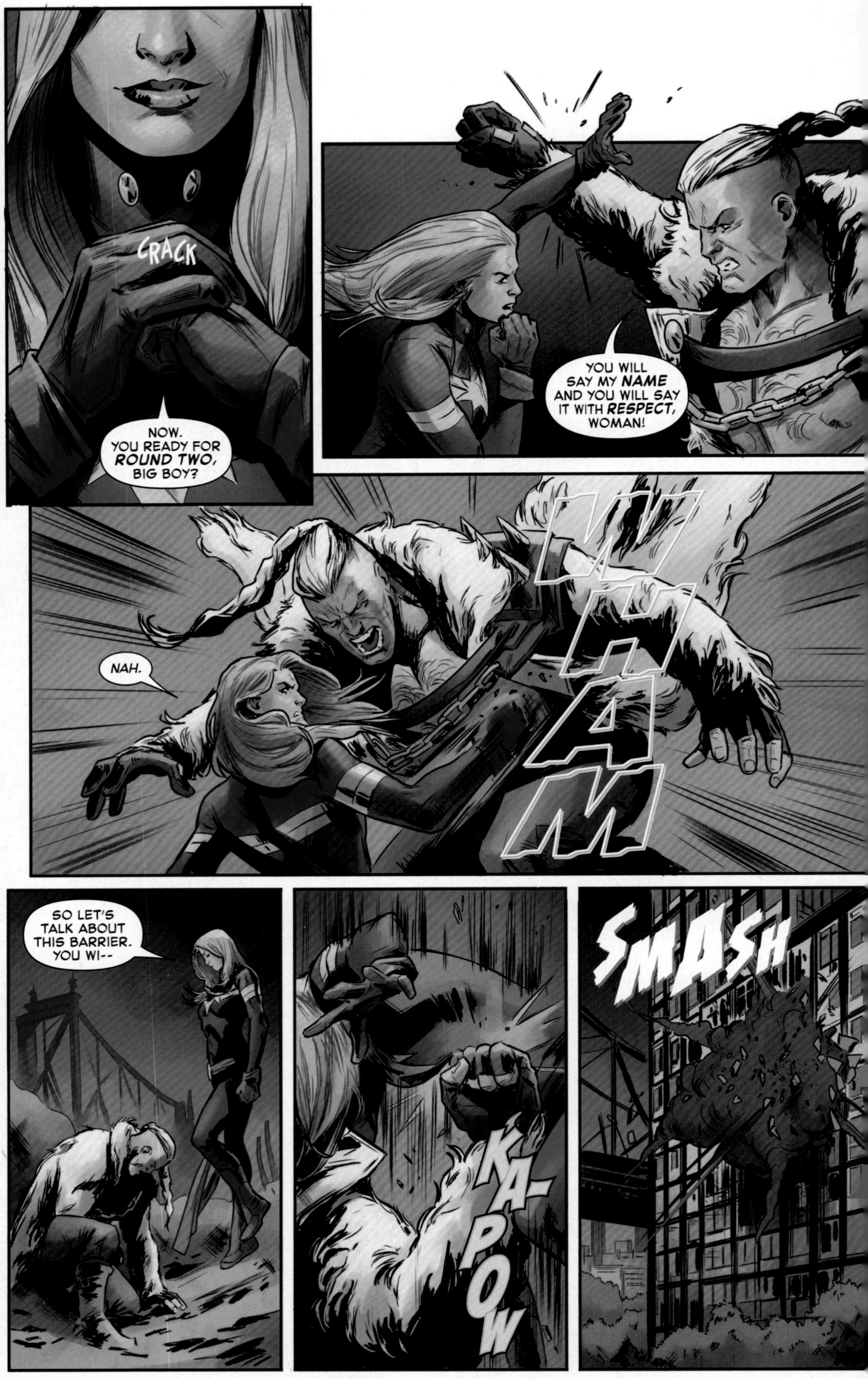
CRACK
NOW. YOU READY FOR ROUND TWO, BIG BOY?
YOU WILL SAY MY NAME AND YOU WILL SAY IT WITH RESPECT, WOMAN!
NAH.
WHAM
SO LET'S TALK ABOUT THIS BARRIER. YOU WI--
KA-POW
SMASH

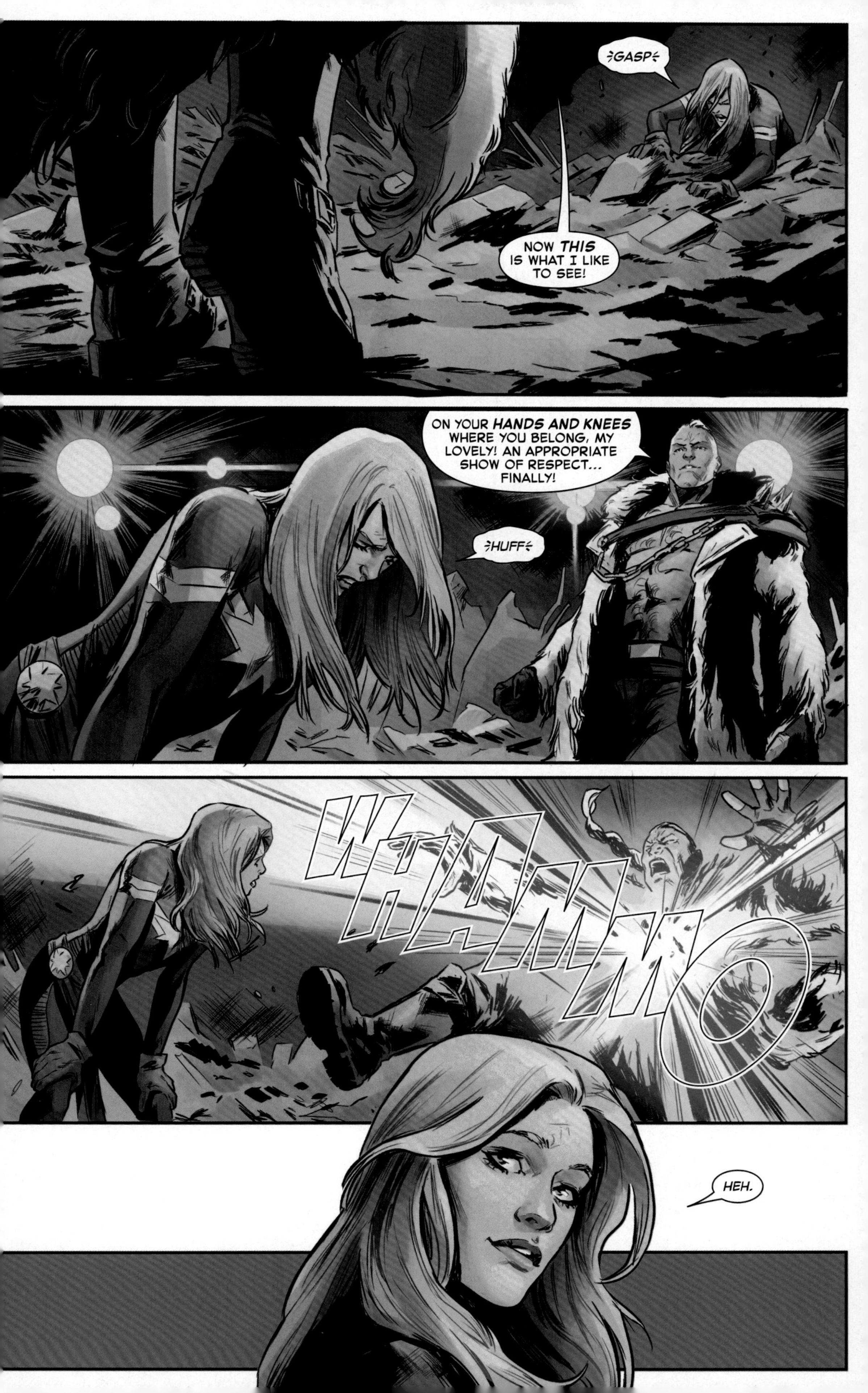

GASP
NOW **THIS** IS WHAT I LIKE TO SEE!
ON YOUR **HANDS AND KNEES** WHERE YOU BELONG, MY LOVELY! AN APPROPRIATE SHOW OF RESPECT... FINALLY!
HUFF
WHAMMO
HEH.

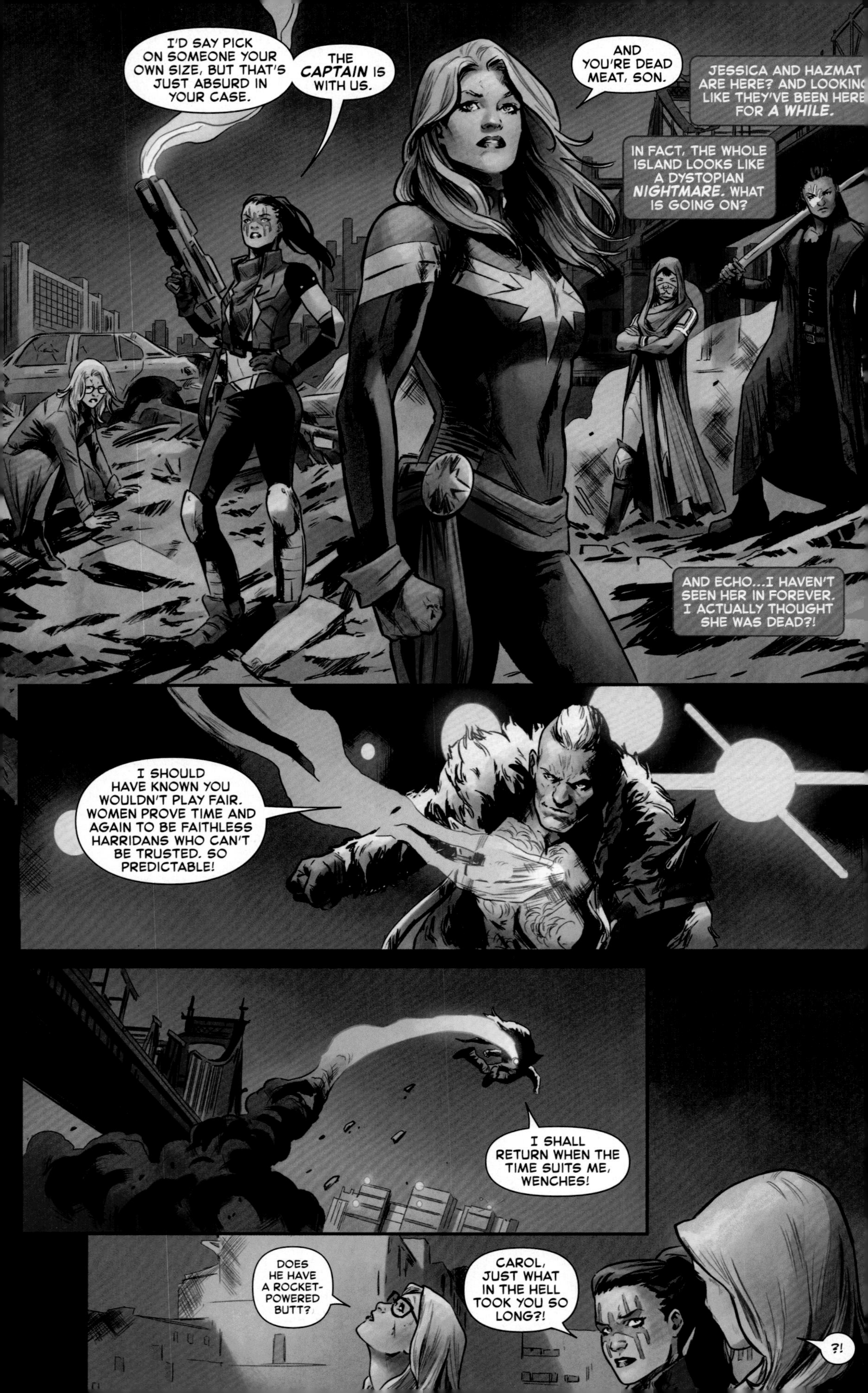

I'D SAY PICK ON SOMEONE YOUR OWN SIZE, BUT THAT'S JUST ABSURD IN YOUR CASE.
THE CAPTAIN IS WITH US.
AND YOU'RE DEAD MEAT, SON.
JESSICA AND HAZMAT ARE HERE? AND LOOKING LIKE THEY'VE BEEN HERE FOR A WHILE.
IN FACT, THE WHOLE ISLAND LOOKS LIKE A DYSTOPIAN NIGHTMARE. WHAT IS GOING ON?
AND ECHO...I HAVEN'T SEEN HER IN FOREVER. I ACTUALLY THOUGHT SHE WAS DEAD?!
I SHOULD HAVE KNOWN YOU WOULDN'T PLAY FAIR. WOMEN PROVE TIME AND AGAIN TO BE FAITHLESS HARRIDANS WHO CAN'T BE TRUSTED. SO PREDICTABLE!
I SHALL RETURN WHEN THE TIME SUITS ME, WENCHES!
DOES HE HAVE A ROCKET-POWERED BUTT?
CAROL, JUST WHAT IN THE HELL TOOK YOU SO LONG?!
?!

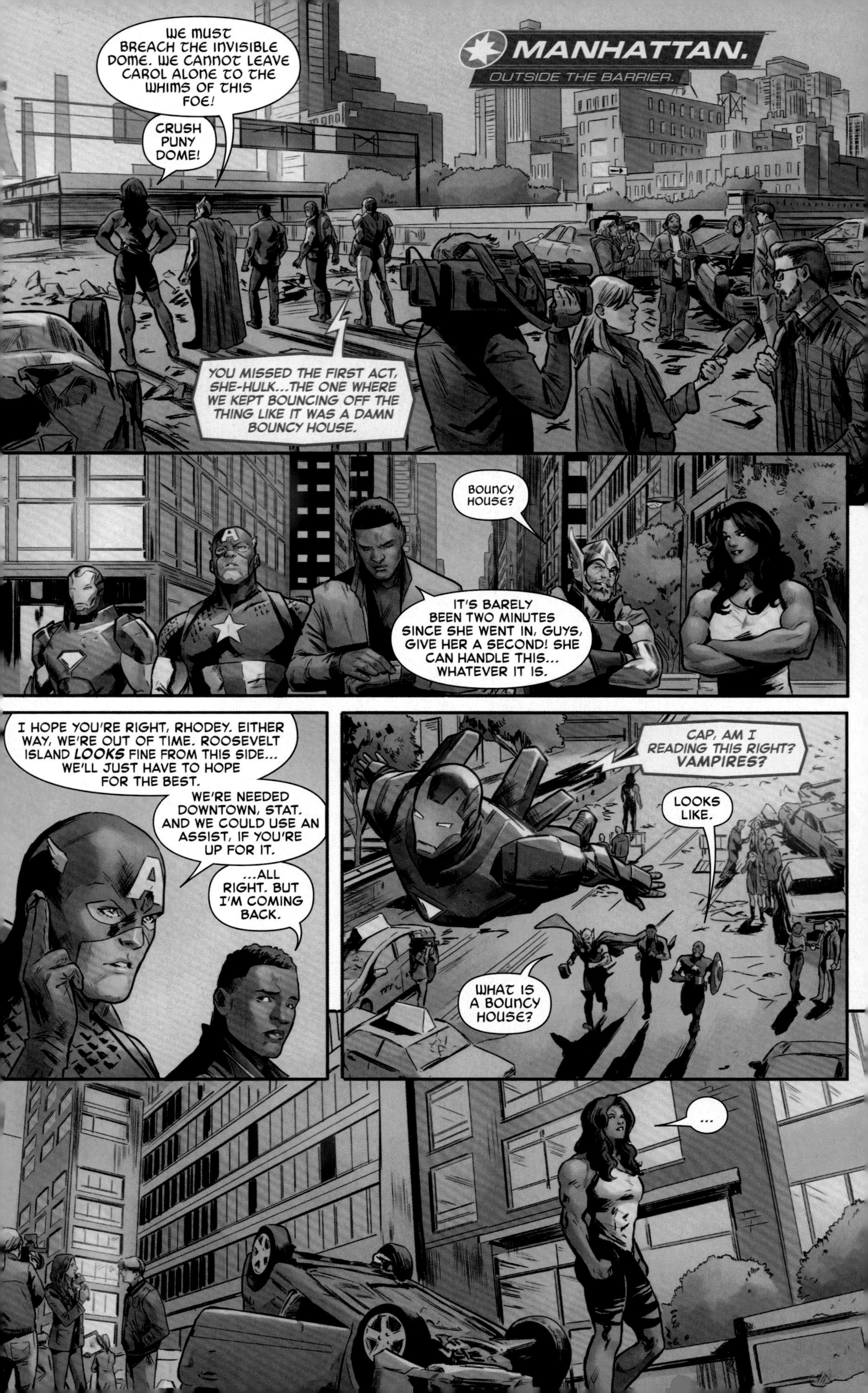
MANHATTAN.
OUTSIDE THE BARRIER.
WE MUST BREACH THE INVISIBLE DOME. WE CANNOT LEAVE CAROL ALONE TO THE WHIMS OF THIS FOE!
CRUSH PUNY DOME!
YOU MISSED THE FIRST ACT, SHE-HULK...THE ONE WHERE WE KEPT BOUNCING OFF THE THING LIKE IT WAS A DAMN BOUNCY HOUSE.
BOUNCY HOUSE?
IT'S BARELY BEEN TWO MINUTES SINCE SHE WENT IN, GUYS, GIVE HER A SECOND! SHE CAN HANDLE THIS... WHATEVER IT IS.
I HOPE YOU'RE RIGHT, RHODEY. EITHER WAY, WE'RE OUT OF TIME. ROOSEVELT ISLAND LOOKS FINE FROM THIS SIDE... WE'LL JUST HAVE TO HOPE FOR THE BEST.
WE'RE NEEDED DOWNTOWN, STAT. AND WE COULD USE AN ASSIST, IF YOU'RE UP FOR IT.
...ALL RIGHT. BUT I'M COMING BACK.
CAP, AM I READING THIS RIGHT? VAMPIRES?
LOOKS LIKE.
WHAT IS A BOUNCY HOUSE?
...

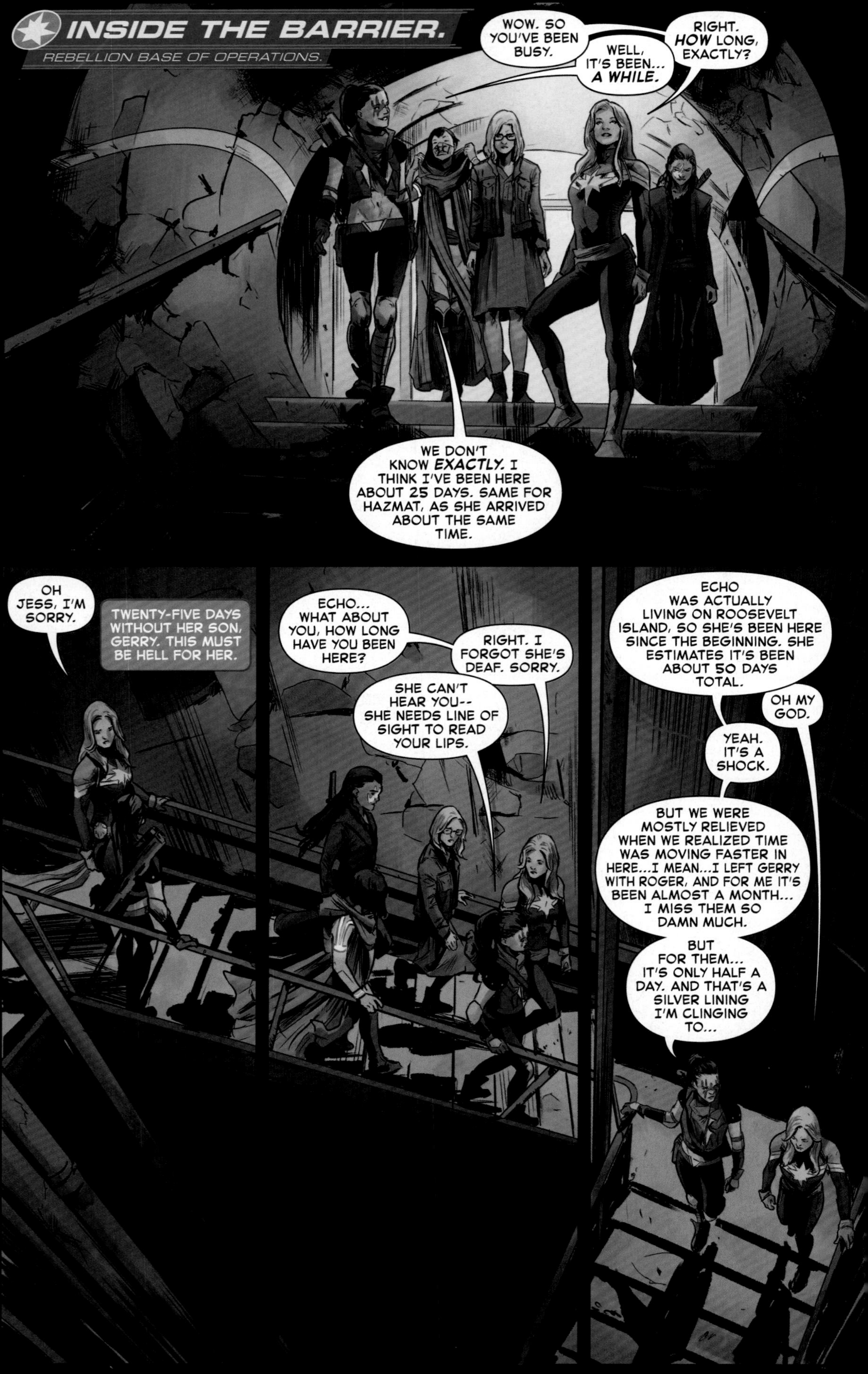
INSIDE THE BARRIER.
REBELLION BASE OF OPERATIONS.
WOW. SO YOU'VE BEEN BUSY.
WELL, IT'S BEEN... A WHILE.
RIGHT. HOW LONG, EXACTLY?
WE DON'T KNOW EXACTLY. I THINK I'VE BEEN HERE ABOUT 25 DAYS. SAME FOR HAZMAT, AS SHE ARRIVED ABOUT THE SAME TIME.
OH JESS, I'M SORRY.
TWENTY-FIVE DAYS WITHOUT HER SON, GERRY. THIS MUST BE HELL FOR HER.
ECHO... WHAT ABOUT YOU, HOW LONG HAVE YOU BEEN HERE?
RIGHT. I FORGOT SHE'S DEAF. SORRY.
SHE CAN'T HEAR YOU-- SHE NEEDS LINE OF SIGHT TO READ YOUR LIPS.
ECHO WAS ACTUALLY LIVING ON ROOSEVELT ISLAND, SO SHE'S BEEN HERE SINCE THE BEGINNING. SHE ESTIMATES IT'S BEEN ABOUT 50 DAYS TOTAL.
OH MY GOD.
YEAH. IT'S A SHOCK.
BUT WE WERE MOSTLY RELIEVED WHEN WE REALIZED TIME WAS MOVING FASTER IN HERE...I MEAN...I LEFT GERRY WITH ROGER, AND FOR ME IT'S BEEN ALMOST A MONTH... I MISS THEM SO DAMN MUCH.
BUT FOR THEM... IT'S ONLY HALF A DAY. AND THAT'S A SILVER LINING I'M CLINGING TO...

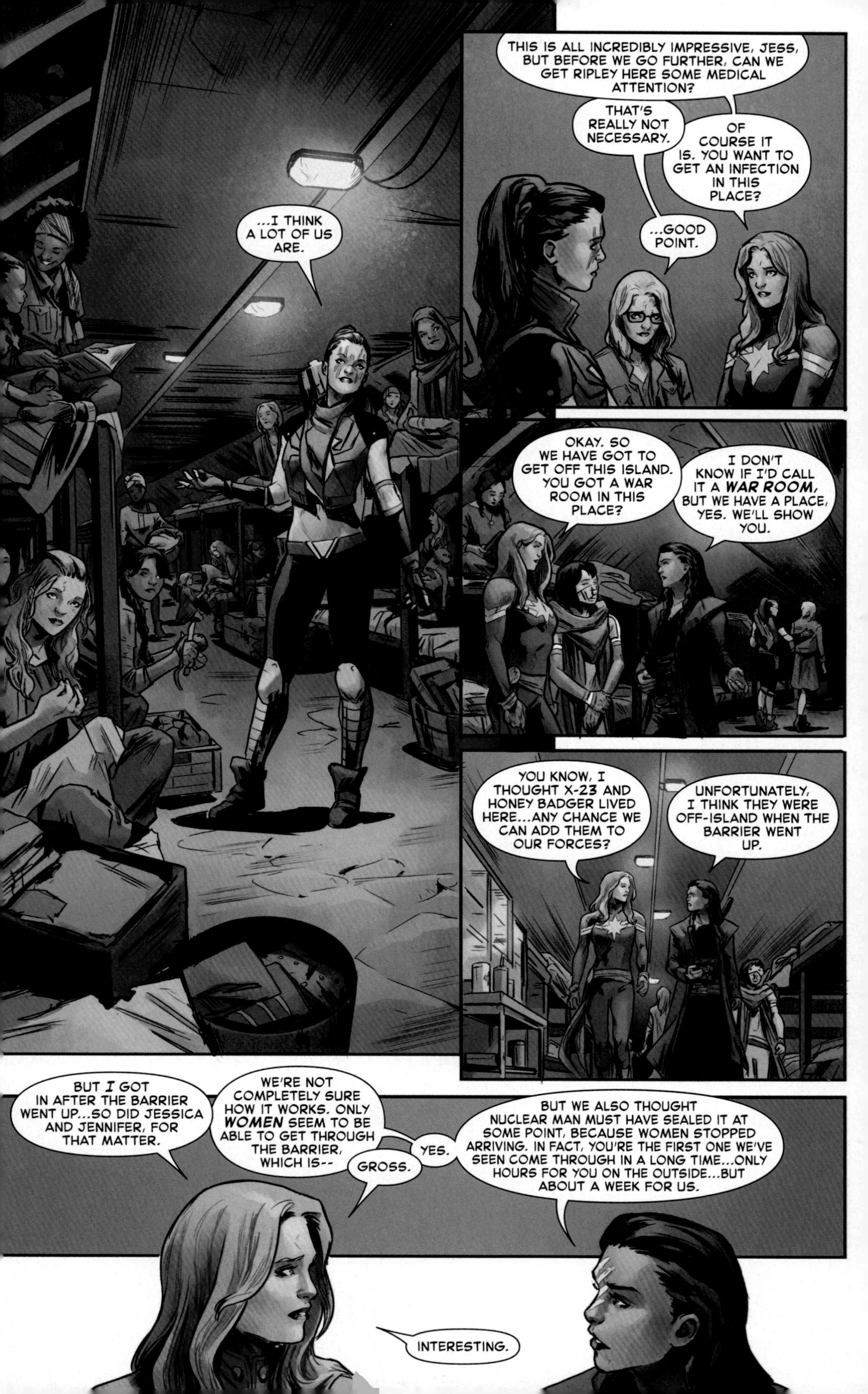
...I THINK A LOT OF US ARE.
THIS IS ALL INCREDIBLY IMPRESSIVE, JESS, BUT BEFORE WE GO FURTHER, CAN WE GET RIPLEY HERE SOME MEDICAL ATTENTION?
THAT'S REALLY NOT NECESSARY.
OF COURSE IT IS. YOU WANT TO GET AN INFECTION IN THIS PLACE?
...GOOD POINT.
OKAY. SO WE HAVE GOT TO GET OFF THIS ISLAND. YOU GOT A WAR ROOM IN THIS PLACE?
I DON'T KNOW IF I'D CALL IT A *WAR ROOM,* BUT WE HAVE A PLACE, YES. WE'LL SHOW YOU.
YOU KNOW, I THOUGHT X-23 AND HONEY BADGER LIVED HERE...ANY CHANCE WE CAN ADD THEM TO OUR FORCES?
UNFORTUNATELY, I THINK THEY WERE OFF-ISLAND WHEN THE BARRIER WENT UP.
BUT *I* GOT IN AFTER THE BARRIER WENT UP...SO DID JESSICA AND JENNIFER, FOR THAT MATTER.
WE'RE NOT COMPLETELY SURE HOW IT WORKS. ONLY ***WOMEN*** SEEM TO BE ABLE TO GET THROUGH THE BARRIER, WHICH IS--
GROSS.
YES.
BUT WE ALSO THOUGHT NUCLEAR MAN MUST HAVE SEALED IT AT SOME POINT, BECAUSE WOMEN STOPPED ARRIVING. IN FACT, YOU'RE THE FIRST ONE WE'VE SEEN COME THROUGH IN A LONG TIME...ONLY HOURS FOR YOU ON THE OUTSIDE...BUT ABOUT A WEEK FOR US.
INTERESTING.

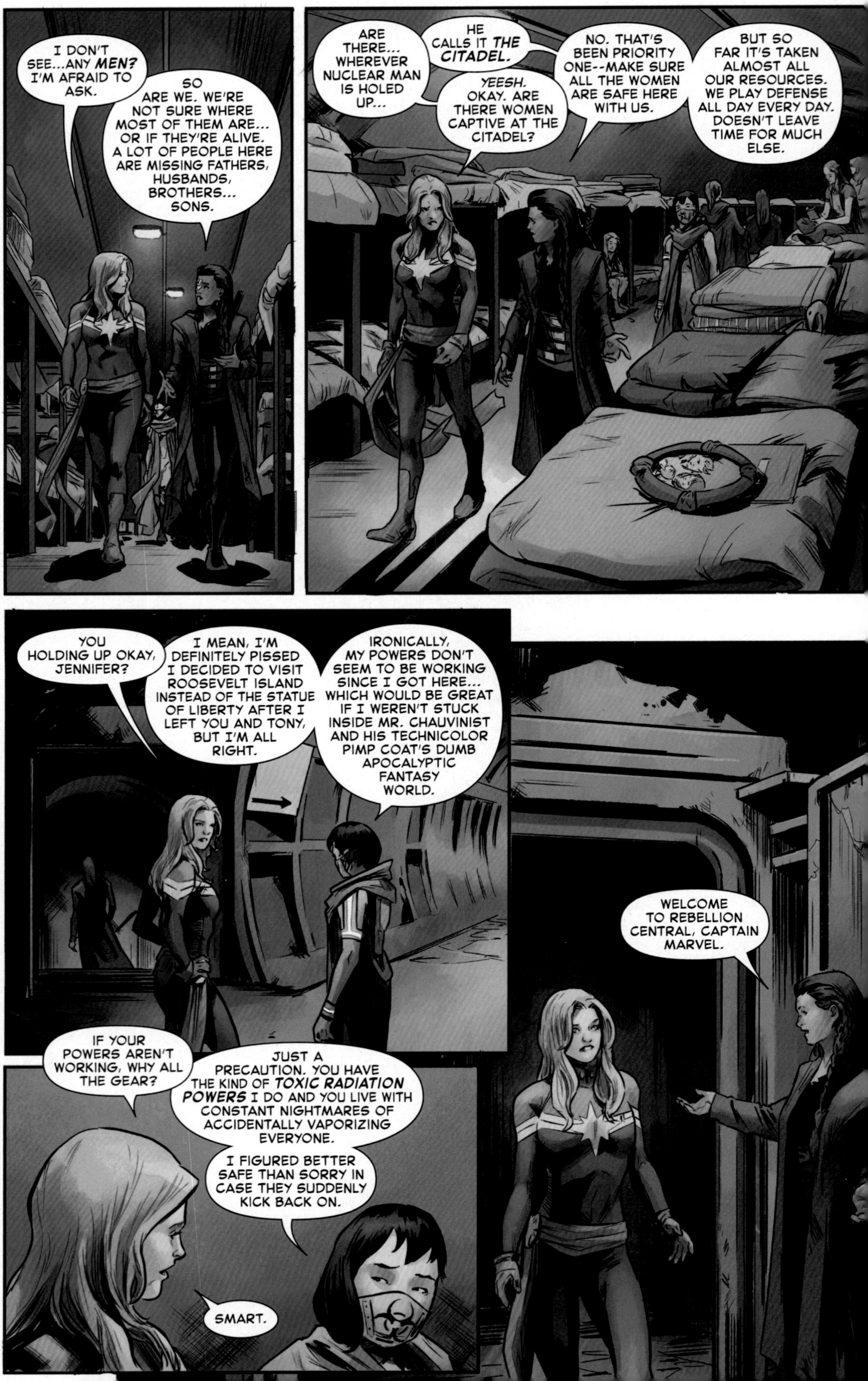
I DON'T SEE...ANY *MEN?* I'M AFRAID TO ASK.
SO ARE WE. WE'RE NOT SURE WHERE MOST OF THEM ARE... OR IF THEY'RE ALIVE. A LOT OF PEOPLE HERE ARE MISSING FATHERS, HUSBANDS, BROTHERS... SONS.
ARE THERE... WHEREVER NUCLEAR MAN IS HOLED UP...
HE CALLS IT *THE CITADEL.*
YEESH. OKAY. ARE THERE WOMEN CAPTIVE AT THE CITADEL?
NO. THAT'S BEEN PRIORITY ONE--MAKE SURE ALL THE WOMEN ARE SAFE HERE WITH US.
BUT SO FAR IT'S TAKEN ALMOST ALL OUR RESOURCES. WE PLAY DEFENSE ALL DAY EVERY DAY. DOESN'T LEAVE TIME FOR MUCH ELSE.
YOU HOLDING UP OKAY, JENNIFER?
I MEAN, I'M DEFINITELY PISSED I DECIDED TO VISIT ROOSEVELT ISLAND INSTEAD OF THE STATUE OF LIBERTY AFTER I LEFT YOU AND TONY, BUT I'M ALL RIGHT.
IRONICALLY, MY POWERS DON'T SEEM TO BE WORKING SINCE I GOT HERE... WHICH WOULD BE GREAT IF I WEREN'T STUCK INSIDE MR. CHAUVINIST AND HIS TECHNICOLOR PIMP COAT'S DUMB APOCALYPTIC FANTASY WORLD.
IF YOUR POWERS AREN'T WORKING, WHY ALL THE GEAR?
JUST A PRECAUTION. YOU HAVE THE KIND OF *TOXIC RADIATION POWERS* I DO AND YOU LIVE WITH CONSTANT NIGHTMARES OF ACCIDENTALLY VAPORIZING EVERYONE.
I FIGURED BETTER SAFE THAN SORRY IN CASE THEY SUDDENLY KICK BACK ON.
SMART.
WELCOME TO REBELLION CENTRAL, CAPTAIN MARVEL.

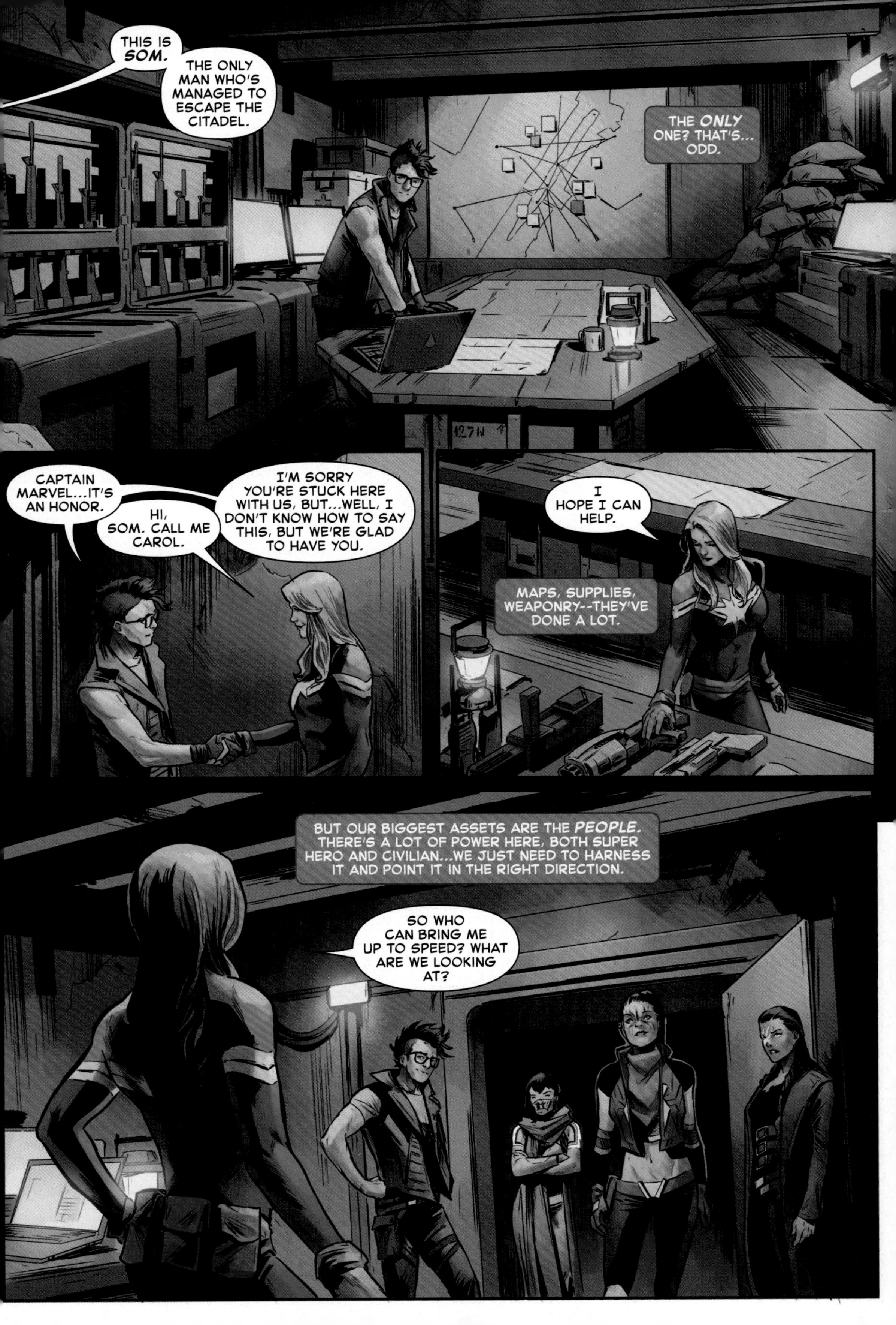
THIS IS SOM.
THE ONLY MAN WHO'S MANAGED TO ESCAPE THE CITADEL.
THE ONLY ONE? THAT'S... ODD.
CAPTAIN MARVEL...IT'S AN HONOR.
HI, SOM. CALL ME CAROL.
I'M SORRY YOU'RE STUCK HERE WITH US, BUT...WELL, I DON'T KNOW HOW TO SAY THIS, BUT WE'RE GLAD TO HAVE YOU.
I HOPE I CAN HELP.
MAPS, SUPPLIES, WEAPONRY--THEY'VE DONE A LOT.
BUT OUR BIGGEST ASSETS ARE THE PEOPLE. THERE'S A LOT OF POWER HERE, BOTH SUPER HERO AND CIVILIAN...WE JUST NEED TO HARNESS IT AND POINT IT IN THE RIGHT DIRECTION.
SO WHO CAN BRING ME UP TO SPEED? WHAT ARE WE LOOKING AT?

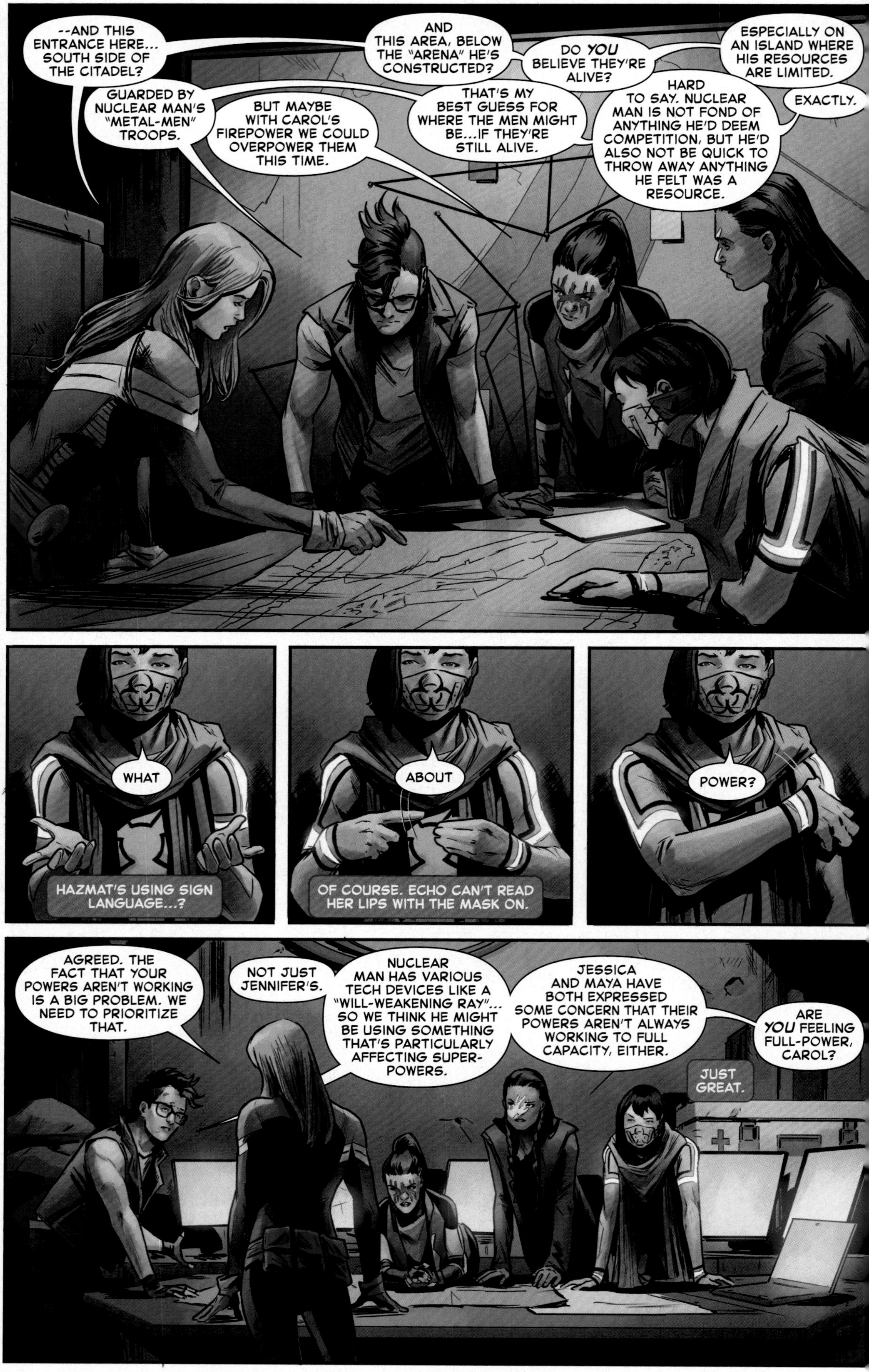
--AND THIS ENTRANCE HERE... SOUTH SIDE OF THE CITADEL?
GUARDED BY NUCLEAR MAN'S "METAL-MEN" TROOPS.
BUT MAYBE WITH CAROL'S FIREPOWER WE COULD OVERPOWER THEM THIS TIME.
AND THIS AREA, BELOW THE "ARENA" HE'S CONSTRUCTED?
THAT'S MY BEST GUESS FOR WHERE THE MEN MIGHT BE...IF THEY'RE STILL ALIVE.
DO YOU BELIEVE THEY'RE ALIVE?
HARD TO SAY. NUCLEAR MAN IS NOT FOND OF ANYTHING HE'D DEEM COMPETITION, BUT HE'D ALSO NOT BE QUICK TO THROW AWAY ANYTHING HE FELT WAS A RESOURCE.
ESPECIALLY ON AN ISLAND WHERE HIS RESOURCES ARE LIMITED.
EXACTLY.
WHAT
HAZMAT'S USING SIGN LANGUAGE...?
ABOUT
OF COURSE. ECHO CAN'T READ HER LIPS WITH THE MASK ON.
POWER?
AGREED. THE FACT THAT YOUR POWERS AREN'T WORKING IS A BIG PROBLEM. WE NEED TO PRIORITIZE THAT.
NOT JUST JENNIFER'S.
NUCLEAR MAN HAS VARIOUS TECH DEVICES LIKE A "WILL-WEAKENING RAY"... SO WE THINK HE MIGHT BE USING SOMETHING THAT'S PARTICULARLY AFFECTING SUPER-POWERS.
JESSICA AND MAYA HAVE BOTH EXPRESSED SOME CONCERN THAT THEIR POWERS AREN'T ALWAYS WORKING TO FULL CAPACITY, EITHER.
ARE YOU FEELING FULL-POWER, CAROL?
JUST GREAT.

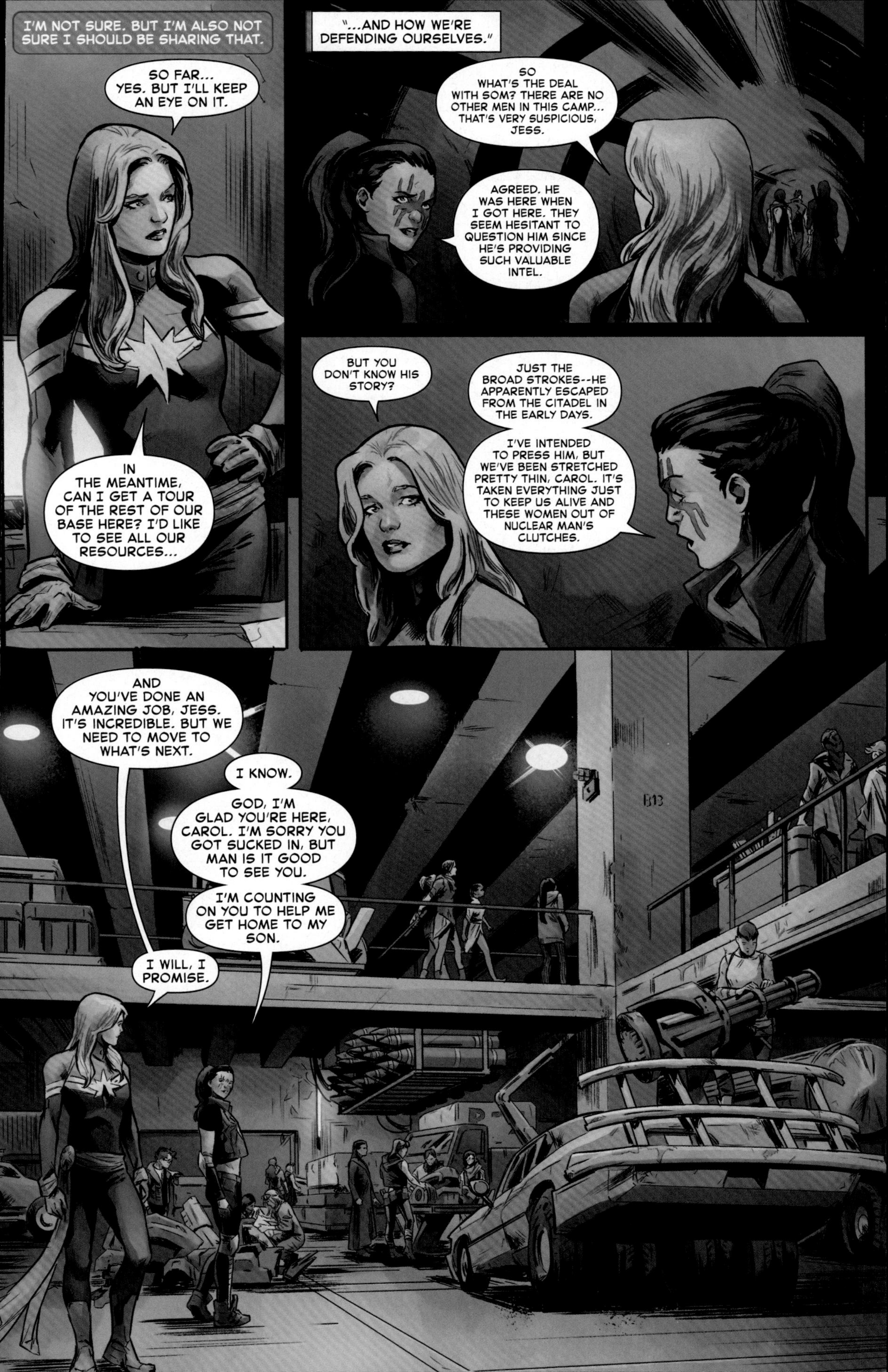
I'M NOT SURE. BUT I'M ALSO NOT SURE I SHOULD BE SHARING THAT.
SO FAR... YES. BUT I'LL KEEP AN EYE ON IT.
IN THE MEANTIME, CAN I GET A TOUR OF THE REST OF OUR BASE HERE? I'D LIKE TO SEE ALL OUR RESOURCES...
"...AND HOW WE'RE DEFENDING OURSELVES."
SO WHAT'S THE DEAL WITH SOM? THERE ARE NO OTHER MEN IN THIS CAMP... THAT'S VERY SUSPICIOUS, JESS.
AGREED. HE WAS HERE WHEN I GOT HERE. THEY SEEM HESITANT TO QUESTION HIM SINCE HE'S PROVIDING SUCH VALUABLE INTEL.
BUT YOU DON'T KNOW HIS STORY?
JUST THE BROAD STROKES--HE APPARENTLY ESCAPED FROM THE CITADEL IN THE EARLY DAYS.
I'VE INTENDED TO PRESS HIM, BUT WE'VE BEEN STRETCHED PRETTY THIN, CAROL. IT'S TAKEN EVERYTHING JUST TO KEEP US ALIVE AND THESE WOMEN OUT OF NUCLEAR MAN'S CLUTCHES.
AND YOU'VE DONE AN AMAZING JOB, JESS. IT'S INCREDIBLE. BUT WE NEED TO MOVE TO WHAT'S NEXT.
I KNOW.
GOD, I'M GLAD YOU'RE HERE, CAROL. I'M SORRY YOU GOT SUCKED IN, BUT MAN IS IT GOOD TO SEE YOU.
I'M COUNTING ON YOU TO HELP ME GET HOME TO MY SON.
I WILL, I PROMISE.
B13

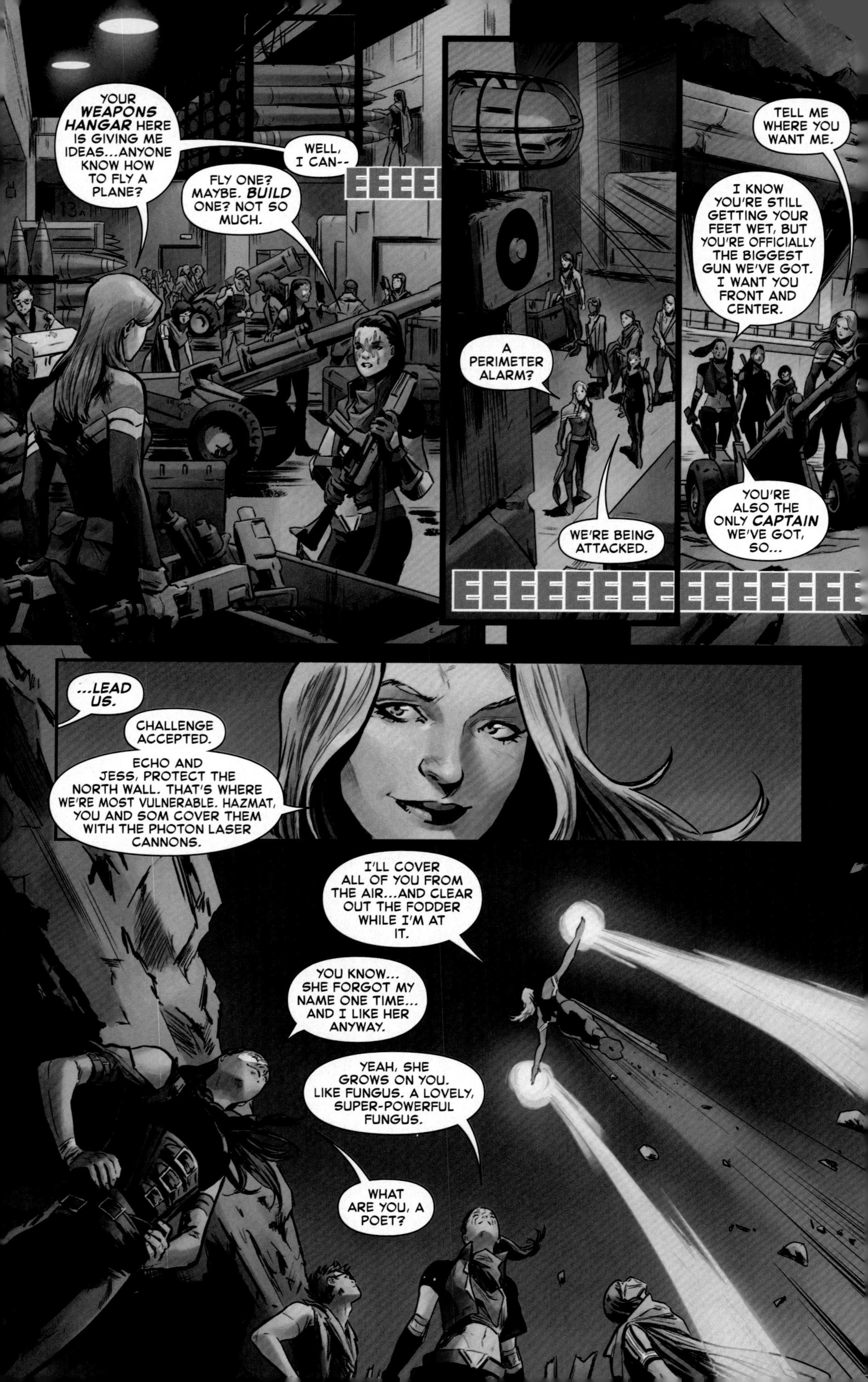
YOUR WEAPONS HANGAR HERE IS GIVING ME IDEAS...ANYONE KNOW HOW TO FLY A PLANE?
WELL, I CAN--
FLY ONE? MAYBE. BUILD ONE? NOT SO MUCH.
EEEE
A PERIMETER ALARM?
WE'RE BEING ATTACKED.
EEEEEEEEEEEEEEEEE
TELL ME WHERE YOU WANT ME.
I KNOW YOU'RE STILL GETTING YOUR FEET WET, BUT YOU'RE OFFICIALLY THE BIGGEST GUN WE'VE GOT. I WANT YOU FRONT AND CENTER.
YOU'RE ALSO THE ONLY CAPTAIN WE'VE GOT, SO...
...LEAD US.
CHALLENGE ACCEPTED.
ECHO AND JESS, PROTECT THE NORTH WALL. THAT'S WHERE WE'RE MOST VULNERABLE. HAZMAT, YOU AND SOM COVER THEM WITH THE PHOTON LASER CANNONS.
I'LL COVER ALL OF YOU FROM THE AIR...AND CLEAR OUT THE FODDER WHILE I'M AT IT.
YOU KNOW... SHE FORGOT MY NAME ONE TIME... AND I LIKE HER ANYWAY.
YEAH, SHE GROWS ON YOU. LIKE FUNGUS. A LOVELY, SUPER-POWERFUL FUNGUS.
WHAT ARE YOU, A POET?

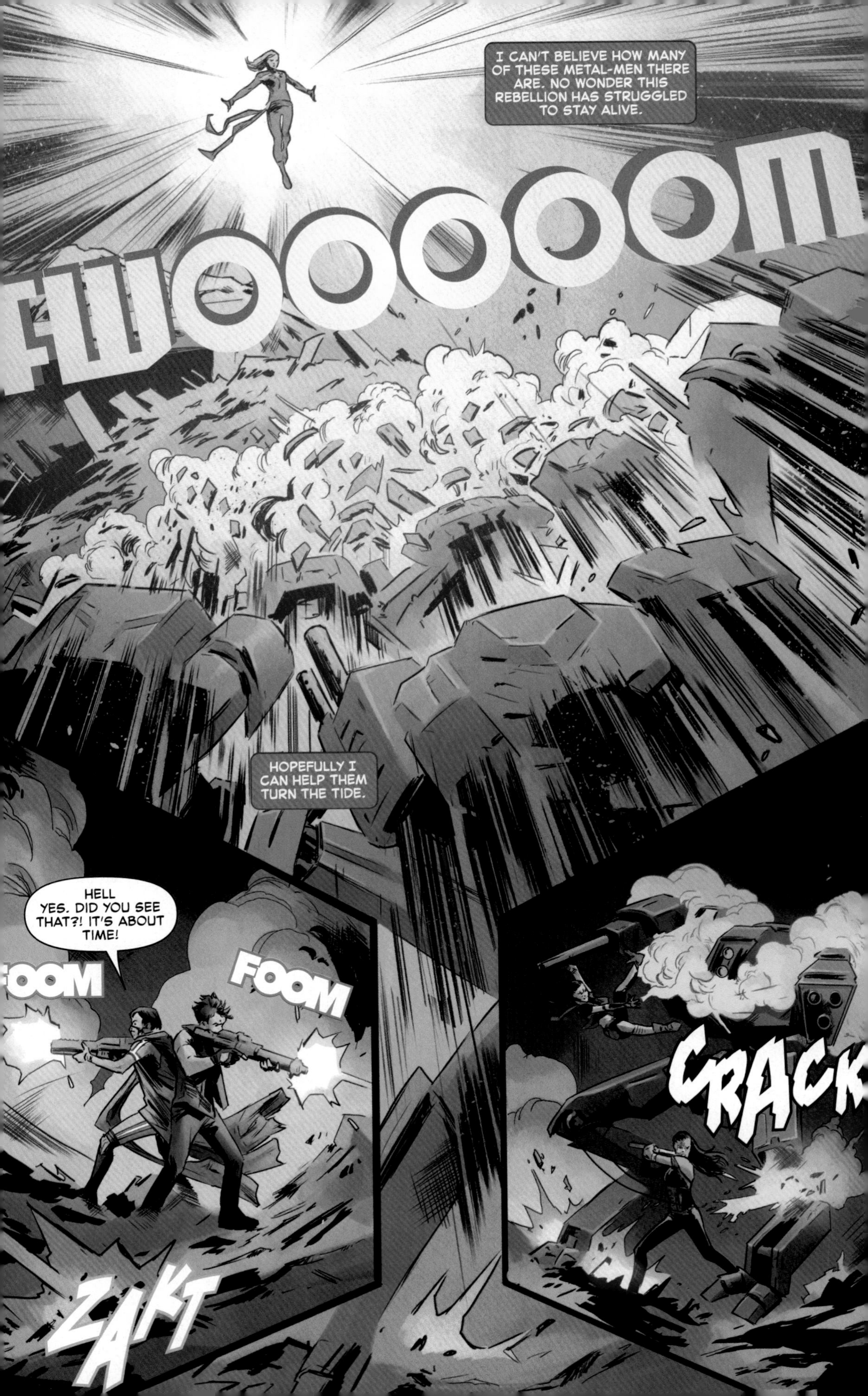
I CAN'T BELIEVE HOW MANY OF THESE METAL-MEN THERE ARE. NO WONDER THIS REBELLION HAS STRUGGLED TO STAY ALIVE.
FWOOOOOOM
HOPEFULLY I CAN HELP THEM TURN THE TIDE.
HELL YES. DID YOU SEE THAT?! IT'S ABOUT TIME!
FOOM
FOOM
ZAKT
CRACK

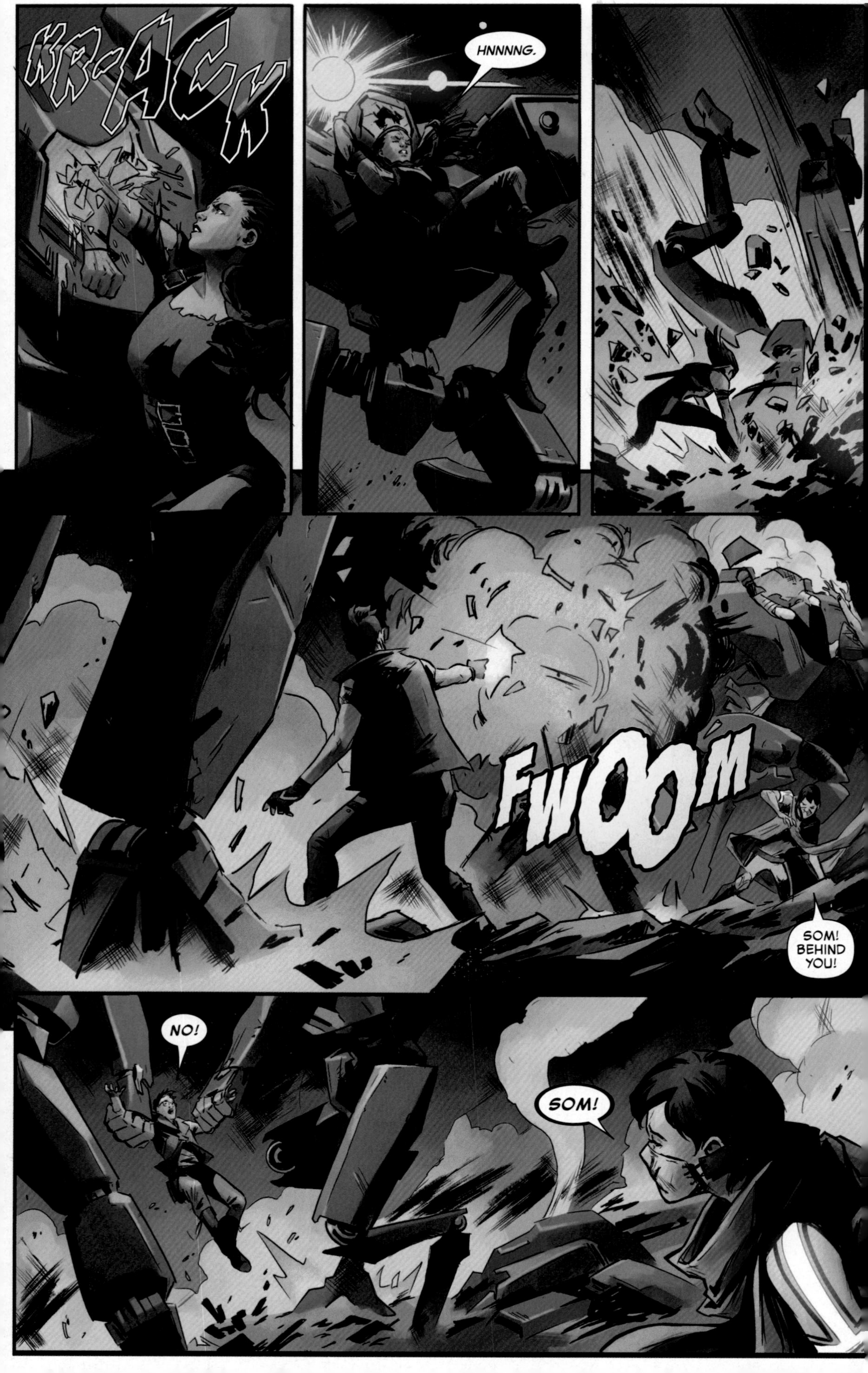
KR-ACK
HNNNNG.
FWOOM
SOM! BEHIND YOU!
NO!
SOM!

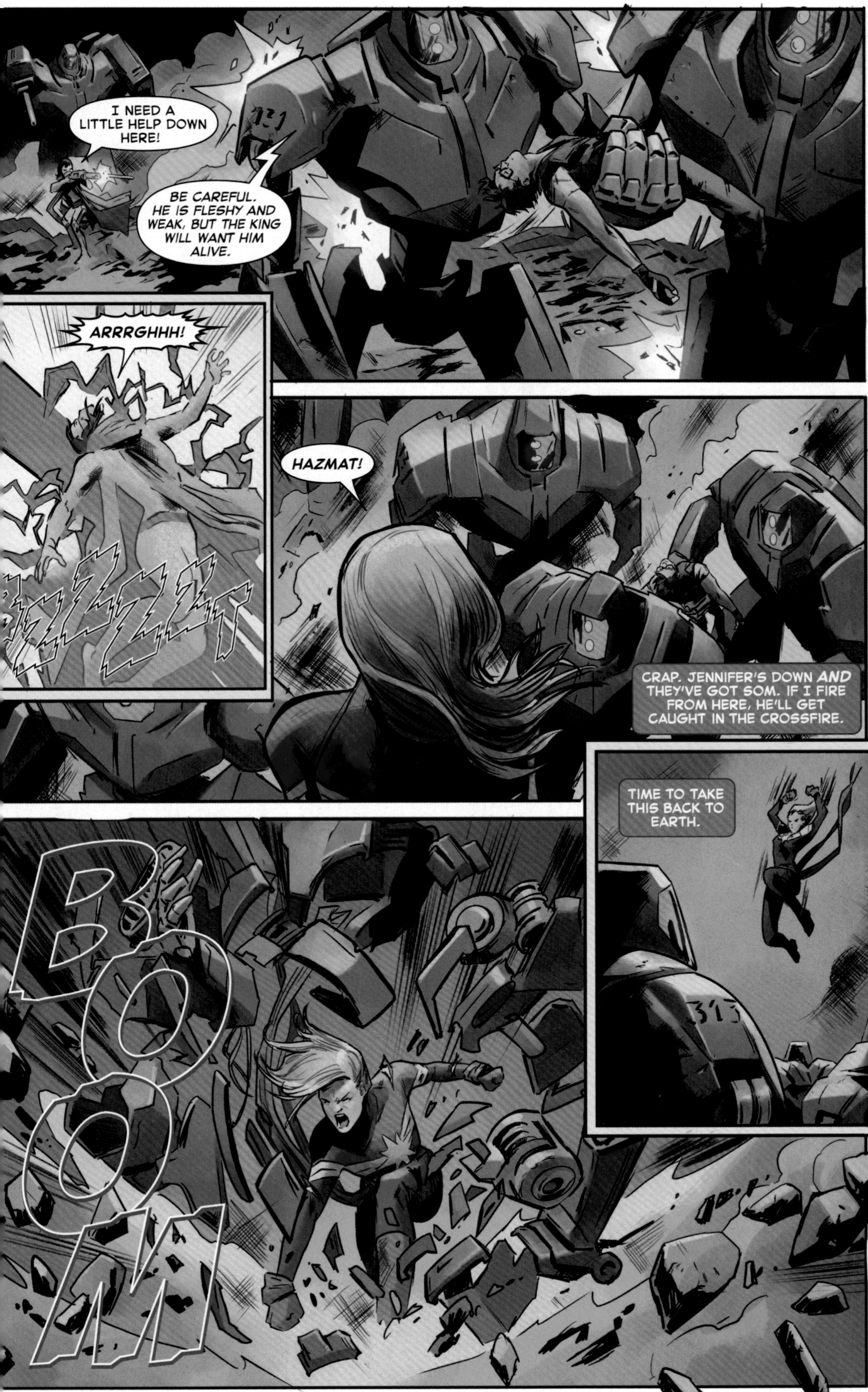
I NEED A LITTLE HELP DOWN HERE!
BE CAREFUL. HE IS FLESHY AND WEAK, BUT THE KING WILL WANT HIM ALIVE.
ARRRGHHH!
ZZZZT
HAZMAT!
CRAP. JENNIFER'S DOWN AND THEY'VE GOT SOM. IF I FIRE FROM HERE, HE'LL GET CAUGHT IN THE CROSSFIRE.
TIME TO TAKE THIS BACK TO EARTH.
BOOOM

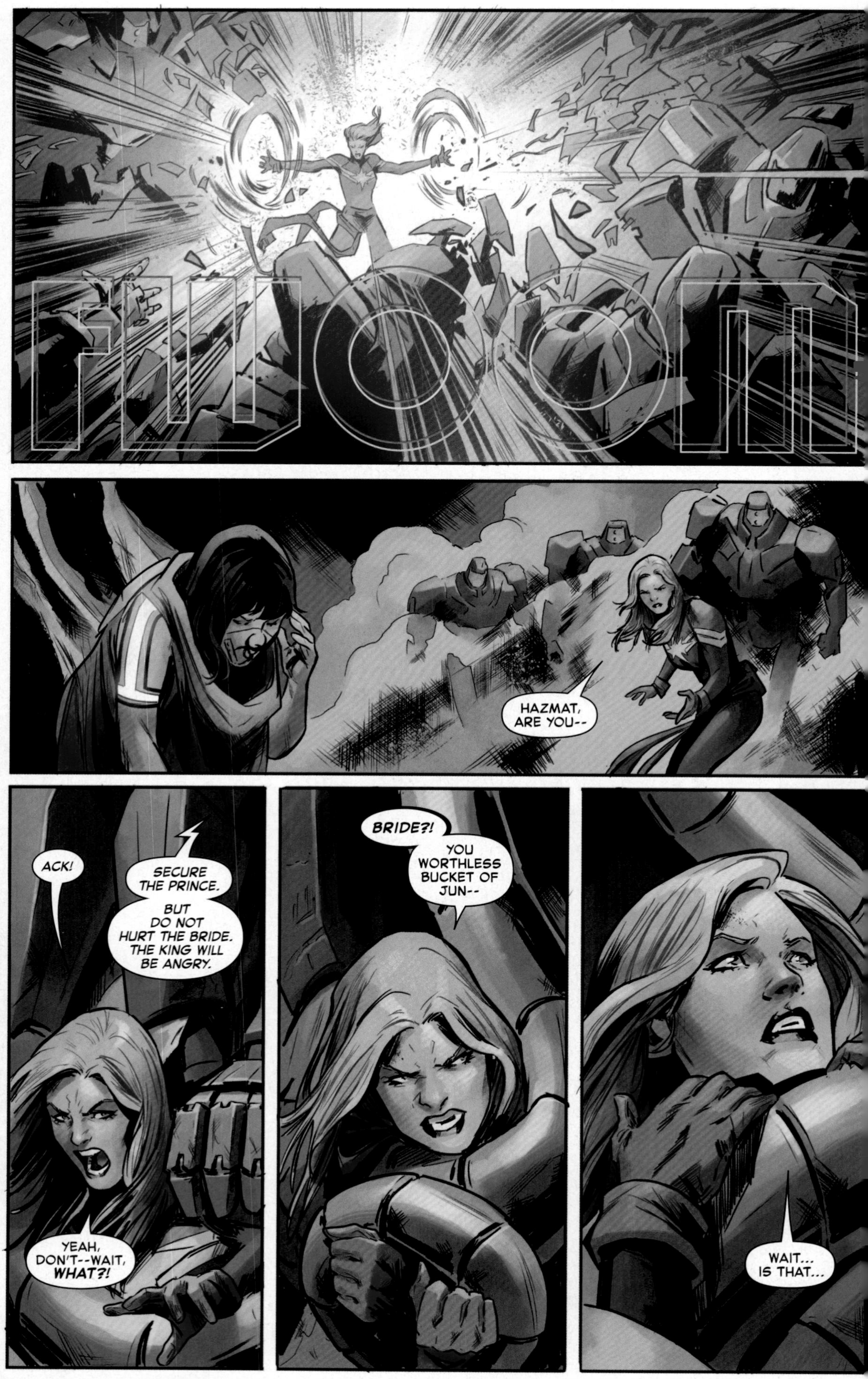
FWOOM
HAZMAT, ARE YOU--
ACK!
SECURE THE PRINCE.
BUT DO NOT HURT THE BRIDE. THE KING WILL BE ANGRY.
YEAH, DON'T--WAIT, WHAT?!
BRIDE?!
YOU WORTHLESS BUCKET OF JUN--
WAIT... IS THAT...

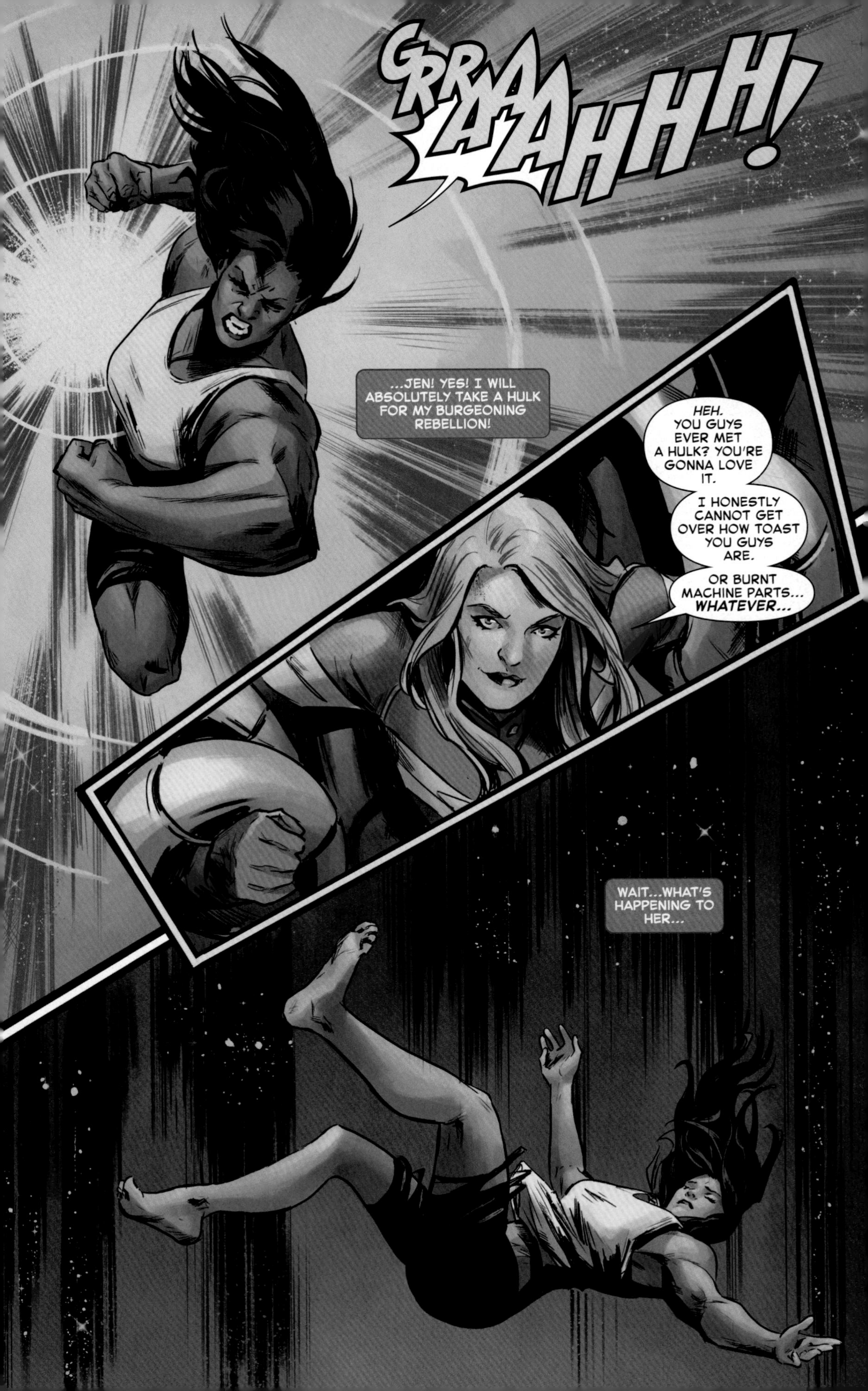
GRRAAAHHH!
...JEN! YES! I WILL ABSOLUTELY TAKE A HULK FOR MY BURGEONING REBELLION!
HEH. YOU GUYS EVER MET A HULK? YOU'RE GONNA LOVE IT.
I HONESTLY CANNOT GET OVER HOW TOAST YOU GUYS ARE.
OR BURNT MACHINE PARTS... WHATEVER...
WAIT...WHAT'S HAPPENING TO HER...

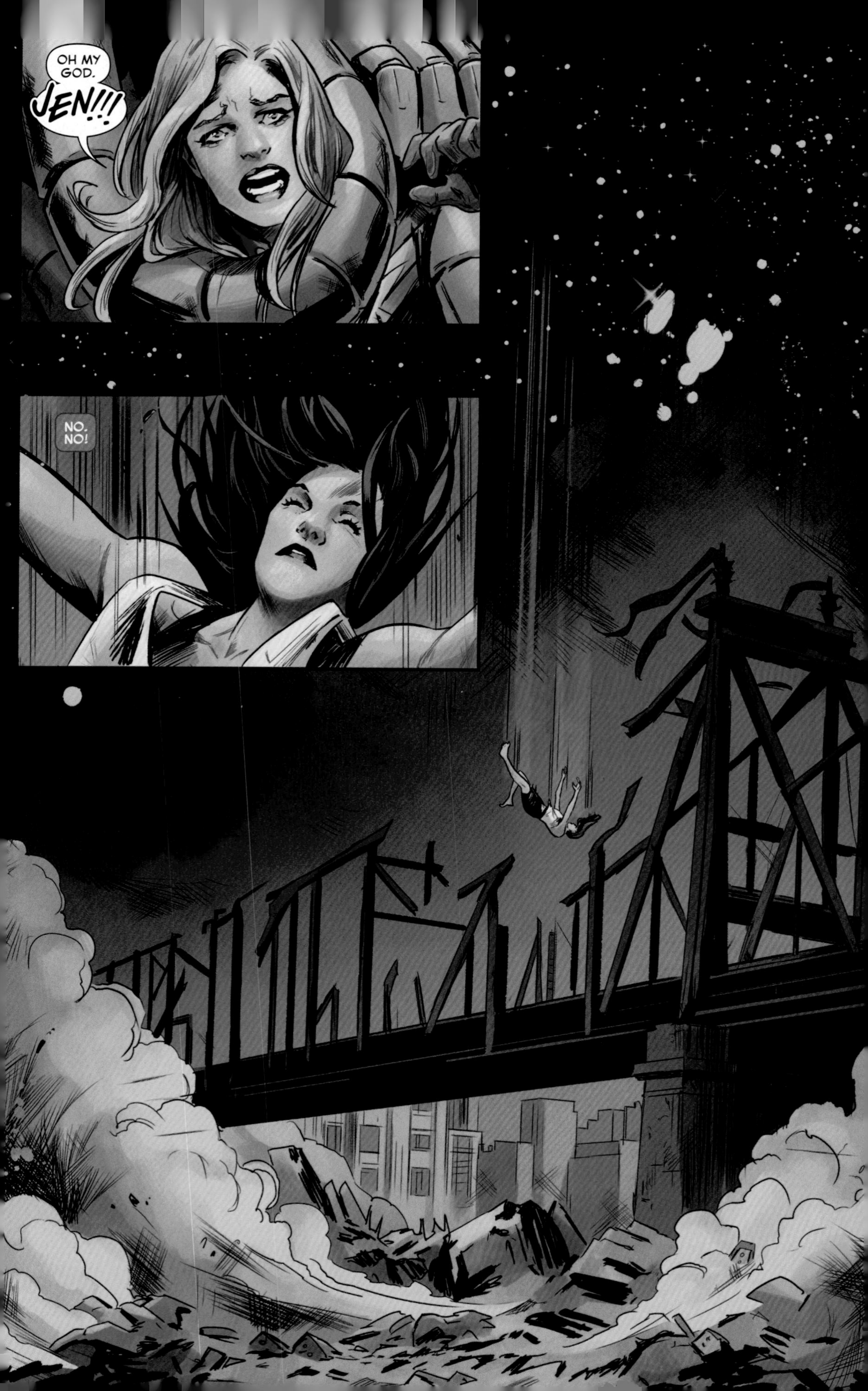
OH MY GOD.
JEN!!!
NO. NO!

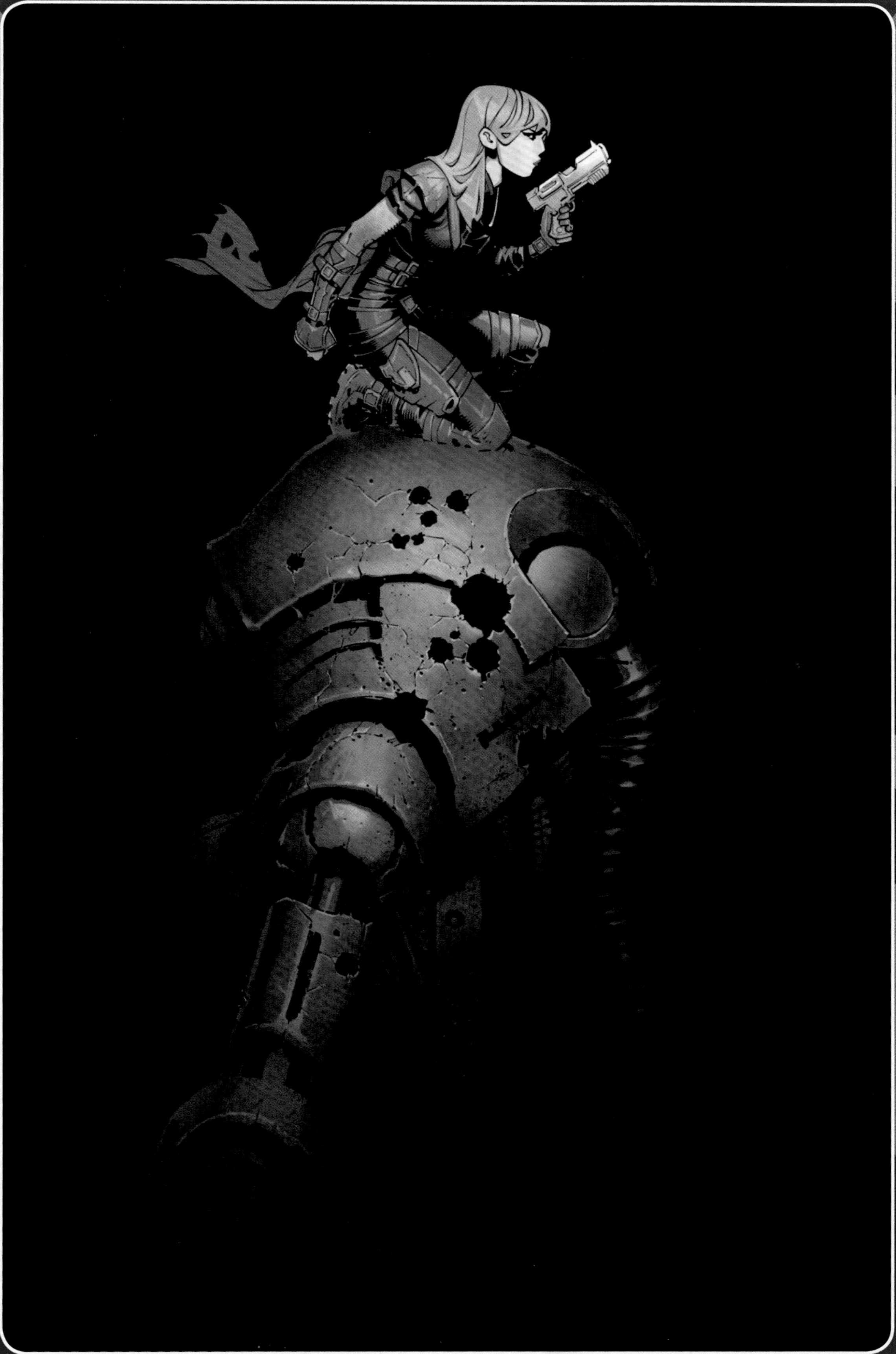

CHRIS BACHALO
2 VARIANT

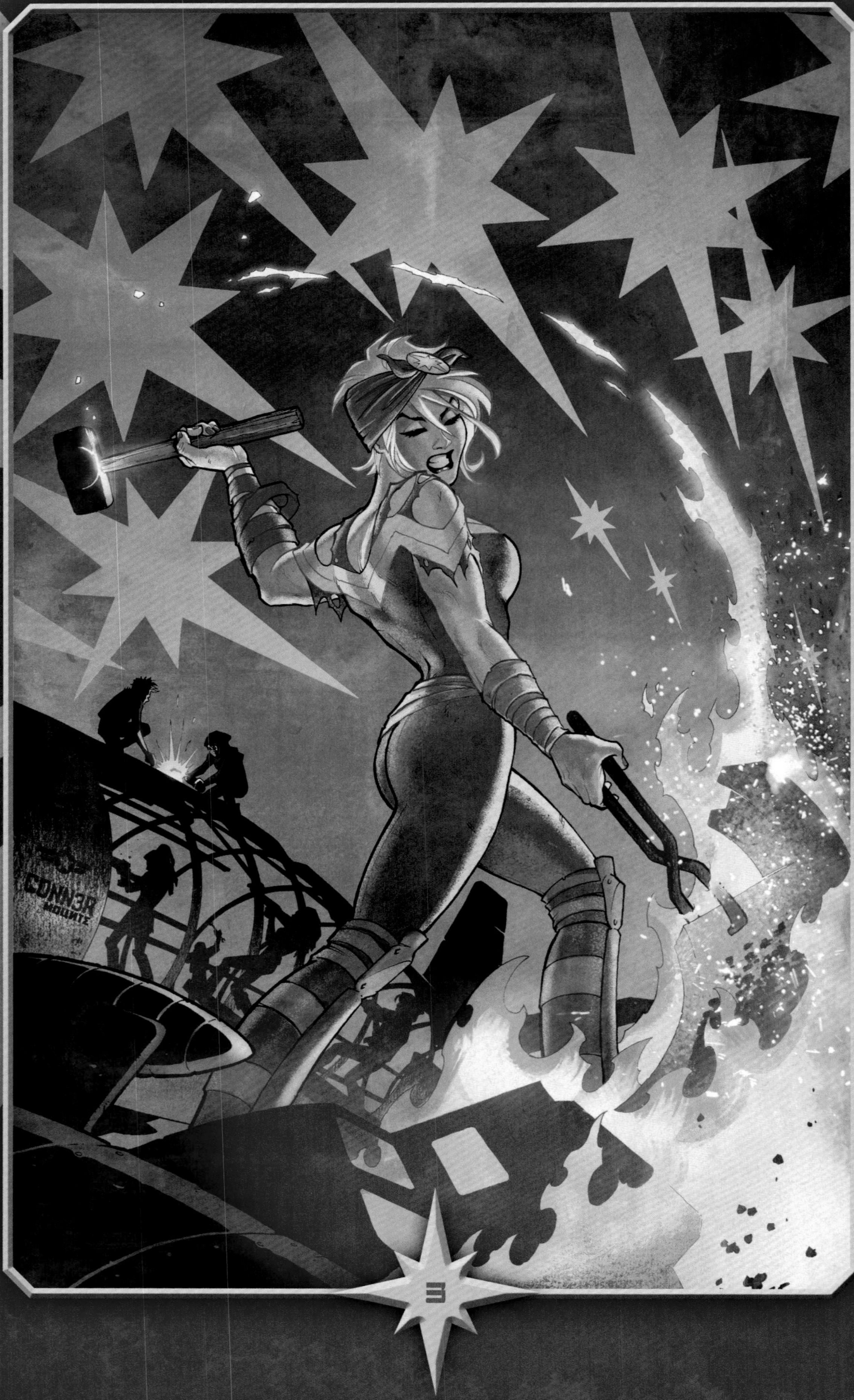
CONN3R
MOUNTZ
3

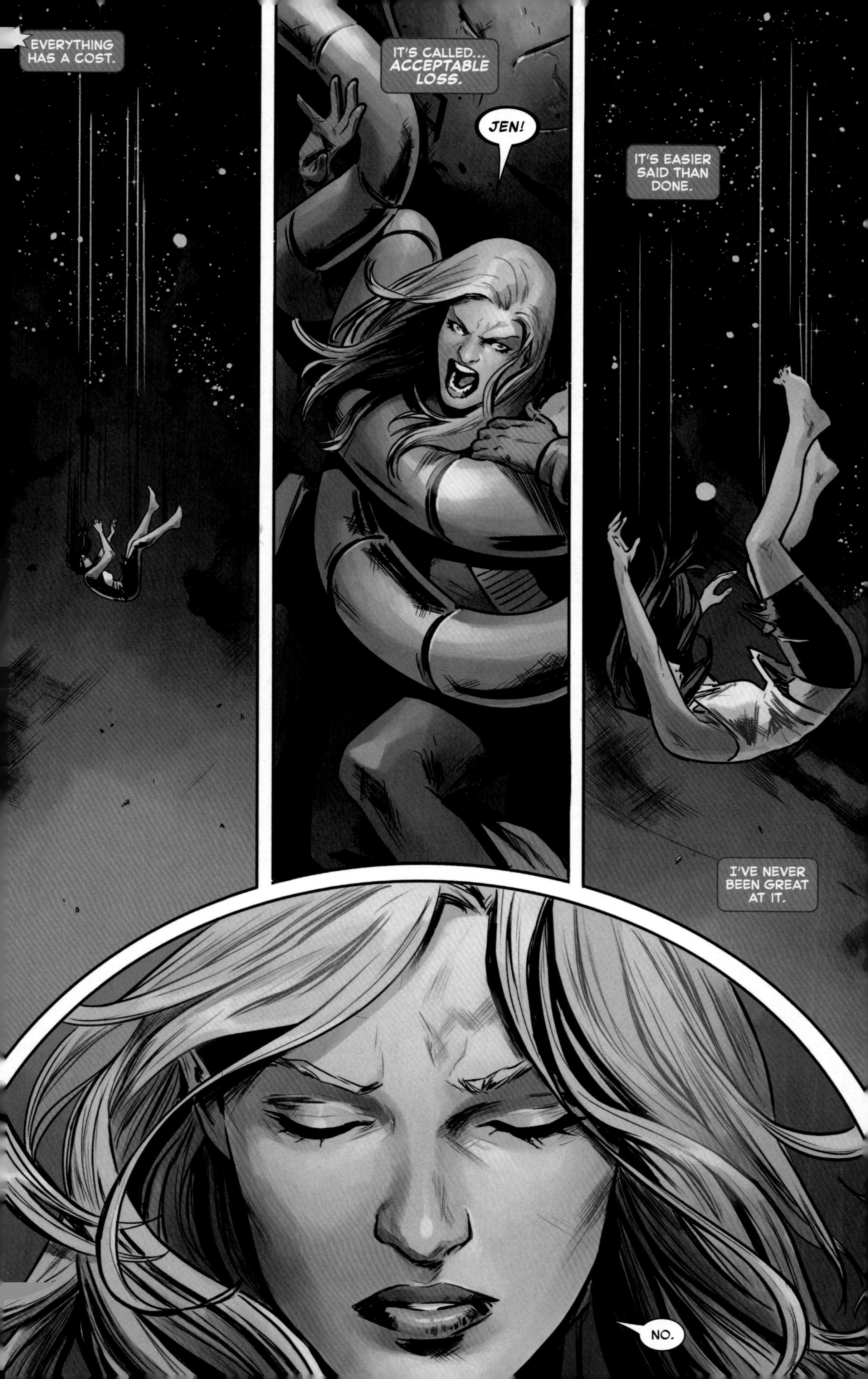
EVERYTHING HAS A COST.
IT'S CALLED... ACCEPTABLE LOSS.
JEN!
IT'S EASIER SAID THAN DONE.
I'VE NEVER BEEN GREAT AT IT.
NO.

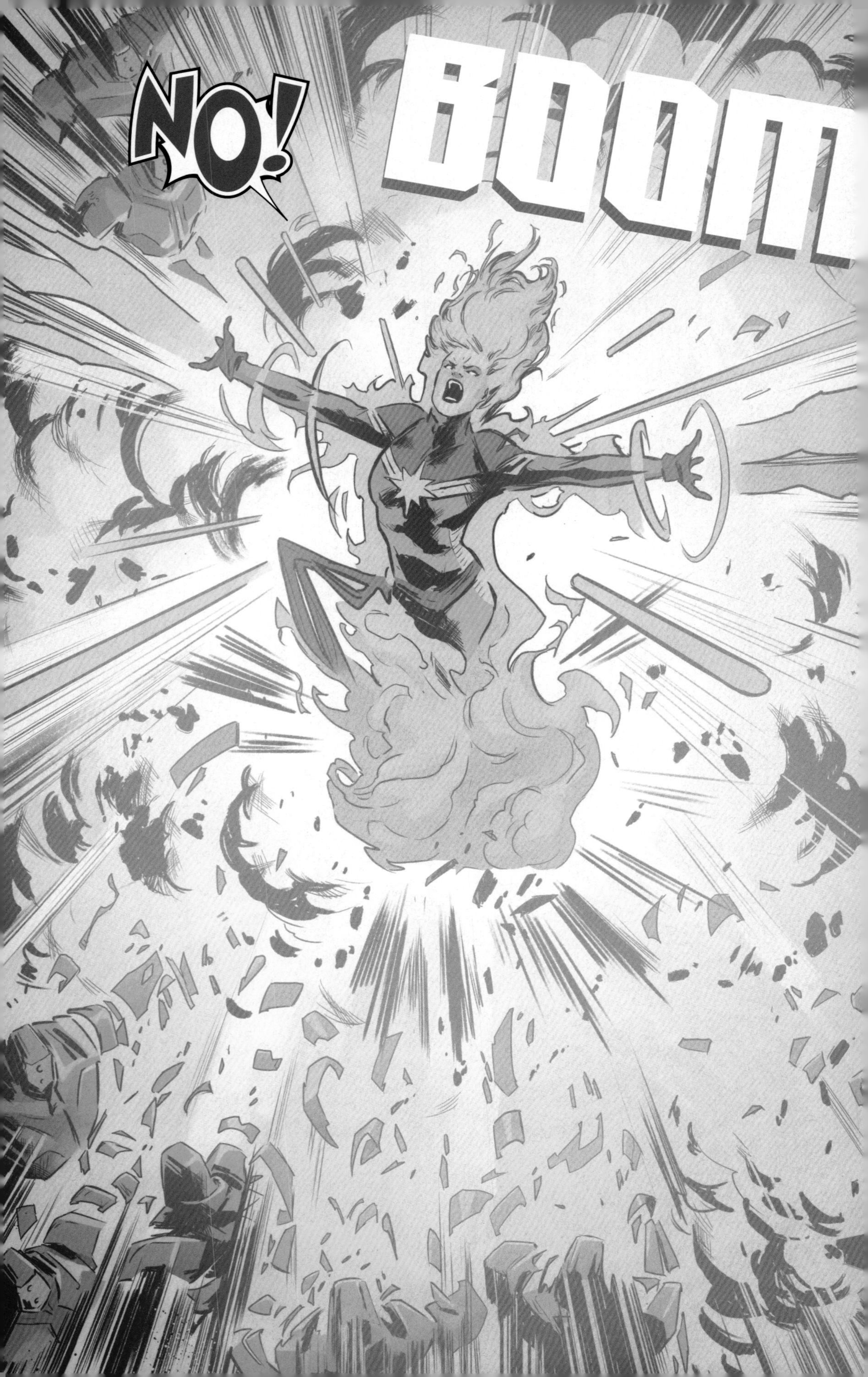
NO!
BOOM

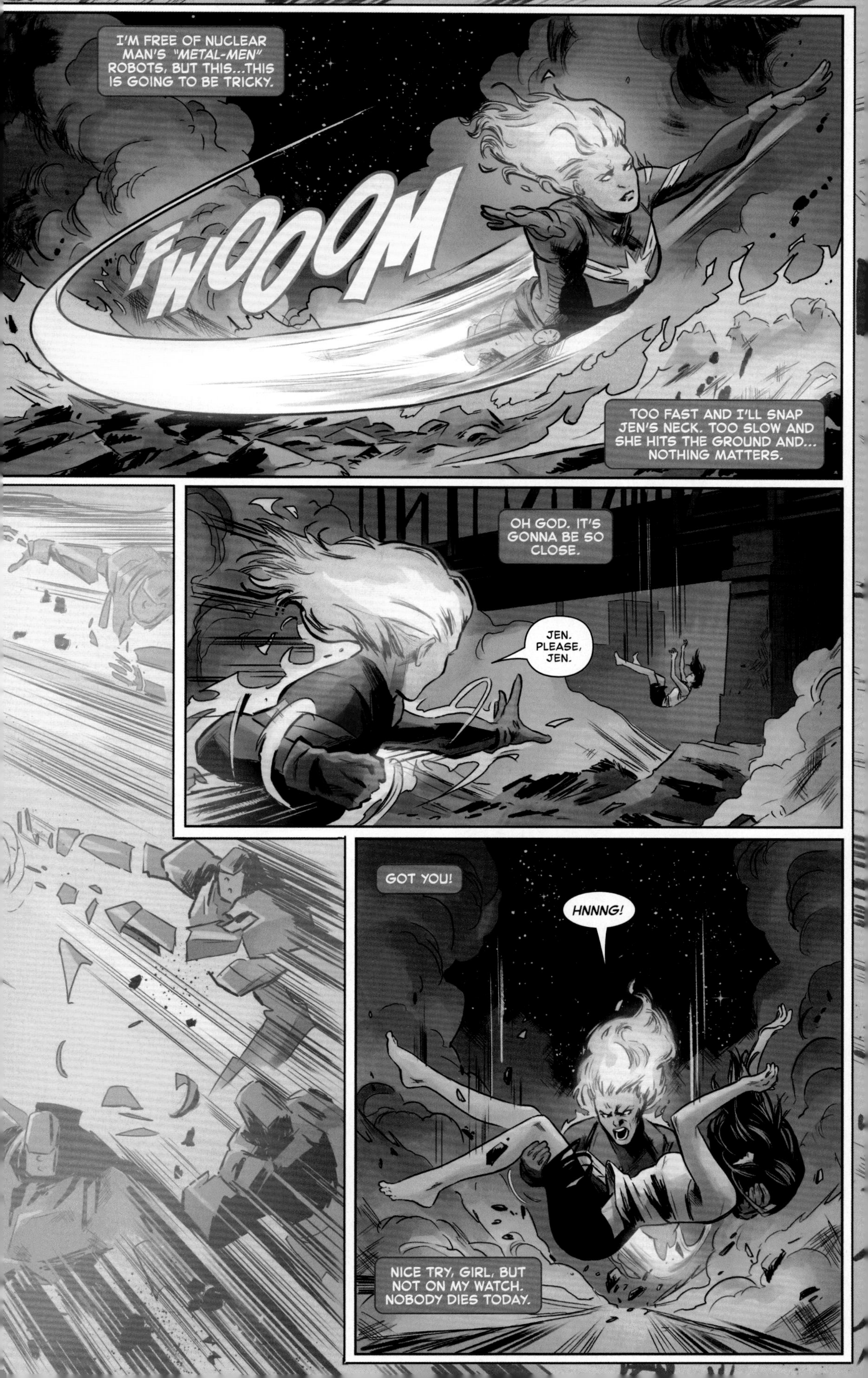
I'M FREE OF NUCLEAR MAN'S "METAL-MEN" ROBOTS, BUT THIS...THIS IS GOING TO BE TRICKY.
FWOOOM
TOO FAST AND I'LL SNAP JEN'S NECK. TOO SLOW AND SHE HITS THE GROUND AND... NOTHING MATTERS.
OH GOD. IT'S GONNA BE SO CLOSE.
JEN. PLEASE, JEN.
GOT YOU!
HNNNG!
NICE TRY, GIRL, BUT NOT ON MY WATCH. NOBODY DIES TODAY.

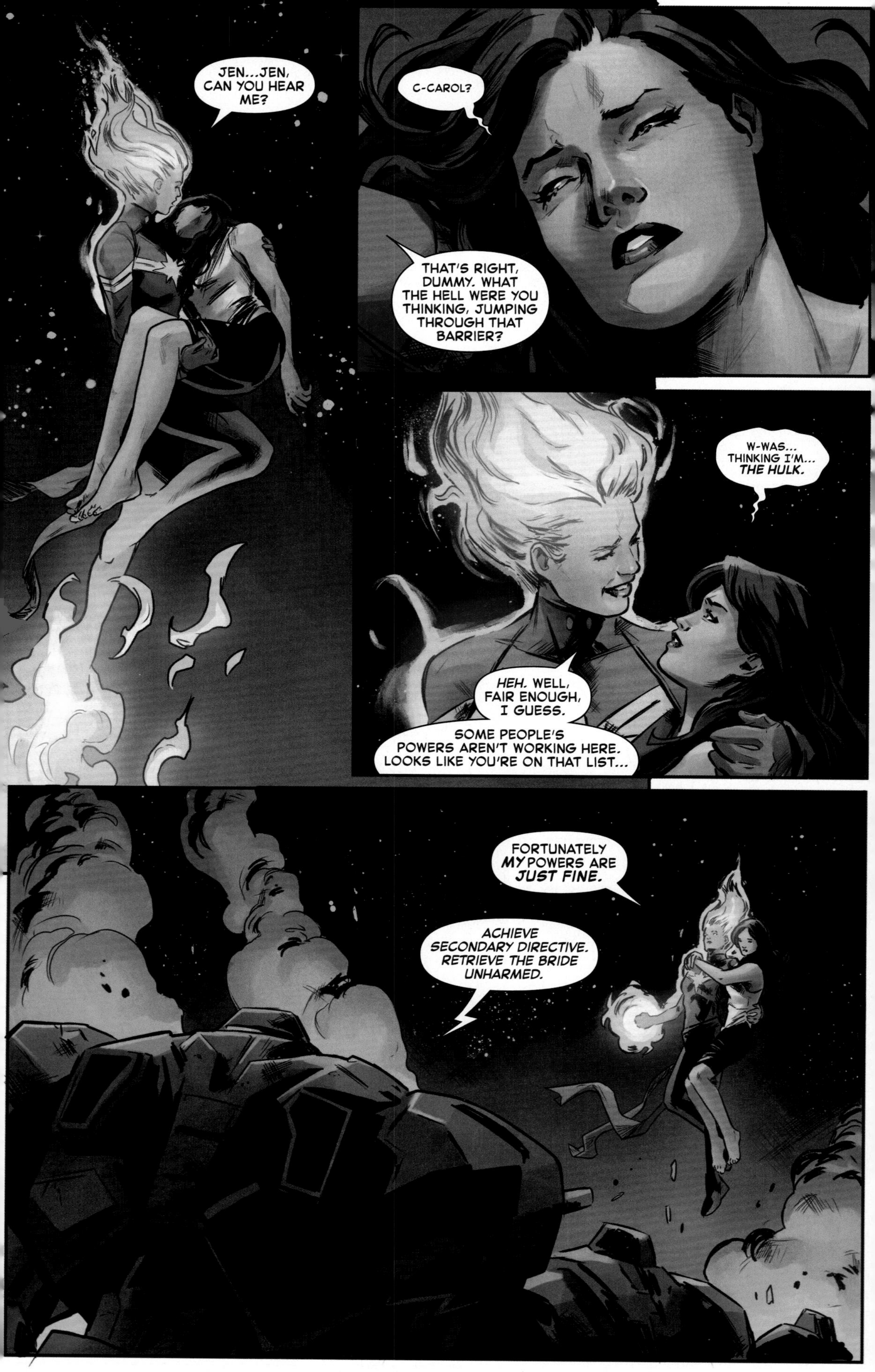
JEN...JEN, CAN YOU HEAR ME?
C-CAROL?
THAT'S RIGHT, DUMMY. WHAT THE HELL WERE YOU THINKING, JUMPING THROUGH THAT BARRIER?
W-WAS... THINKING I'M... THE HULK.
HEH. WELL, FAIR ENOUGH, I GUESS.
SOME PEOPLE'S POWERS AREN'T WORKING HERE. LOOKS LIKE YOU'RE ON THAT LIST...
FORTUNATELY MY POWERS ARE JUST FINE.
ACHIEVE SECONDARY DIRECTIVE. RETRIEVE THE BRIDE UNHARMED.

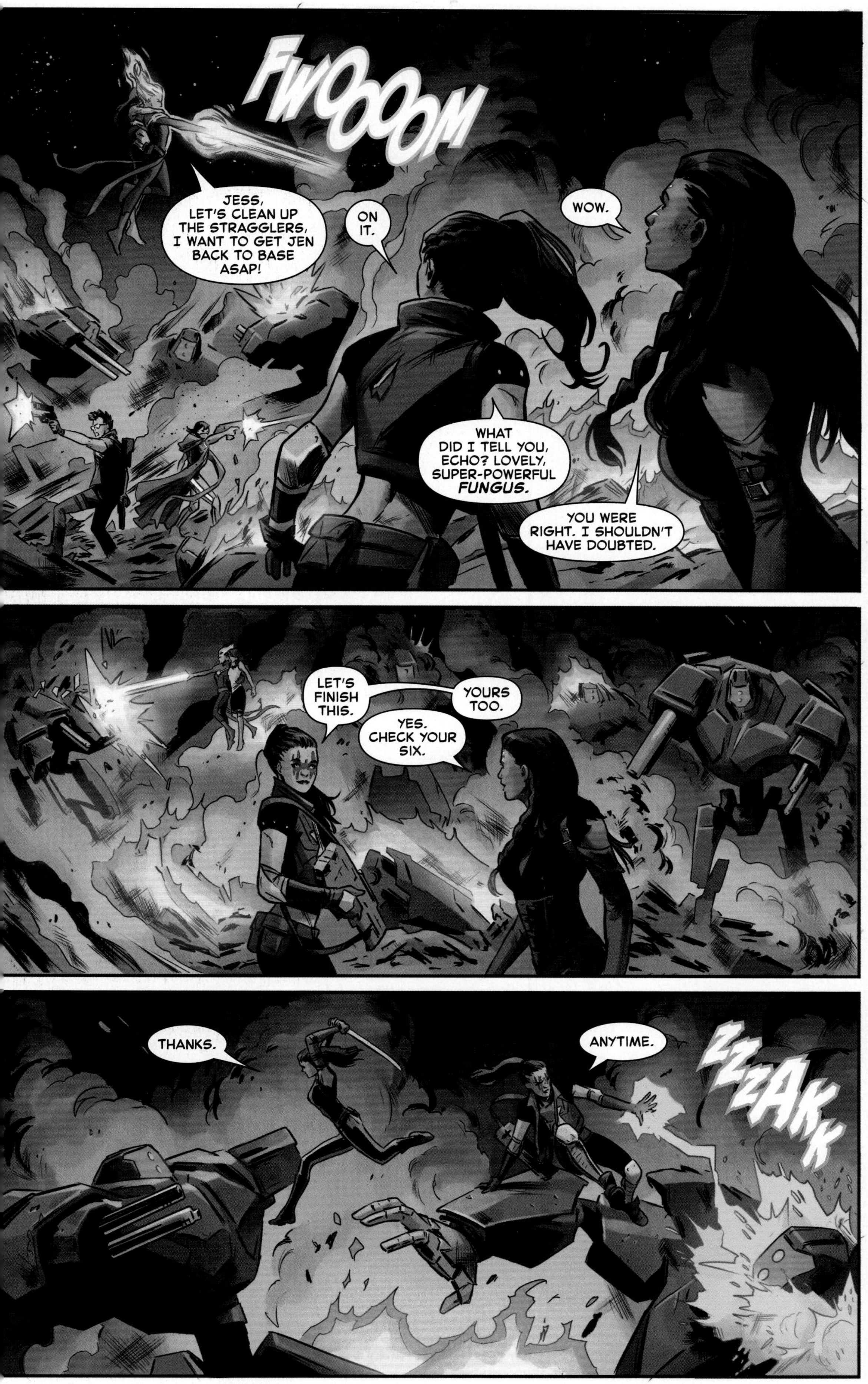
FWOOOOM
JESS, LET'S CLEAN UP THE STRAGGLERS, I WANT TO GET JEN BACK TO BASE ASAP!
ON IT.
WOW.
WHAT DID I TELL YOU, ECHO? LOVELY, SUPER-POWERFUL *FUNGUS.*
YOU WERE RIGHT. I SHOULDN'T HAVE DOUBTED.
LET'S FINISH THIS.
YES. CHECK YOUR SIX.
YOURS TOO.
THANKS.
ANYTIME.
ZZZAKK

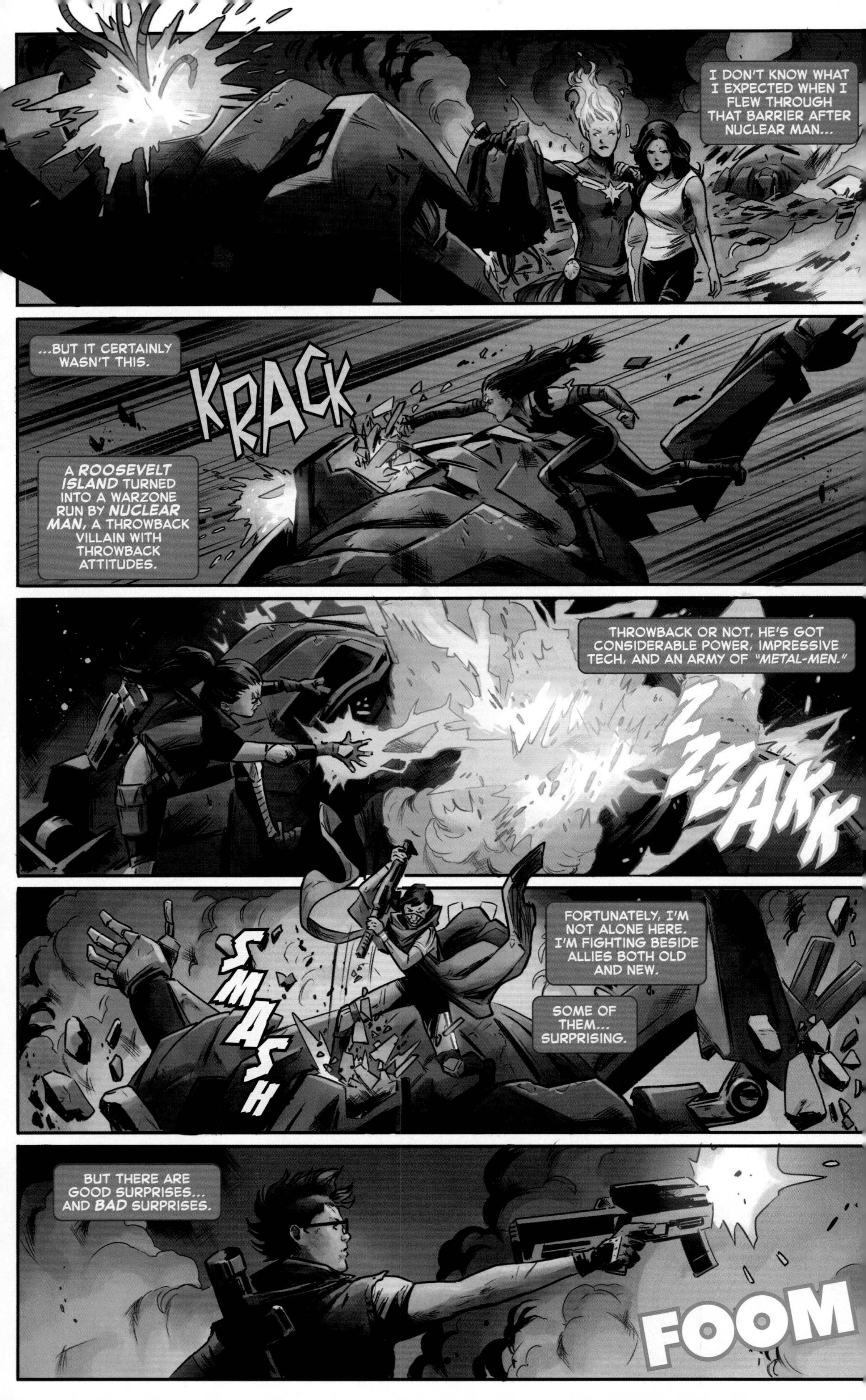
I DON'T KNOW WHAT I EXPECTED WHEN I FLEW THROUGH THAT BARRIER AFTER NUCLEAR MAN...
...BUT IT CERTAINLY WASN'T THIS.
KRACK
A ROOSEVELT ISLAND TURNED INTO A WARZONE RUN BY NUCLEAR MAN, A THROWBACK VILLAIN WITH THROWBACK ATTITUDES.
THROWBACK OR NOT, HE'S GOT CONSIDERABLE POWER, IMPRESSIVE TECH, AND AN ARMY OF "METAL-MEN."
ZZZAKK
SMASH
FORTUNATELY, I'M NOT ALONE HERE. I'M FIGHTING BESIDE ALLIES BOTH OLD AND NEW.
SOME OF THEM... SURPRISING.
BUT THERE ARE GOOD SURPRISES... AND BAD SURPRISES.
FOOM

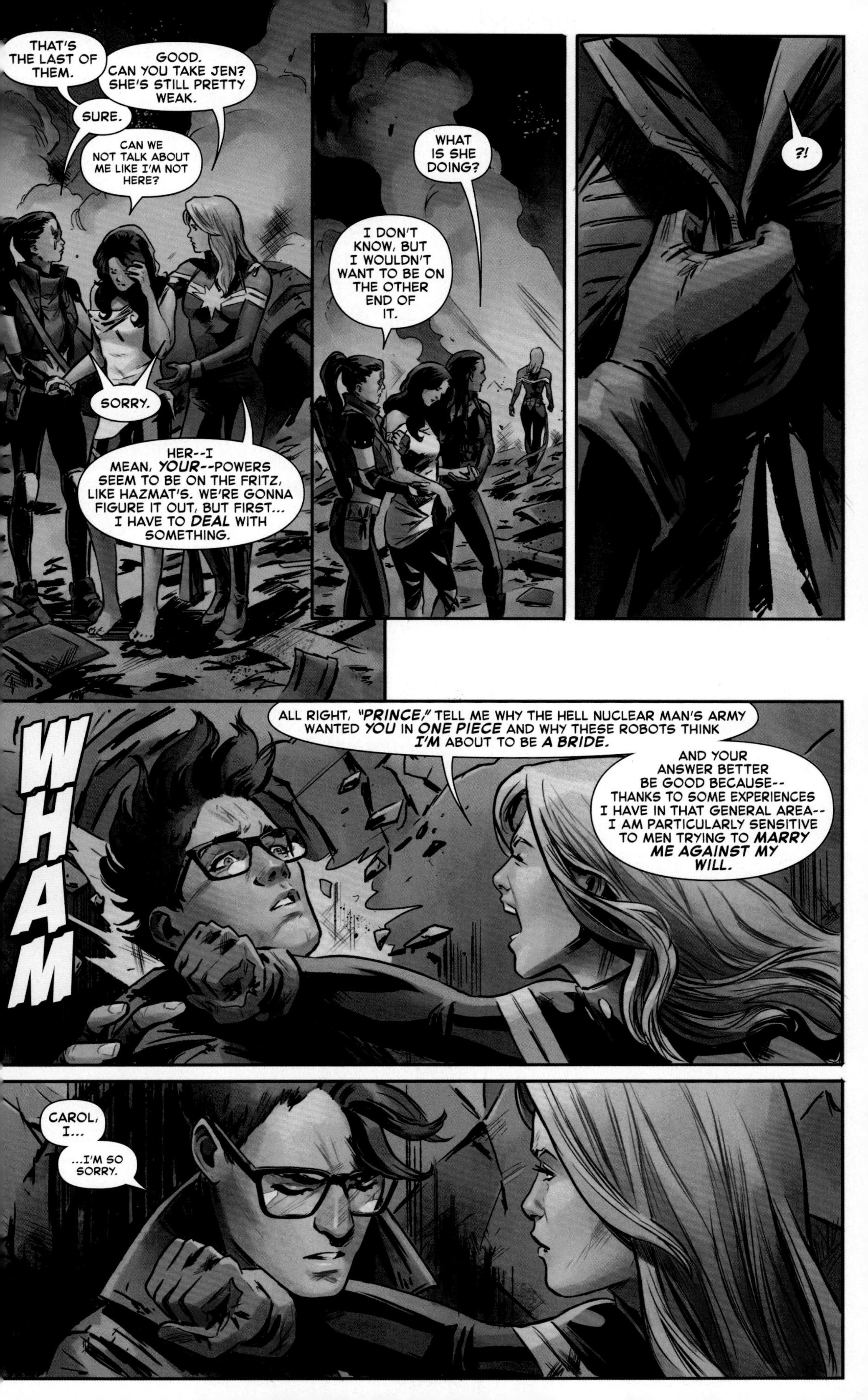
THAT'S THE LAST OF THEM.
GOOD. CAN YOU TAKE JEN? SHE'S STILL PRETTY WEAK.
SURE.
CAN WE NOT TALK ABOUT ME LIKE I'M NOT HERE?
SORRY.
HER--I MEAN, YOUR--POWERS SEEM TO BE ON THE FRITZ, LIKE HAZMAT'S. WE'RE GONNA FIGURE IT OUT, BUT FIRST... I HAVE TO DEAL WITH SOMETHING.
WHAT IS SHE DOING?
I DON'T KNOW, BUT I WOULDN'T WANT TO BE ON THE OTHER END OF IT.
?!
WHAM
ALL RIGHT, "PRINCE," TELL ME WHY THE HELL NUCLEAR MAN'S ARMY WANTED YOU IN ONE PIECE AND WHY THESE ROBOTS THINK I'M ABOUT TO BE A BRIDE.
AND YOUR ANSWER BETTER BE GOOD BECAUSE--THANKS TO SOME EXPERIENCES I HAVE IN THAT GENERAL AREA--I AM PARTICULARLY SENSITIVE TO MEN TRYING TO MARRY ME AGAINST MY WILL.
CAROL, I...
...I'M SO SORRY.

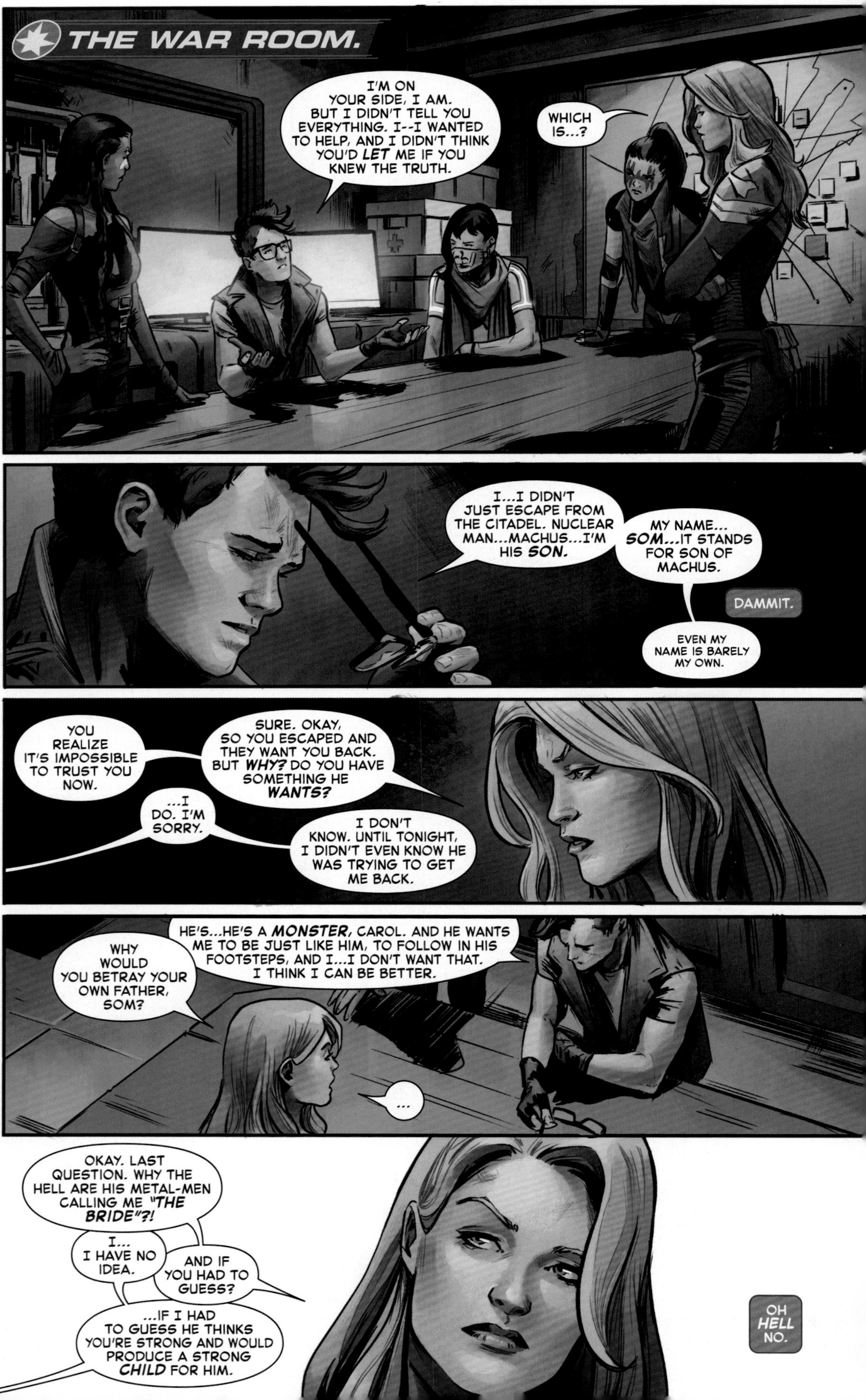
THE WAR ROOM.
I'M ON YOUR SIDE, I AM. BUT I DIDN'T TELL YOU EVERYTHING. I--I WANTED TO HELP, AND I DIDN'T THINK YOU'D LET ME IF YOU KNEW THE TRUTH.
WHICH IS...?
I...I DIDN'T JUST ESCAPE FROM THE CITADEL. NUCLEAR MAN...MACHUS...I'M HIS SON.
MY NAME... SOM...IT STANDS FOR SON OF MACHUS.
DAMMIT.
EVEN MY NAME IS BARELY MY OWN.
SURE. OKAY, SO YOU ESCAPED AND THEY WANT YOU BACK. BUT WHY? DO YOU HAVE SOMETHING HE WANTS?
I DON'T KNOW. UNTIL TONIGHT, I DIDN'T EVEN KNOW HE WAS TRYING TO GET ME BACK.
YOU REALIZE IT'S IMPOSSIBLE TO TRUST YOU NOW.
...I DO. I'M SORRY.
WHY WOULD YOU BETRAY YOUR OWN FATHER, SOM?
HE'S...HE'S A MONSTER, CAROL. AND HE WANTS ME TO BE JUST LIKE HIM, TO FOLLOW IN HIS FOOTSTEPS, AND I...I DON'T WANT THAT. I THINK I CAN BE BETTER.
...
OKAY. LAST QUESTION. WHY THE HELL ARE HIS METAL-MEN CALLING ME "THE BRIDE"?!
I... I HAVE NO IDEA.
AND IF YOU HAD TO GUESS?
...IF I HAD TO GUESS HE THINKS YOU'RE STRONG AND WOULD PRODUCE A STRONG CHILD FOR HIM.
OH HELL NO.

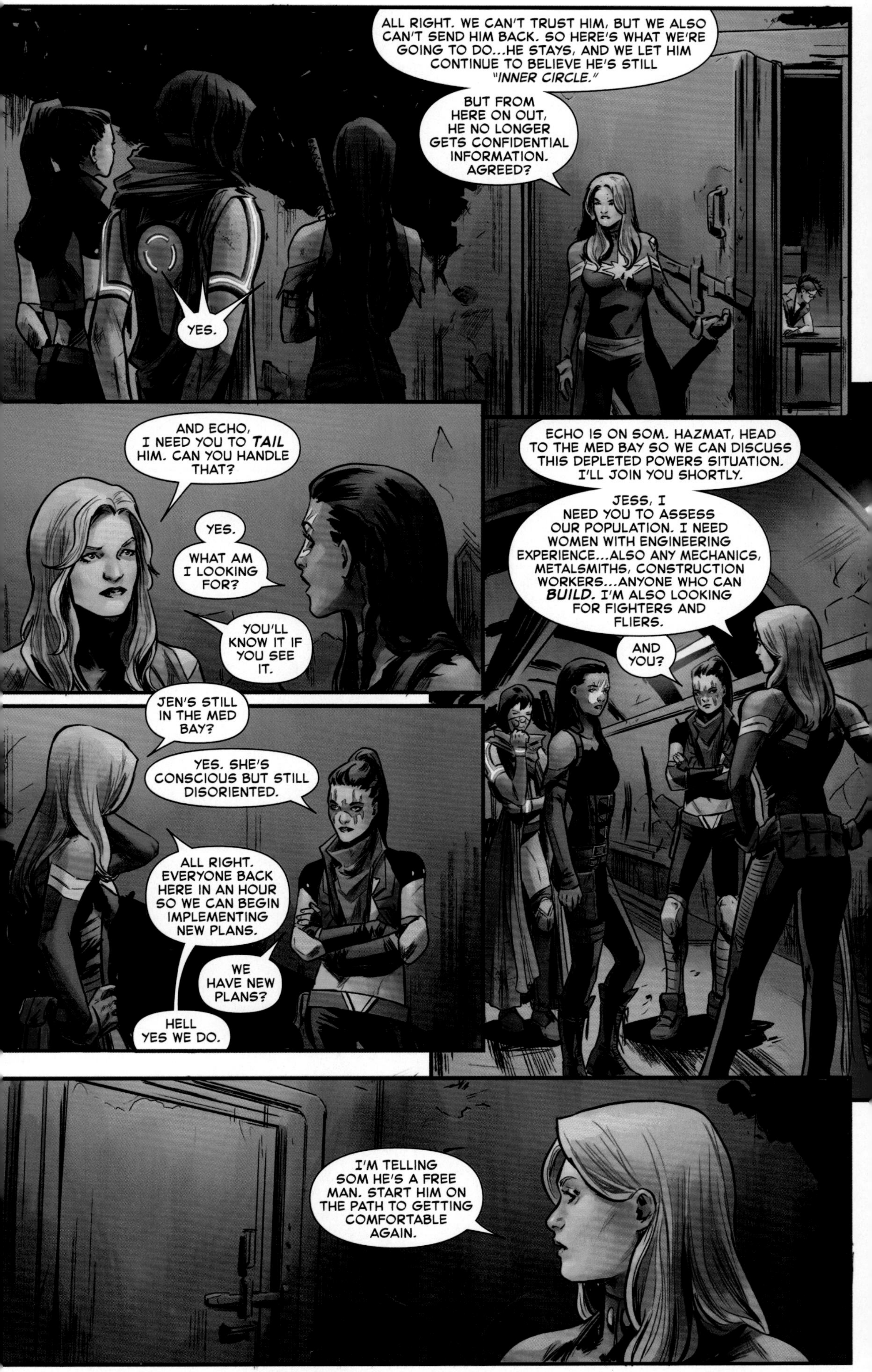
ALL RIGHT. WE CAN'T TRUST HIM, BUT WE ALSO CAN'T SEND HIM BACK. SO HERE'S WHAT WE'RE GOING TO DO...HE STAYS, AND WE LET HIM CONTINUE TO BELIEVE HE'S STILL "INNER CIRCLE."
BUT FROM HERE ON OUT, HE NO LONGER GETS CONFIDENTIAL INFORMATION. AGREED?
YES.
AND ECHO, I NEED YOU TO TAIL HIM. CAN YOU HANDLE THAT?
YES.
WHAT AM I LOOKING FOR?
YOU'LL KNOW IT IF YOU SEE IT.
ECHO IS ON SOM. HAZMAT, HEAD TO THE MED BAY SO WE CAN DISCUSS THIS DEPLETED POWERS SITUATION. I'LL JOIN YOU SHORTLY.
JESS, I NEED YOU TO ASSESS OUR POPULATION. I NEED WOMEN WITH ENGINEERING EXPERIENCE...ALSO ANY MECHANICS, METALSMITHS, CONSTRUCTION WORKERS...ANYONE WHO CAN BUILD. I'M ALSO LOOKING FOR FIGHTERS AND FLIERS.
AND YOU?
JEN'S STILL IN THE MED BAY?
YES. SHE'S CONSCIOUS BUT STILL DISORIENTED.
ALL RIGHT. EVERYONE BACK HERE IN AN HOUR SO WE CAN BEGIN IMPLEMENTING NEW PLANS.
WE HAVE NEW PLANS?
HELL YES WE DO.
I'M TELLING SOM HE'S A FREE MAN. START HIM ON THE PATH TO GETTING COMFORTABLE AGAIN.

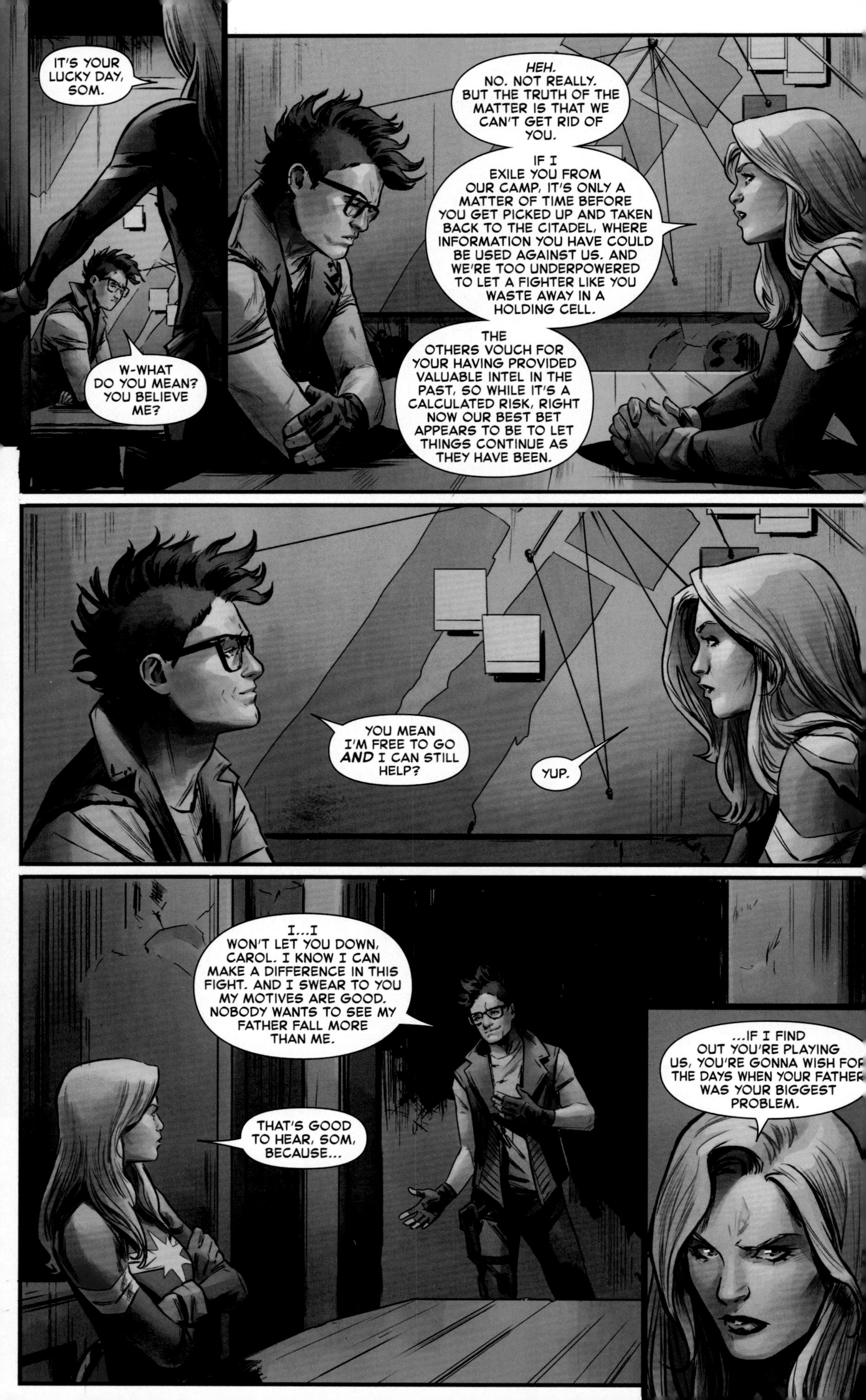
IT'S YOUR LUCKY DAY, SOM.
W-WHAT DO YOU MEAN? YOU BELIEVE ME?
HEH. NO. NOT REALLY. BUT THE TRUTH OF THE MATTER IS THAT WE CAN'T GET RID OF YOU.
IF I EXILE YOU FROM OUR CAMP, IT'S ONLY A MATTER OF TIME BEFORE YOU GET PICKED UP AND TAKEN BACK TO THE CITADEL, WHERE INFORMATION YOU HAVE COULD BE USED AGAINST US. AND WE'RE TOO UNDERPOWERED TO LET A FIGHTER LIKE YOU WASTE AWAY IN A HOLDING CELL.
THE OTHERS VOUCH FOR YOUR HAVING PROVIDED VALUABLE INTEL IN THE PAST, SO WHILE IT'S A CALCULATED RISK, RIGHT NOW OUR BEST BET APPEARS TO BE TO LET THINGS CONTINUE AS THEY HAVE BEEN.
YOU MEAN I'M FREE TO GO ***AND*** I CAN STILL HELP?
YUP.
I...I WON'T LET YOU DOWN, CAROL. I KNOW I CAN MAKE A DIFFERENCE IN THIS FIGHT. AND I SWEAR TO YOU MY MOTIVES ARE GOOD. NOBODY WANTS TO SEE MY FATHER FALL MORE THAN ME.
THAT'S GOOD TO HEAR, SOM, BECAUSE...
...IF I FIND OUT YOU'RE PLAYING US, YOU'RE GONNA WISH FOR THE DAYS WHEN YOUR FATHER WAS YOUR BIGGEST PROBLEM.

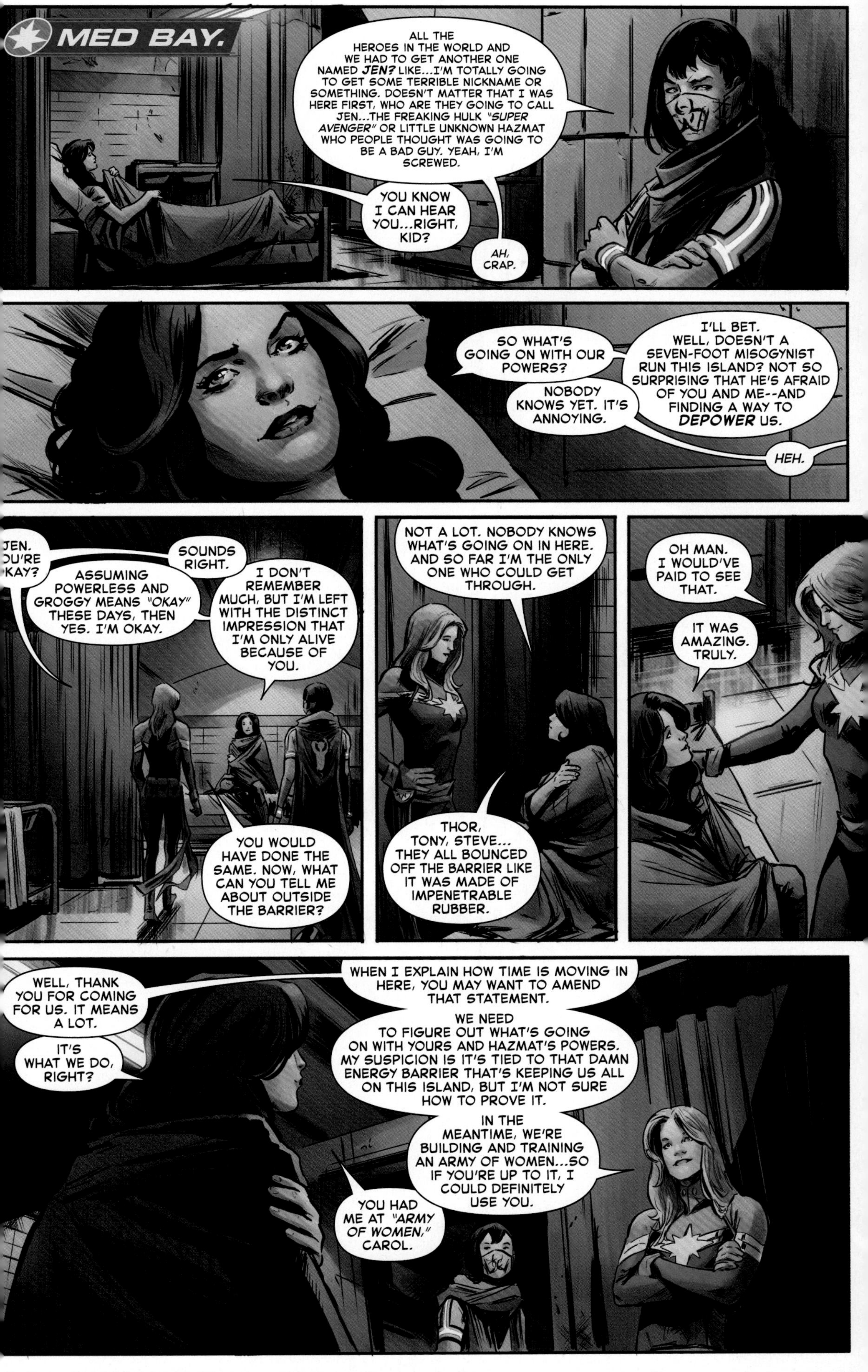
MED BAY.
ALL THE HEROES IN THE WORLD AND WE HAD TO GET ANOTHER ONE NAMED JEN? LIKE...I'M TOTALLY GOING TO GET SOME TERRIBLE NICKNAME OR SOMETHING. DOESN'T MATTER THAT I WAS HERE FIRST, WHO ARE THEY GOING TO CALL JEN...THE FREAKING HULK "SUPER AVENGER" OR LITTLE UNKNOWN HAZMAT WHO PEOPLE THOUGHT WAS GOING TO BE A BAD GUY. YEAH, I'M SCREWED.
YOU KNOW I CAN HEAR YOU...RIGHT, KID?
AH, CRAP.
SO WHAT'S GOING ON WITH OUR POWERS?
NOBODY KNOWS YET. IT'S ANNOYING.
I'LL BET. WELL, DOESN'T A SEVEN-FOOT MISOGYNIST RUN THIS ISLAND? NOT SO SURPRISING THAT HE'S AFRAID OF YOU AND ME--AND FINDING A WAY TO DEPOWER US.
HEH.
JEN.
ASSUMING POWERLESS AND GROGGY MEANS "OKAY" THESE DAYS, THEN YES. I'M OKAY.
SOUNDS RIGHT.
I DON'T REMEMBER MUCH, BUT I'M LEFT WITH THE DISTINCT IMPRESSION THAT I'M ONLY ALIVE BECAUSE OF YOU.
YOU WOULD HAVE DONE THE SAME. NOW, WHAT CAN YOU TELL ME ABOUT OUTSIDE THE BARRIER?
NOT A LOT. NOBODY KNOWS WHAT'S GOING ON IN HERE. AND SO FAR I'M THE ONLY ONE WHO COULD GET THROUGH.
THOR, TONY, STEVE... THEY ALL BOUNCED OFF THE BARRIER LIKE IT WAS MADE OF IMPENETRABLE RUBBER.
OH MAN. I WOULD'VE PAID TO SEE THAT.
IT WAS AMAZING. TRULY.
WELL, THANK YOU FOR COMING FOR US. IT MEANS A LOT.
IT'S WHAT WE DO, RIGHT?
WHEN I EXPLAIN HOW TIME IS MOVING IN HERE, YOU MAY WANT TO AMEND THAT STATEMENT.
WE NEED TO FIGURE OUT WHAT'S GOING ON WITH YOURS AND HAZMAT'S POWERS. MY SUSPICION IS IT'S TIED TO THAT DAMN ENERGY BARRIER THAT'S KEEPING US ALL ON THIS ISLAND, BUT I'M NOT SURE HOW TO PROVE IT.
IN THE MEANTIME, WE'RE BUILDING AND TRAINING AN ARMY OF WOMEN...SO IF YOU'RE UP TO IT, I COULD DEFINITELY USE YOU.
YOU HAD ME AT "ARMY OF WOMEN," CAROL.

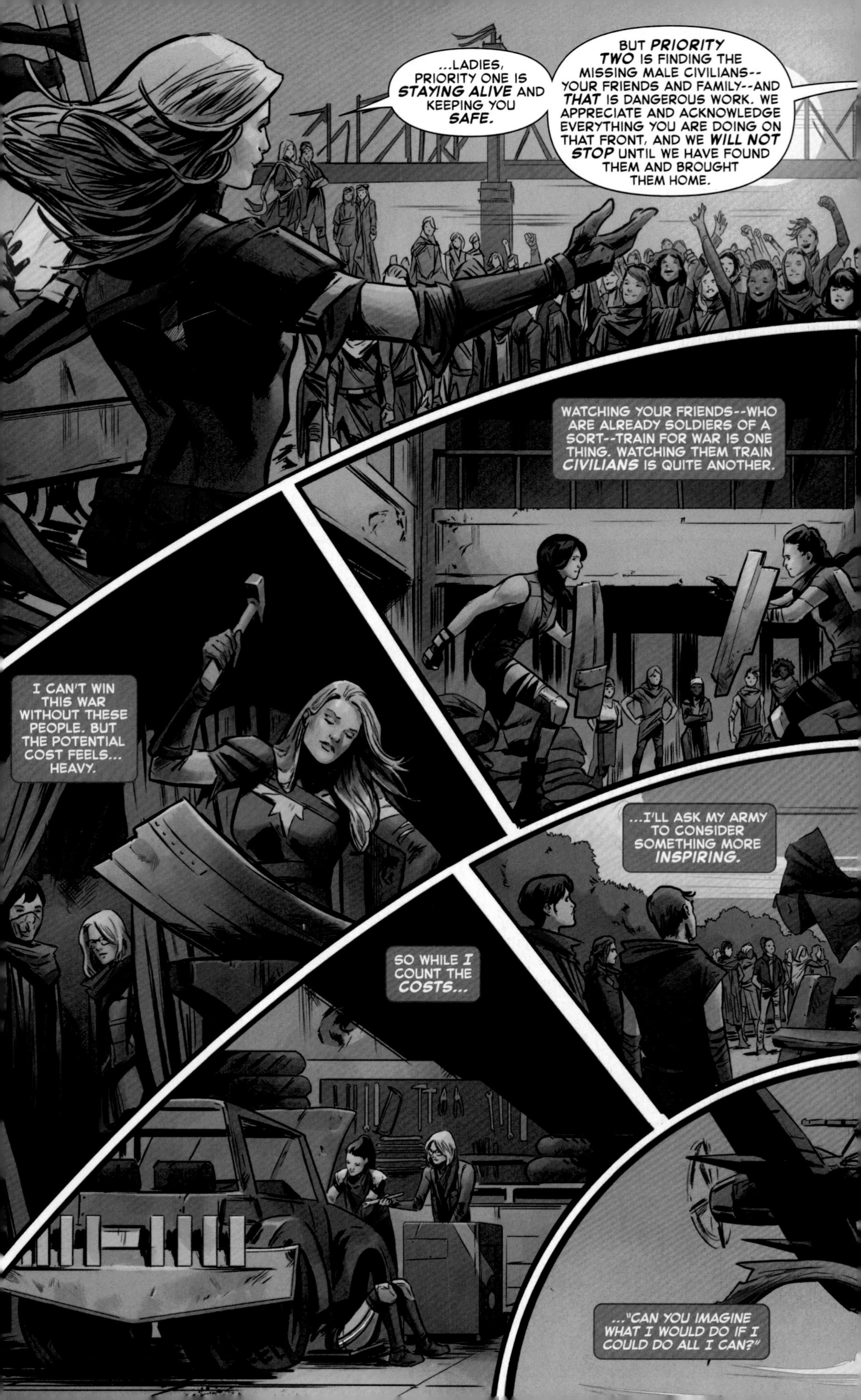
...LADIES, PRIORITY ONE IS STAYING ALIVE AND KEEPING YOU SAFE.
BUT PRIORITY TWO IS FINDING THE MISSING MALE CIVILIANS--YOUR FRIENDS AND FAMILY--AND THAT IS DANGEROUS WORK. WE APPRECIATE AND ACKNOWLEDGE EVERYTHING YOU ARE DOING ON THAT FRONT, AND WE WILL NOT STOP UNTIL WE HAVE FOUND THEM AND BROUGHT THEM HOME.
WATCHING YOUR FRIENDS--WHO ARE ALREADY SOLDIERS OF A SORT--TRAIN FOR WAR IS ONE THING. WATCHING THEM TRAIN CIVILIANS IS QUITE ANOTHER.
I CAN'T WIN THIS WAR WITHOUT THESE PEOPLE. BUT THE POTENTIAL COST FEELS... HEAVY.
SO WHILE I COUNT THE COSTS...
...I'LL ASK MY ARMY TO CONSIDER SOMETHING MORE INSPIRING.
..."CAN YOU IMAGINE WHAT I WOULD DO IF I COULD DO ALL I CAN?"

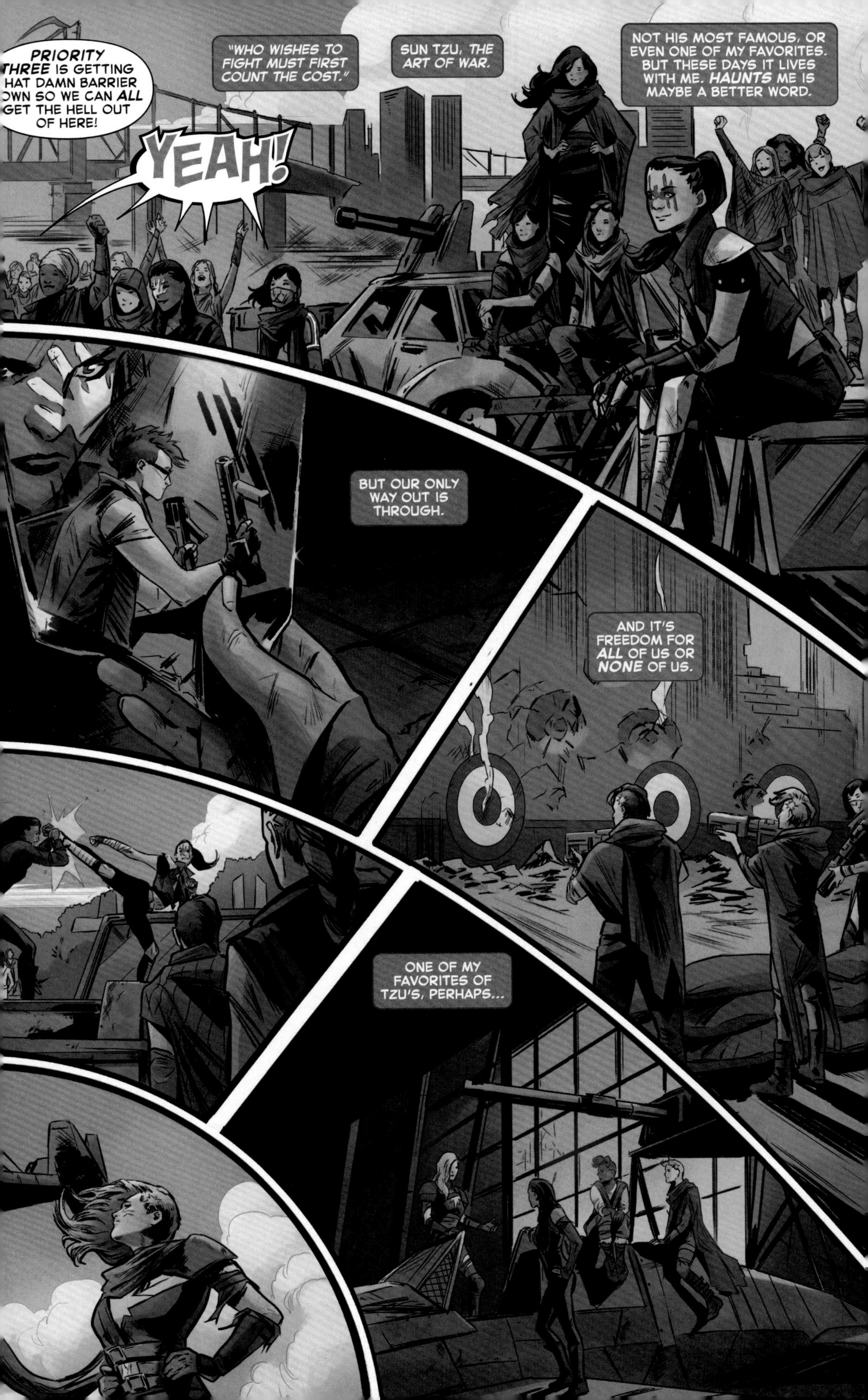
PRIORITY THREE IS GETTING HAT DAMN BARRIER OWN SO WE CAN ALL GET THE HELL OUT OF HERE!
YEAH!
"WHO WISHES TO FIGHT MUST FIRST COUNT THE COST."
SUN TZU, THE ART OF WAR.
NOT HIS MOST FAMOUS, OR EVEN ONE OF MY FAVORITES. BUT THESE DAYS IT LIVES WITH ME. HAUNTS ME IS MAYBE A BETTER WORD.
BUT OUR ONLY WAY OUT IS THROUGH.
AND IT'S FREEDOM FOR ALL OF US OR NONE OF US.
ONE OF MY FAVORITES OF TZU'S, PERHAPS...

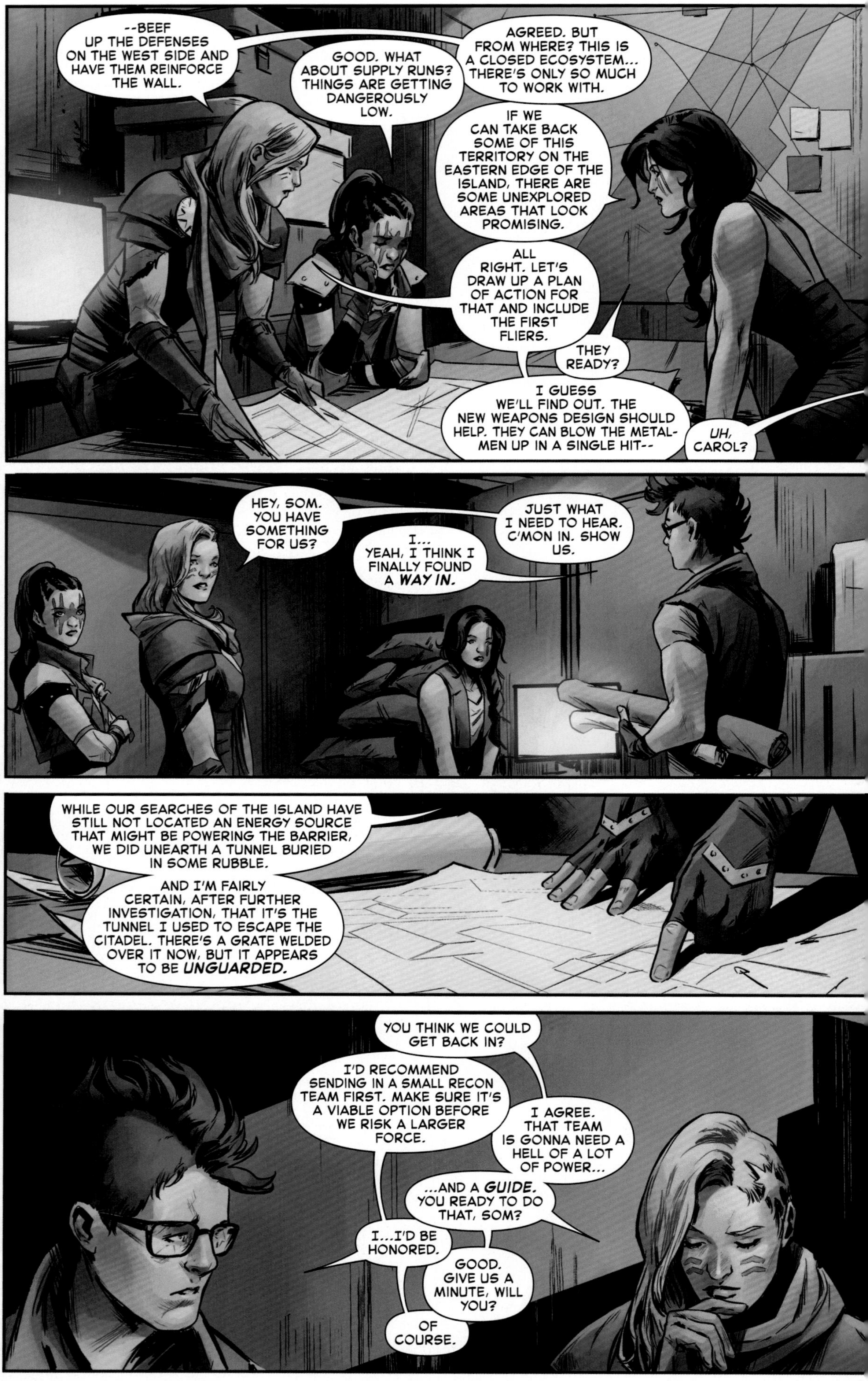
--BEEF UP THE DEFENSES ON THE WEST SIDE AND HAVE THEM REINFORCE THE WALL.
AGREED. BUT FROM WHERE? THIS IS A CLOSED ECOSYSTEM... THERE'S ONLY SO MUCH TO WORK WITH.
GOOD. WHAT ABOUT SUPPLY RUNS? THINGS ARE GETTING DANGEROUSLY LOW.
IF WE CAN TAKE BACK SOME OF THIS TERRITORY ON THE EASTERN EDGE OF THE ISLAND, THERE ARE SOME UNEXPLORED AREAS THAT LOOK PROMISING.
ALL RIGHT. LET'S DRAW UP A PLAN OF ACTION FOR THAT AND INCLUDE THE FIRST FLIERS.
THEY READY?
I GUESS WE'LL FIND OUT. THE NEW WEAPONS DESIGN SHOULD HELP. THEY CAN BLOW THE METAL-MEN UP IN A SINGLE HIT--
UH, CAROL?
HEY, SOM. YOU HAVE SOMETHING FOR US?
JUST WHAT I NEED TO HEAR. C'MON IN. SHOW US.
I... YEAH, I THINK I FINALLY FOUND A ***WAY IN.***
WHILE OUR SEARCHES OF THE ISLAND HAVE STILL NOT LOCATED AN ENERGY SOURCE THAT MIGHT BE POWERING THE BARRIER, WE DID UNEARTH A TUNNEL BURIED IN SOME RUBBLE.
AND I'M FAIRLY CERTAIN, AFTER FURTHER INVESTIGATION, THAT IT'S THE TUNNEL I USED TO ESCAPE THE CITADEL. THERE'S A GRATE WELDED OVER IT NOW, BUT IT APPEARS TO BE ***UNGUARDED.***
YOU THINK WE COULD GET BACK IN?
I'D RECOMMEND SENDING IN A SMALL RECON TEAM FIRST. MAKE SURE IT'S A VIABLE OPTION BEFORE WE RISK A LARGER FORCE.
I AGREE. THAT TEAM IS GONNA NEED A HELL OF A LOT OF POWER...
...AND A ***GUIDE.*** YOU READY TO DO THAT, SOM?
I...I'D BE HONORED.
GOOD. GIVE US A MINUTE, WILL YOU?
OF COURSE.

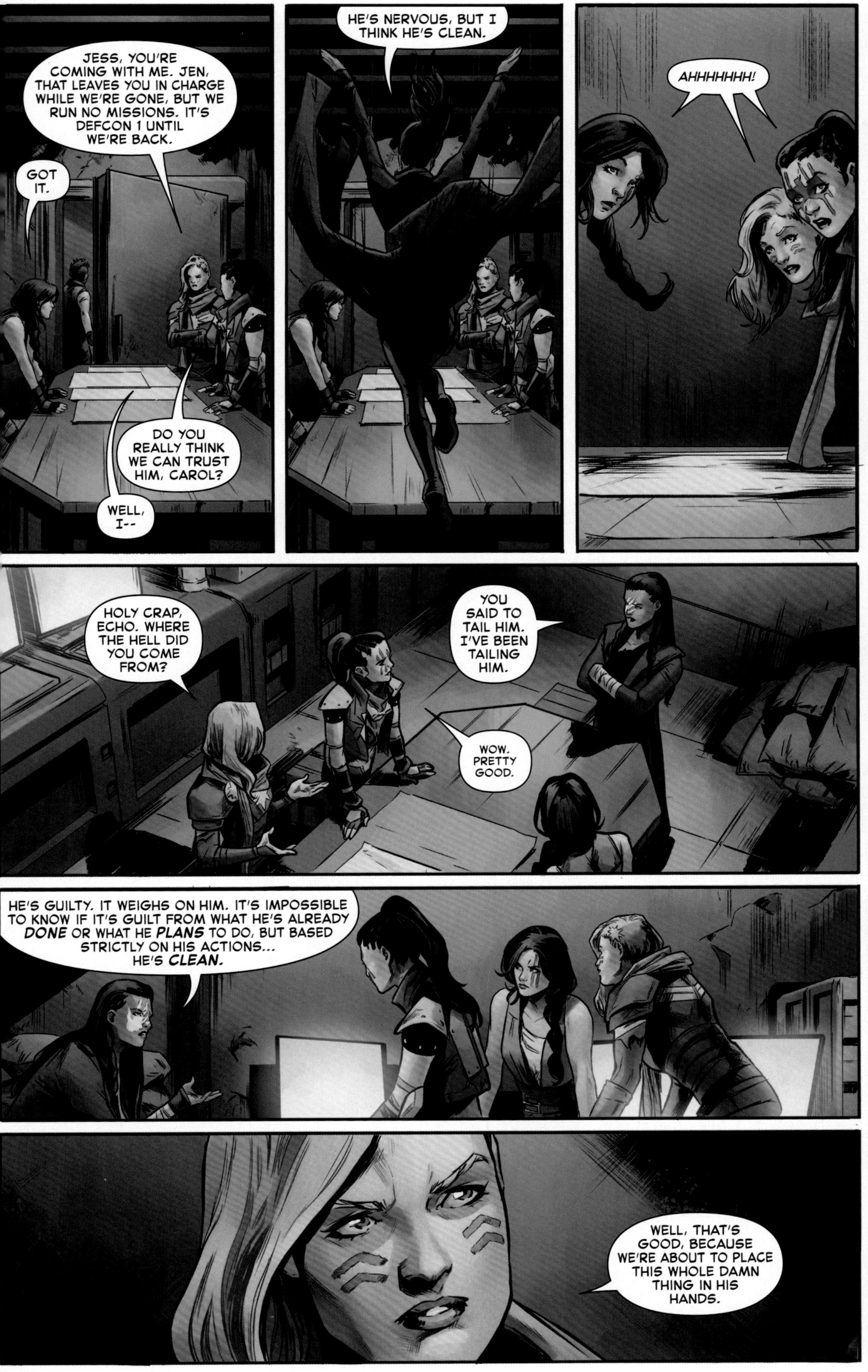
JESS, YOU'RE COMING WITH ME. JEN, THAT LEAVES YOU IN CHARGE WHILE WE'RE GONE, BUT WE RUN NO MISSIONS. IT'S DEFCON 1 UNTIL WE'RE BACK.
GOT IT.
DO YOU REALLY THINK WE CAN TRUST HIM, CAROL?
WELL, I--
HE'S NERVOUS, BUT I THINK HE'S CLEAN.
AHHHHHHH!
HOLY CRAP, ECHO. WHERE THE HELL DID YOU COME FROM?
YOU SAID TO TAIL HIM. I'VE BEEN TAILING HIM.
WOW. PRETTY GOOD.
HE'S GUILTY. IT WEIGHS ON HIM. IT'S IMPOSSIBLE TO KNOW IF IT'S GUILT FROM WHAT HE'S ALREADY DONE OR WHAT HE PLANS TO DO, BUT BASED STRICTLY ON HIS ACTIONS... HE'S CLEAN.
WELL, THAT'S GOOD, BECAUSE WE'RE ABOUT TO PLACE THIS WHOLE DAMN THING IN HIS HANDS.

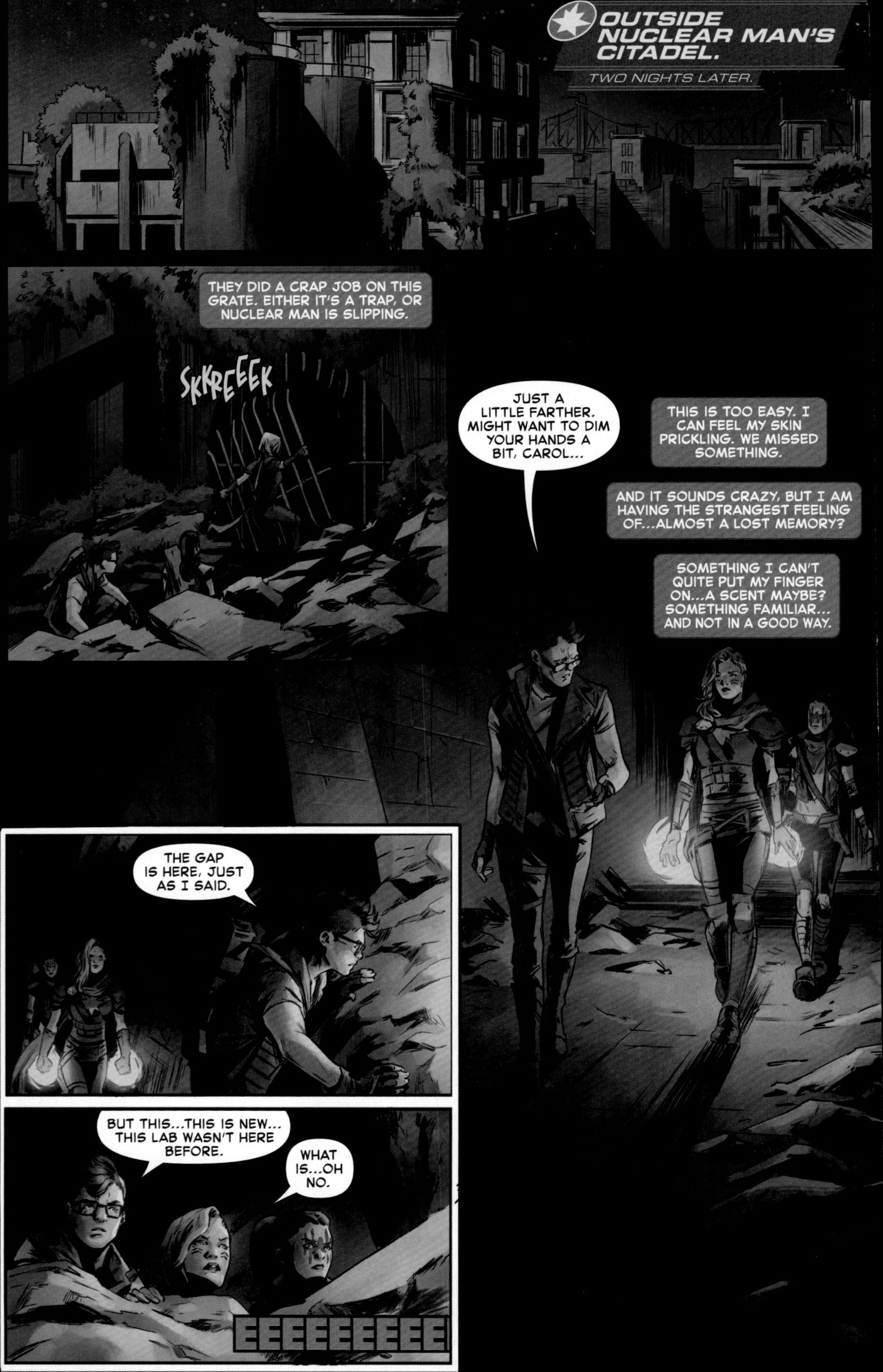

OUTSIDE NUCLEAR MAN'S CITADEL.
TWO NIGHTS LATER.
THEY DID A CRAP JOB ON THIS GRATE. EITHER IT'S A TRAP, OR NUCLEAR MAN IS SLIPPING.
SKKREEEEK
JUST A LITTLE FARTHER. MIGHT WANT TO DIM YOUR HANDS A BIT, CAROL...
THIS IS TOO EASY. I CAN FEEL MY SKIN PRICKLING. WE MISSED SOMETHING.
AND IT SOUNDS CRAZY, BUT I AM HAVING THE STRANGEST FEELING OF...ALMOST A LOST MEMORY?
SOMETHING I CAN'T QUITE PUT MY FINGER ON...A SCENT MAYBE? SOMETHING FAMILIAR... AND NOT IN A GOOD WAY.
THE GAP IS HERE, JUST AS I SAID.
BUT THIS...THIS IS NEW... THIS LAB WASN'T HERE BEFORE.
WHAT IS...OH NO.
EEEEEEEEE

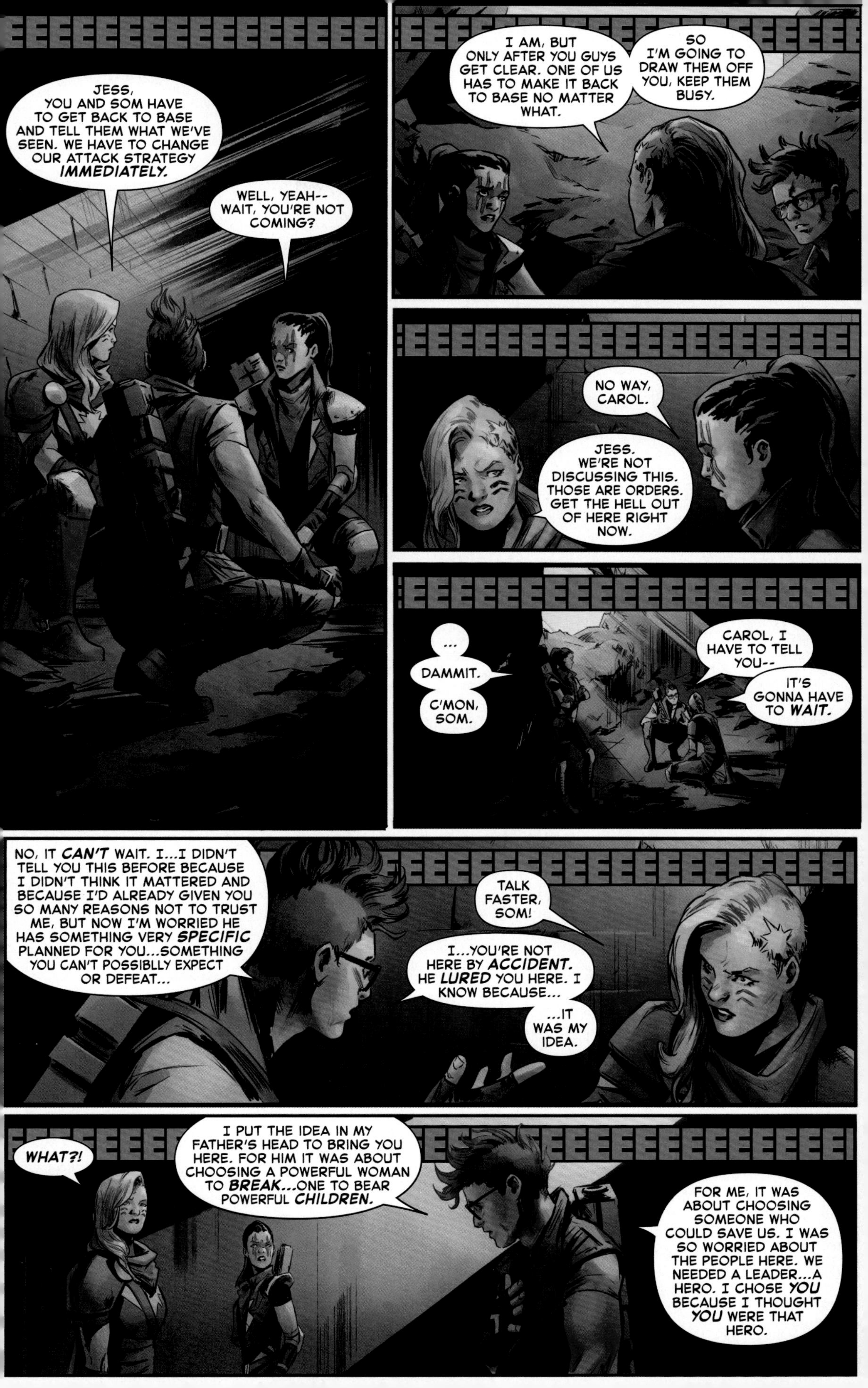
EEEEEEEEEEEEEEEEEE
JESS, YOU AND SOM HAVE TO GET BACK TO BASE AND TELL THEM WHAT WE'VE SEEN. WE HAVE TO CHANGE OUR ATTACK STRATEGY *IMMEDIATELY.*
WELL, YEAH-- WAIT, YOU'RE NOT COMING?
I AM, BUT ONLY AFTER YOU GUYS GET CLEAR. ONE OF US HAS TO MAKE IT BACK TO BASE NO MATTER WHAT.
SO I'M GOING TO DRAW THEM OFF YOU, KEEP THEM BUSY.
EEEEEEEEEEEEEEEEEE
NO WAY, CAROL.
JESS. WE'RE NOT DISCUSSING THIS. THOSE ARE ORDERS. GET THE HELL OUT OF HERE RIGHT NOW.
EEEEEEEEEEEEEEEEEE
...
DAMMIT.
C'MON, SOM.
CAROL, I HAVE TO TELL YOU--
IT'S GONNA HAVE TO *WAIT.*
NO, IT *CAN'T* WAIT. I...I DIDN'T TELL YOU THIS BEFORE BECAUSE I DIDN'T THINK IT MATTERED AND BECAUSE I'D ALREADY GIVEN YOU SO MANY REASONS NOT TO TRUST ME, BUT NOW I'M WORRIED HE HAS SOMETHING VERY *SPECIFIC* PLANNED FOR YOU...SOMETHING YOU CAN'T POSSIBLLY EXPECT OR DEFEAT...
TALK FASTER, SOM!
I...YOU'RE NOT HERE BY *ACCIDENT.* HE *LURED* YOU HERE. I KNOW BECAUSE...
...IT WAS MY IDEA.
WHAT?!
I PUT THE IDEA IN MY FATHER'S HEAD TO BRING YOU HERE. FOR HIM IT WAS ABOUT CHOOSING A POWERFUL WOMAN TO *BREAK...*ONE TO BEAR POWERFUL *CHILDREN.*
FOR ME, IT WAS ABOUT CHOOSING SOMEONE WHO COULD SAVE US. I WAS SO WORRIED ABOUT THE PEOPLE HERE. WE NEEDED A LEADER...A HERO. I CHOSE *YOU* BECAUSE I THOUGHT *YOU* WERE THAT HERO.

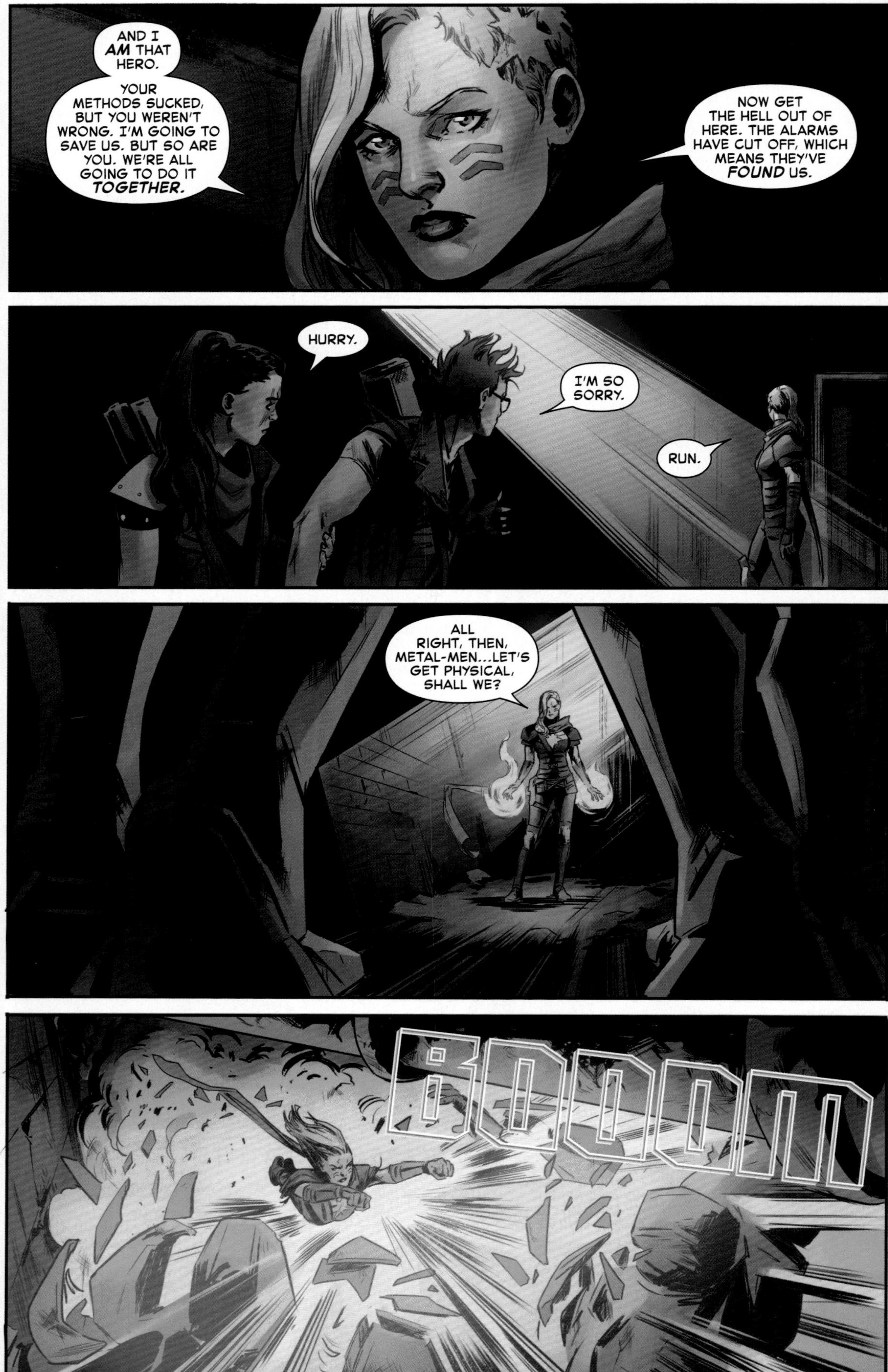
AND I AM THAT HERO.
YOUR METHODS SUCKED, BUT YOU WEREN'T WRONG. I'M GOING TO SAVE US. BUT SO ARE YOU. WE'RE ALL GOING TO DO IT TOGETHER.
NOW GET THE HELL OUT OF HERE. THE ALARMS HAVE CUT OFF, WHICH MEANS THEY'VE FOUND US.
HURRY.
I'M SO SORRY.
RUN.
ALL RIGHT, THEN, METAL-MEN...LET'S GET PHYSICAL, SHALL WE?
BOOOM

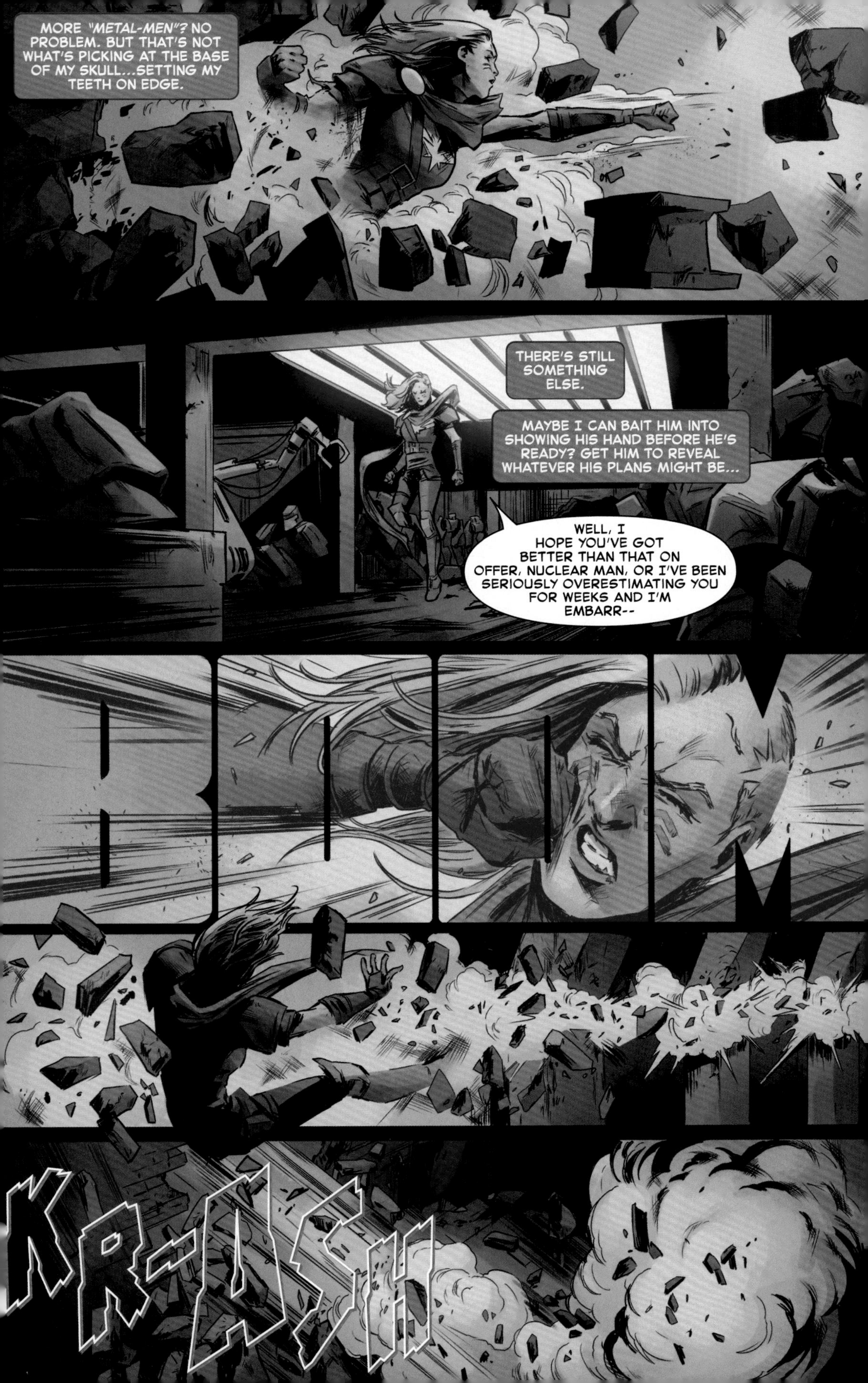

MORE "METAL-MEN"? NO PROBLEM. BUT THAT'S NOT WHAT'S PICKING AT THE BASE OF MY SKULL...SETTING MY TEETH ON EDGE.
THERE'S STILL SOMETHING ELSE.
MAYBE I CAN BAIT HIM INTO SHOWING HIS HAND BEFORE HE'S READY? GET HIM TO REVEAL WHATEVER HIS PLANS MIGHT BE...
WELL, I HOPE YOU'VE GOT BETTER THAN THAT ON OFFER, NUCLEAR MAN, OR I'VE BEEN SERIOUSLY OVERESTIMATING YOU FOR WEEKS AND I'M EMBARR--
BOOM
KR-ASH

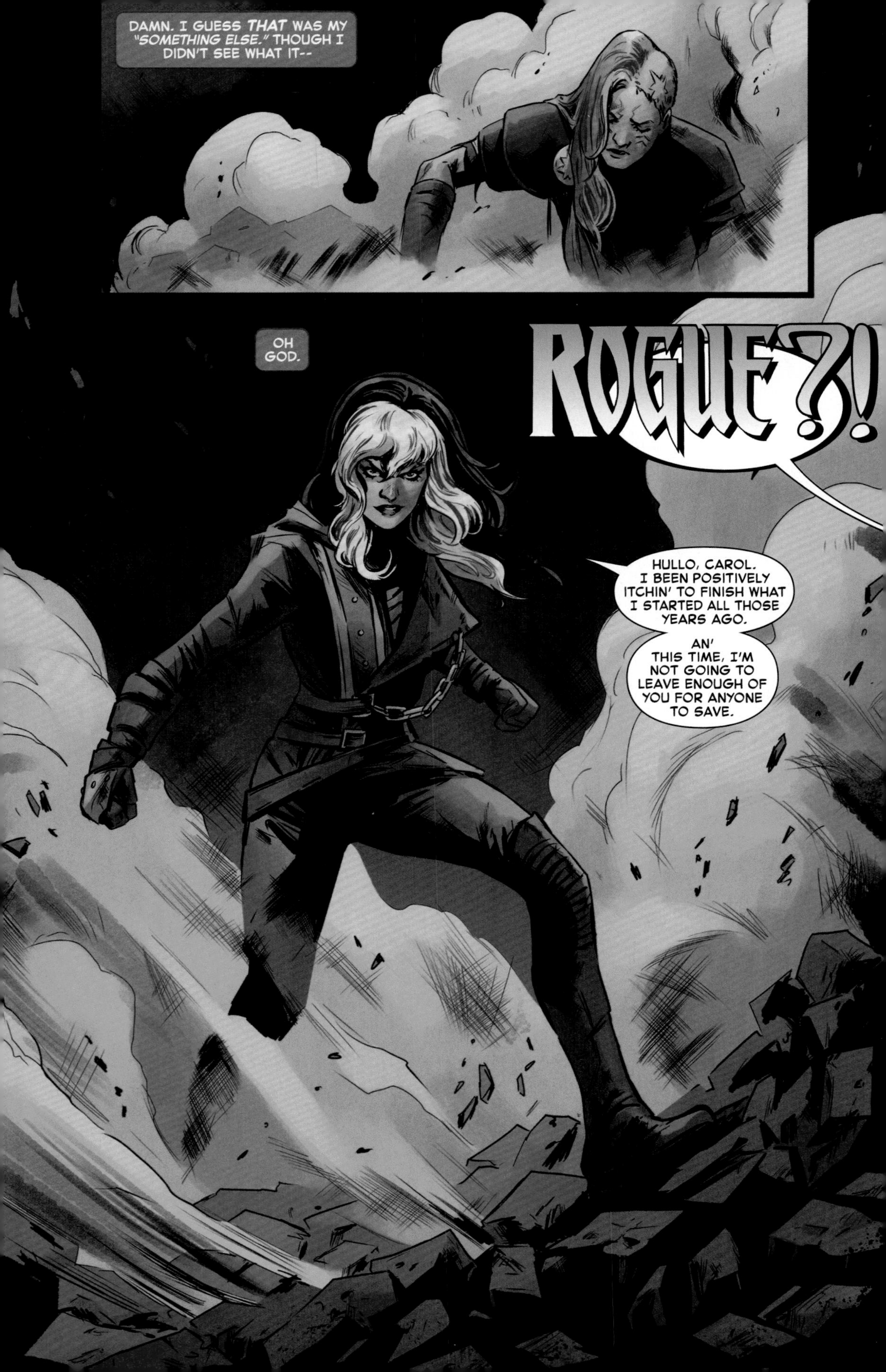
DAMN. I GUESS THAT WAS MY "SOMETHING ELSE." THOUGH I DIDN'T SEE WHAT IT--
OH GOD.
ROGUE?!
HULLO, CAROL. I BEEN POSITIVELY ITCHIN' TO FINISH WHAT I STARTED ALL THOSE YEARS AGO.
AN' THIS TIME, I'M NOT GOING TO LEAVE ENOUGH OF YOU FOR ANYONE TO SAVE.

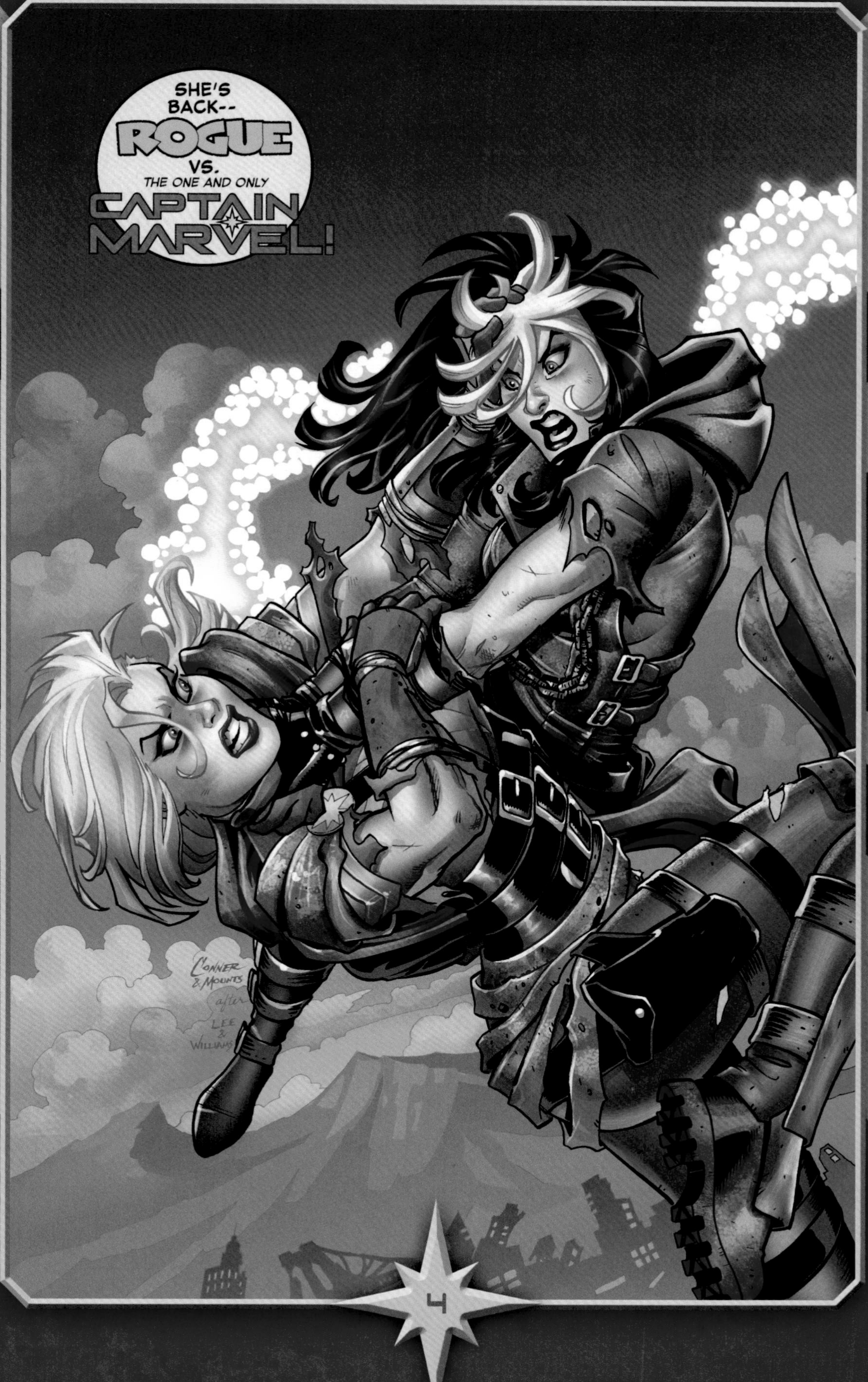
SHE'S BACK--
ROGUE
VS.
THE ONE AND ONLY
CAPTAIN MARVEL!
CONNER & MOUNTS after LEE & WILLIAMS
4

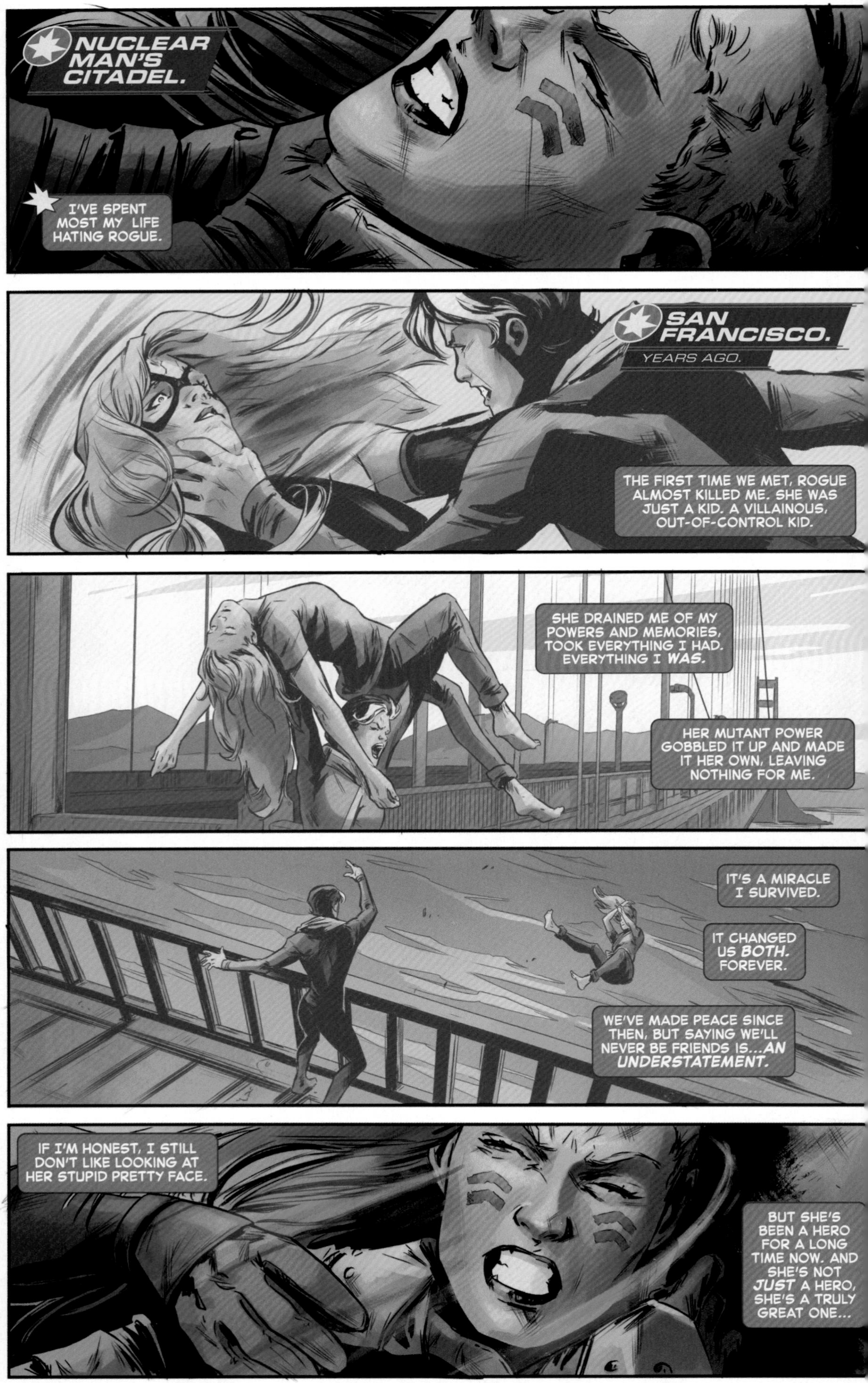
NUCLEAR MAN'S CITADEL.
I'VE SPENT MOST MY LIFE HATING ROGUE.
SAN FRANCISCO.
YEARS AGO.
THE FIRST TIME WE MET, ROGUE ALMOST KILLED ME. SHE WAS JUST A KID. A VILLAINOUS, OUT-OF-CONTROL KID.
SHE DRAINED ME OF MY POWERS AND MEMORIES, TOOK EVERYTHING I HAD. EVERYTHING I *WAS.*
HER MUTANT POWER GOBBLED IT UP AND MADE IT HER OWN, LEAVING NOTHING FOR ME.
IT'S A MIRACLE I SURVIVED.
IT CHANGED US *BOTH.* FOREVER.
WE'VE MADE PEACE SINCE THEN, BUT SAYING WE'LL NEVER BE FRIENDS IS...*AN UNDERSTATEMENT.*
IF I'M HONEST, I STILL DON'T LIKE LOOKING AT HER STUPID PRETTY FACE.
BUT SHE'S BEEN A HERO FOR A LONG TIME NOW. AND SHE'S NOT *JUST* A HERO, SHE'S A TRULY GREAT ONE...

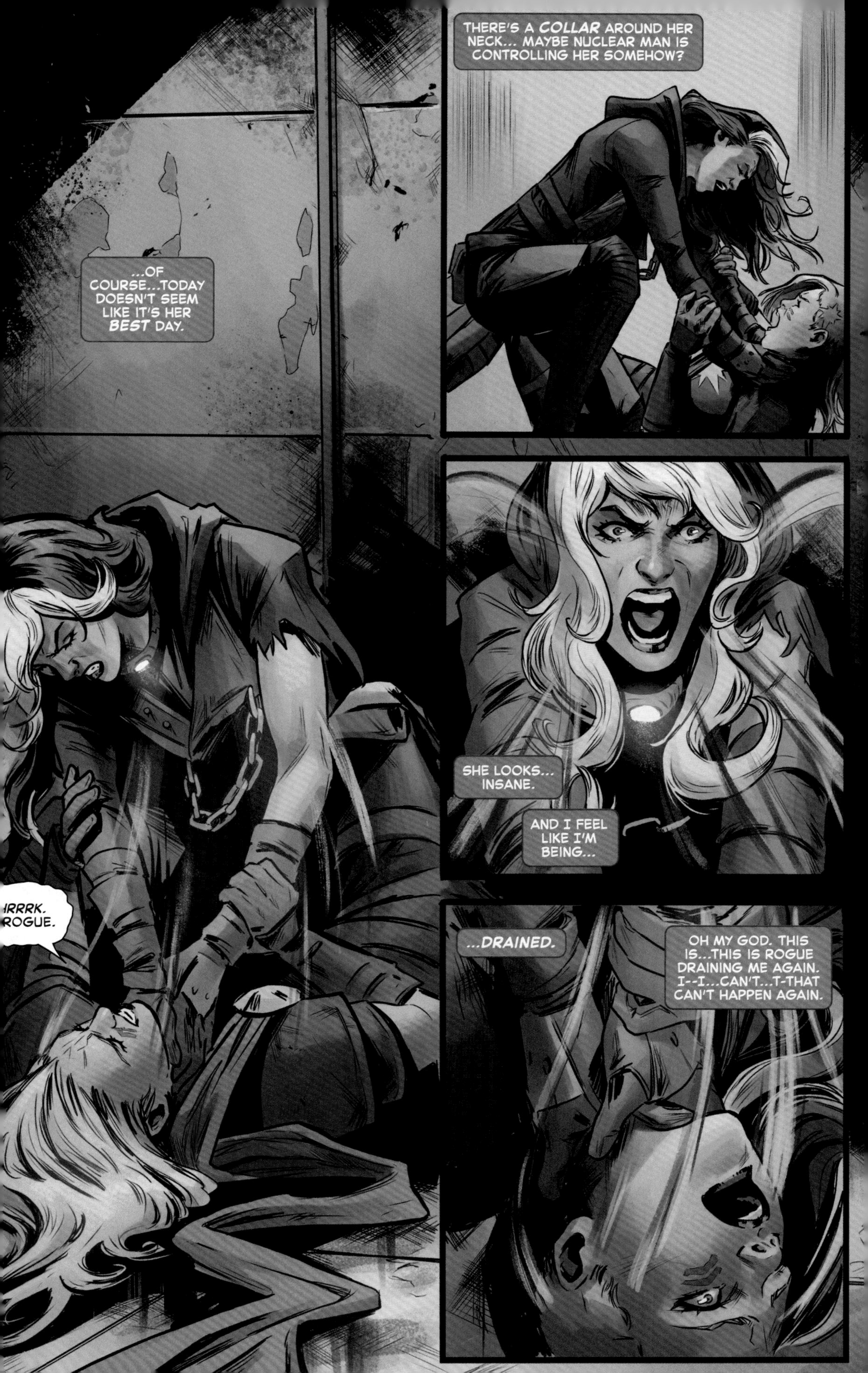
...OF COURSE...TODAY DOESN'T SEEM LIKE IT'S HER BEST DAY.
THERE'S A COLLAR AROUND HER NECK... MAYBE NUCLEAR MAN IS CONTROLLING HER SOMEHOW?
IRRRK. ROGUE.
SHE LOOKS... INSANE.
AND I FEEL LIKE I'M BEING...
...DRAINED.
OH MY GOD. THIS IS...THIS IS ROGUE DRAINING ME AGAIN. I--I...CAN'T...T-THAT CAN'T HAPPEN AGAIN.

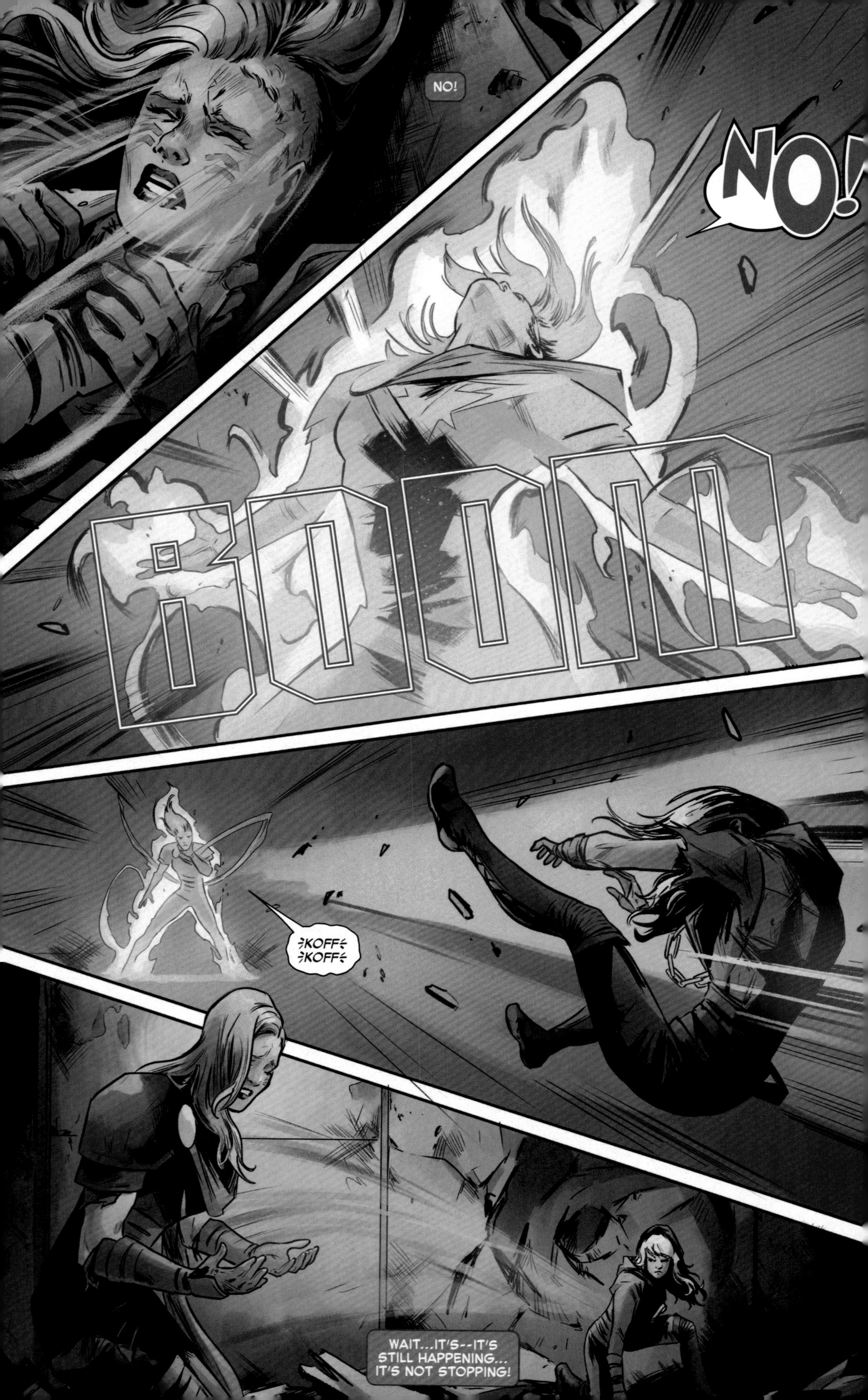
NO!
NO!
BOOM
KOFF KOFF
WAIT...IT'S--IT'S STILL HAPPENING... IT'S NOT STOPPING!

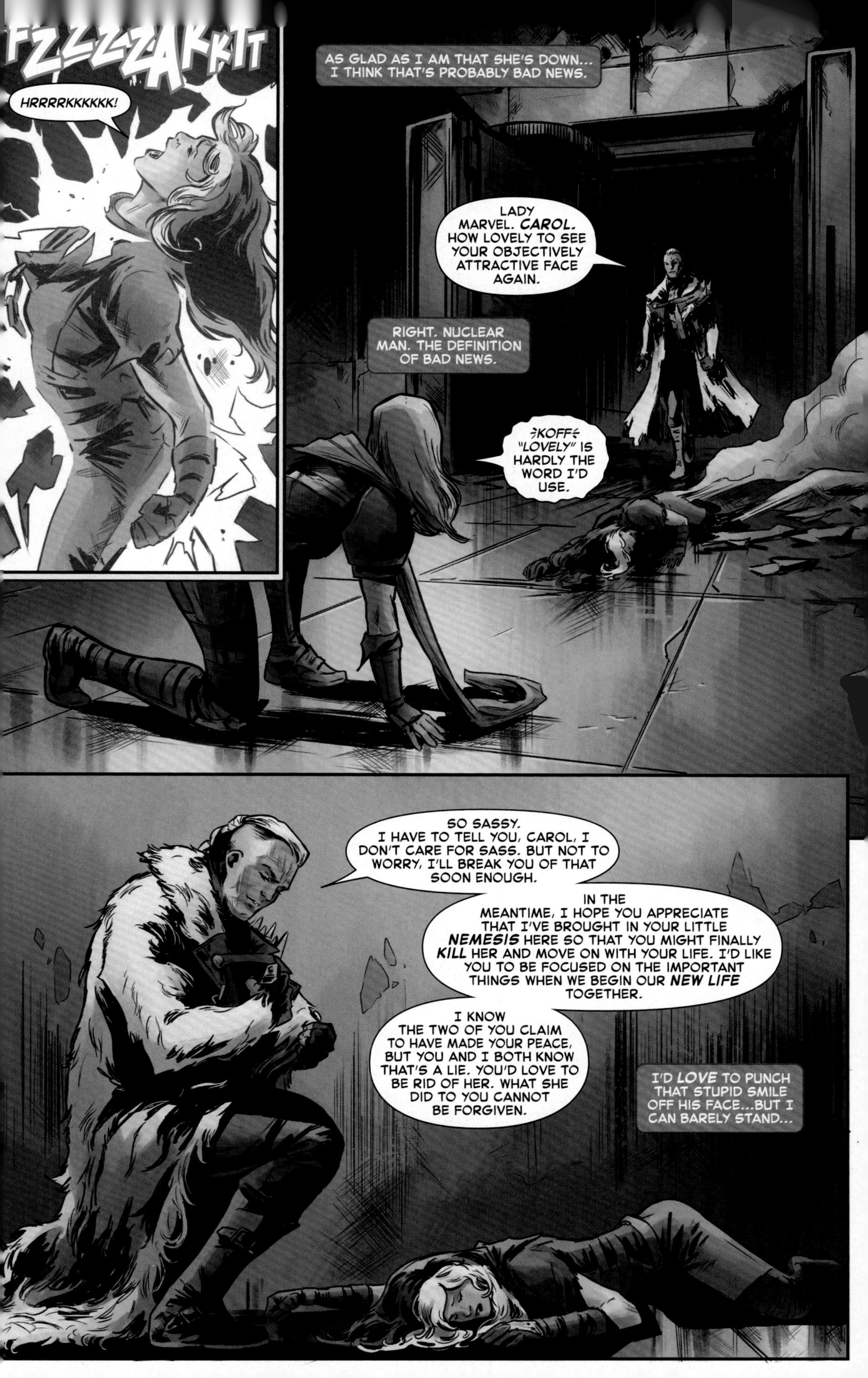
FZZZZZAKKTT
HRRRRKKKKKK!
AS GLAD AS I AM THAT SHE'S DOWN... I THINK THAT'S PROBABLY BAD NEWS.
LADY MARVEL. CAROL. HOW LOVELY TO SEE YOUR OBJECTIVELY ATTRACTIVE FACE AGAIN.
RIGHT. NUCLEAR MAN. THE DEFINITION OF BAD NEWS.
KOFF "LOVELY" IS HARDLY THE WORD I'D USE.
SO SASSY. I HAVE TO TELL YOU, CAROL, I DON'T CARE FOR SASS. BUT NOT TO WORRY, I'LL BREAK YOU OF THAT SOON ENOUGH.
IN THE MEANTIME, I HOPE YOU APPRECIATE THAT I'VE BROUGHT IN YOUR LITTLE NEMESIS HERE SO THAT YOU MIGHT FINALLY KILL HER AND MOVE ON WITH YOUR LIFE. I'D LIKE YOU TO BE FOCUSED ON THE IMPORTANT THINGS WHEN WE BEGIN OUR NEW LIFE TOGETHER.
I KNOW THE TWO OF YOU CLAIM TO HAVE MADE YOUR PEACE, BUT YOU AND I BOTH KNOW THAT'S A LIE. YOU'D LOVE TO BE RID OF HER. WHAT SHE DID TO YOU CANNOT BE FORGIVEN.
I'D LOVE TO PUNCH THAT STUPID SMILE OFF HIS FACE...BUT I CAN BARELY STAND...

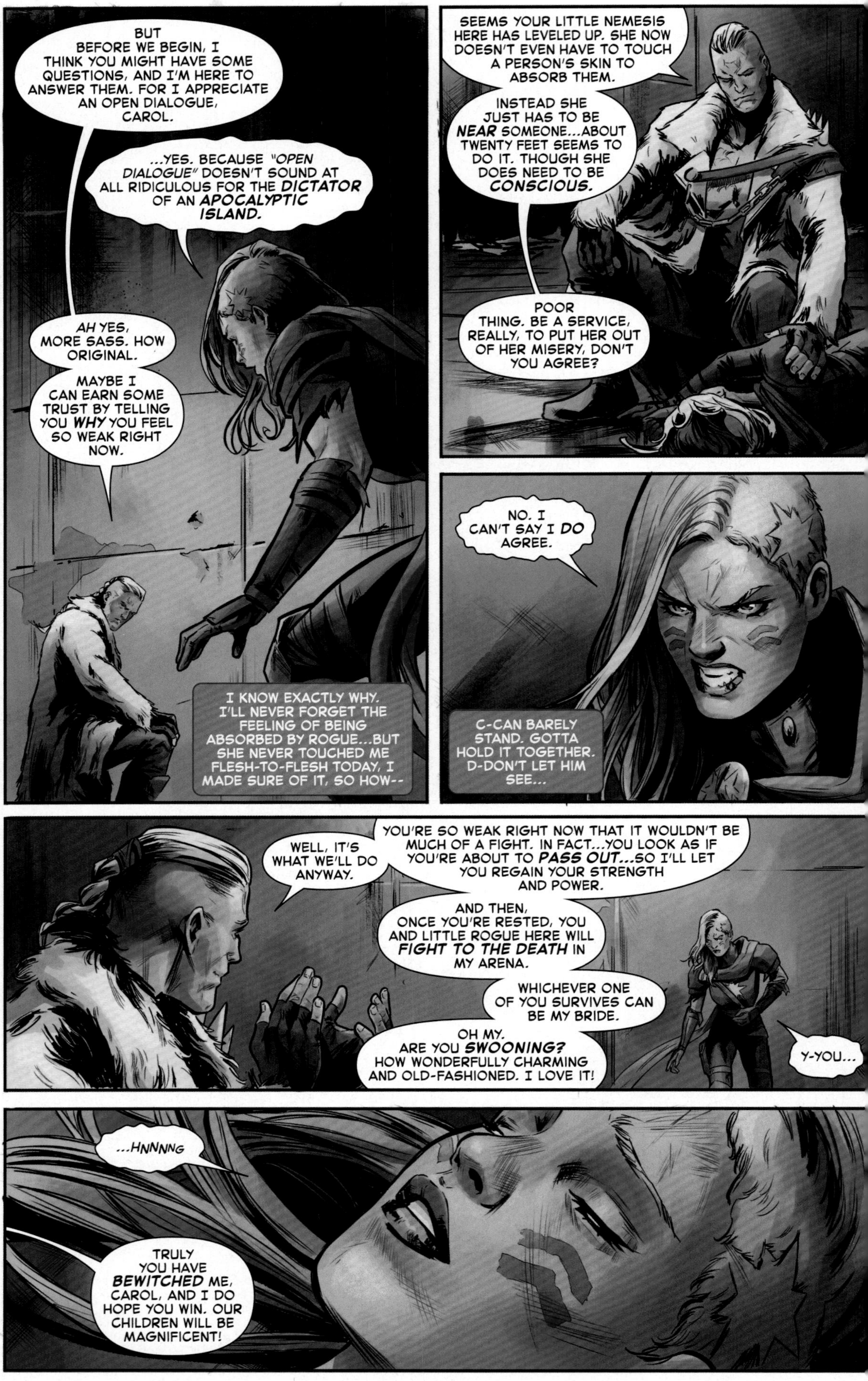

BUT BEFORE WE BEGIN, I THINK YOU MIGHT HAVE SOME QUESTIONS, AND I'M HERE TO ANSWER THEM. FOR I APPRECIATE AN OPEN DIALOGUE, CAROL.
...YES. BECAUSE "OPEN DIALOGUE" DOESN'T SOUND AT ALL RIDICULOUS FOR THE DICTATOR OF AN APOCALYPTIC ISLAND.
AH YES, MORE SASS. HOW ORIGINAL.
MAYBE I CAN EARN SOME TRUST BY TELLING YOU WHY YOU FEEL SO WEAK RIGHT NOW.
I KNOW EXACTLY WHY. I'LL NEVER FORGET THE FEELING OF BEING ABSORBED BY ROGUE...BUT SHE NEVER TOUCHED ME FLESH-TO-FLESH TODAY, I MADE SURE OF IT, SO HOW--
SEEMS YOUR LITTLE NEMESIS HERE HAS LEVELED UP. SHE NOW DOESN'T EVEN HAVE TO TOUCH A PERSON'S SKIN TO ABSORB THEM.
INSTEAD SHE JUST HAS TO BE NEAR SOMEONE...ABOUT TWENTY FEET SEEMS TO DO IT. THOUGH SHE DOES NEED TO BE CONSCIOUS.
POOR THING. BE A SERVICE, REALLY, TO PUT HER OUT OF HER MISERY, DON'T YOU AGREE?
NO. I CAN'T SAY I DO AGREE.
C-CAN BARELY STAND. GOTTA HOLD IT TOGETHER. D-DON'T LET HIM SEE...
WELL, IT'S WHAT WE'LL DO ANYWAY.
YOU'RE SO WEAK RIGHT NOW THAT IT WOULDN'T BE MUCH OF A FIGHT. IN FACT...YOU LOOK AS IF YOU'RE ABOUT TO PASS OUT...SO I'LL LET YOU REGAIN YOUR STRENGTH AND POWER.
AND THEN, ONCE YOU'RE RESTED, YOU AND LITTLE ROGUE HERE WILL FIGHT TO THE DEATH IN MY ARENA.
WHICHEVER ONE OF YOU SURVIVES CAN BE MY BRIDE.
Y-YOU...
OH MY. ARE YOU SWOONING? HOW WONDERFULLY CHARMING AND OLD-FASHIONED. I LOVE IT!
...HNNNNG
TRULY YOU HAVE BEWITCHED ME, CAROL, AND I DO HOPE YOU WIN. OUR CHILDREN WILL BE MAGNIFICENT!

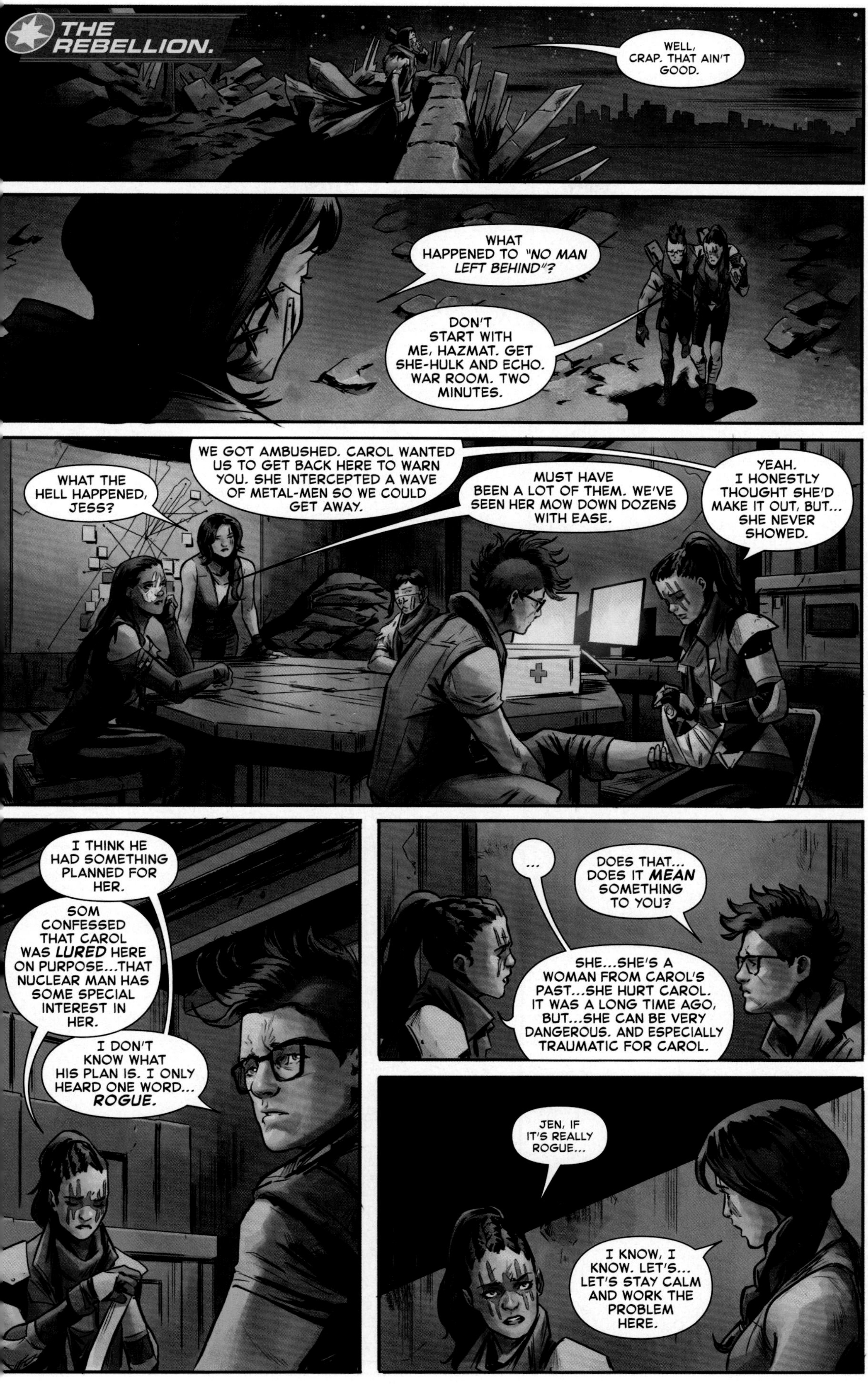
THE REBELLION.
WELL, CRAP. THAT AIN'T GOOD.
WHAT HAPPENED TO "NO MAN LEFT BEHIND"?
DON'T START WITH ME, HAZMAT. GET SHE-HULK AND ECHO. WAR ROOM. TWO MINUTES.
WHAT THE HELL HAPPENED, JESS?
WE GOT AMBUSHED. CAROL WANTED US TO GET BACK HERE TO WARN YOU. SHE INTERCEPTED A WAVE OF METAL-MEN SO WE COULD GET AWAY.
MUST HAVE BEEN A LOT OF THEM. WE'VE SEEN HER MOW DOWN DOZENS WITH EASE.
YEAH. I HONESTLY THOUGHT SHE'D MAKE IT OUT, BUT... SHE NEVER SHOWED.
I THINK HE HAD SOMETHING PLANNED FOR HER.
SOM CONFESSED THAT CAROL WAS LURED HERE ON PURPOSE...THAT NUCLEAR MAN HAS SOME SPECIAL INTEREST IN HER.
I DON'T KNOW WHAT HIS PLAN IS. I ONLY HEARD ONE WORD... ROGUE.
...
DOES THAT... DOES IT MEAN SOMETHING TO YOU?
SHE...SHE'S A WOMAN FROM CAROL'S PAST...SHE HURT CAROL. IT WAS A LONG TIME AGO, BUT...SHE CAN BE VERY DANGEROUS. AND ESPECIALLY TRAUMATIC FOR CAROL.
JEN, IF IT'S REALLY ROGUE...
I KNOW, I KNOW. LET'S... LET'S STAY CALM AND WORK THE PROBLEM HERE.

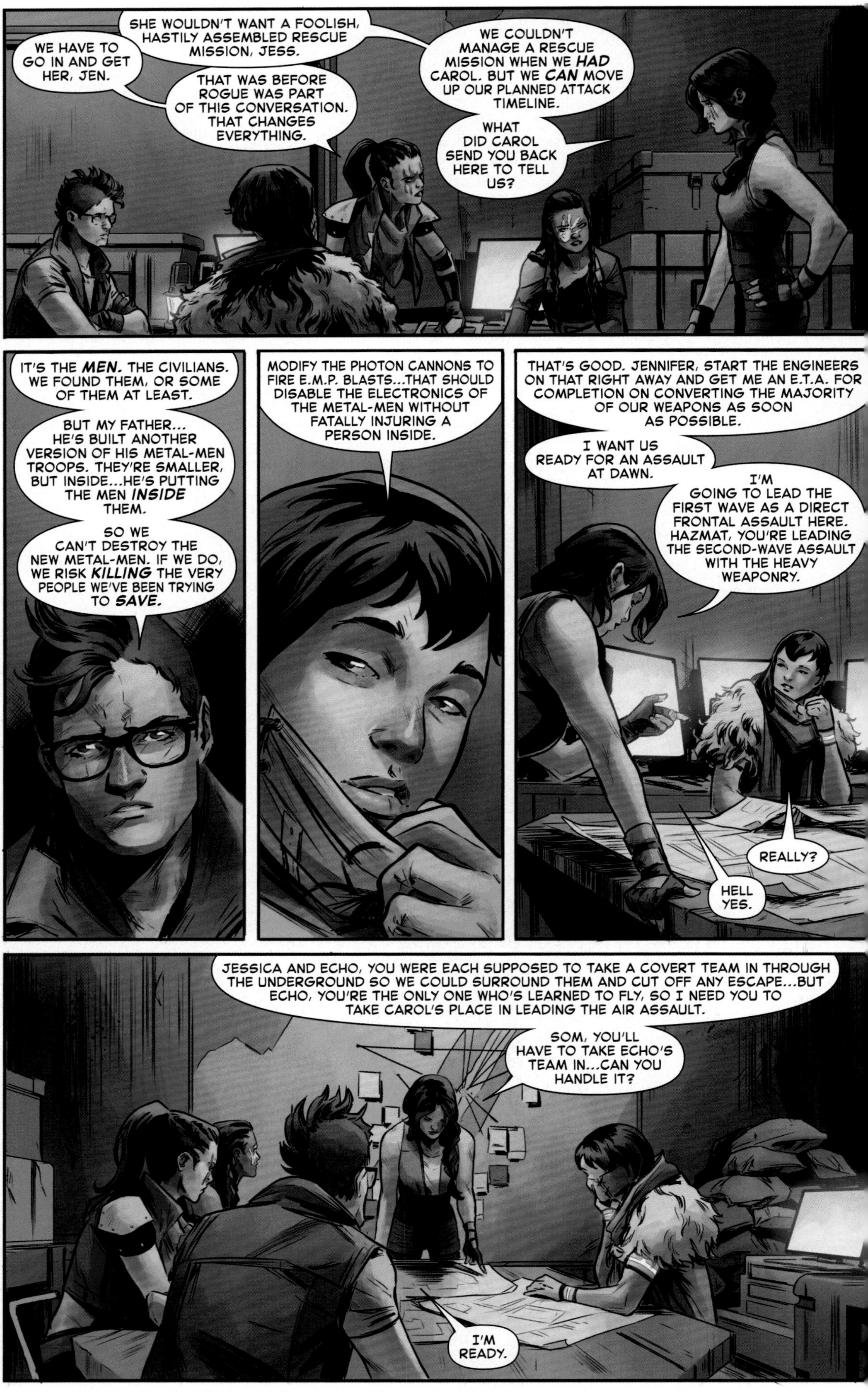

WE HAVE TO GO IN AND GET HER, JEN.
SHE WOULDN'T WANT A FOOLISH, HASTILY ASSEMBLED RESCUE MISSION, JESS.
THAT WAS BEFORE ROGUE WAS PART OF THIS CONVERSATION. THAT CHANGES EVERYTHING.
WE COULDN'T MANAGE A RESCUE MISSION WHEN WE HAD CAROL. BUT WE CAN MOVE UP OUR PLANNED ATTACK TIMELINE.
WHAT DID CAROL SEND YOU BACK HERE TO TELL US?
IT'S THE MEN. THE CIVILIANS. WE FOUND THEM, OR SOME OF THEM AT LEAST.
BUT MY FATHER... HE'S BUILT ANOTHER VERSION OF HIS METAL-MEN TROOPS. THEY'RE SMALLER, BUT INSIDE... HE'S PUTTING THE MEN INSIDE THEM.
SO WE CAN'T DESTROY THE NEW METAL-MEN. IF WE DO, WE RISK KILLING THE VERY PEOPLE WE'VE BEEN TRYING TO SAVE.
MODIFY THE PHOTON CANNONS TO FIRE E.M.P. BLASTS...THAT SHOULD DISABLE THE ELECTRONICS OF THE METAL-MEN WITHOUT FATALLY INJURING A PERSON INSIDE.
THAT'S GOOD. JENNIFER, START THE ENGINEERS ON THAT RIGHT AWAY AND GET ME AN E.T.A. FOR COMPLETION ON CONVERTING THE MAJORITY OF OUR WEAPONS AS SOON AS POSSIBLE.
I WANT US READY FOR AN ASSAULT AT DAWN.
I'M GOING TO LEAD THE FIRST WAVE AS A DIRECT FRONTAL ASSAULT HERE. HAZMAT, YOU'RE LEADING THE SECOND-WAVE ASSAULT WITH THE HEAVY WEAPONRY.
REALLY?
HELL YES.
JESSICA AND ECHO, YOU WERE EACH SUPPOSED TO TAKE A COVERT TEAM IN THROUGH THE UNDERGROUND SO WE COULD SURROUND THEM AND CUT OFF ANY ESCAPE...BUT ECHO, YOU'RE THE ONLY ONE WHO'S LEARNED TO FLY, SO I NEED YOU TO TAKE CAROL'S PLACE IN LEADING THE AIR ASSAULT.
SOM, YOU'LL HAVE TO TAKE ECHO'S TEAM IN...CAN YOU HANDLE IT?
I'M READY.

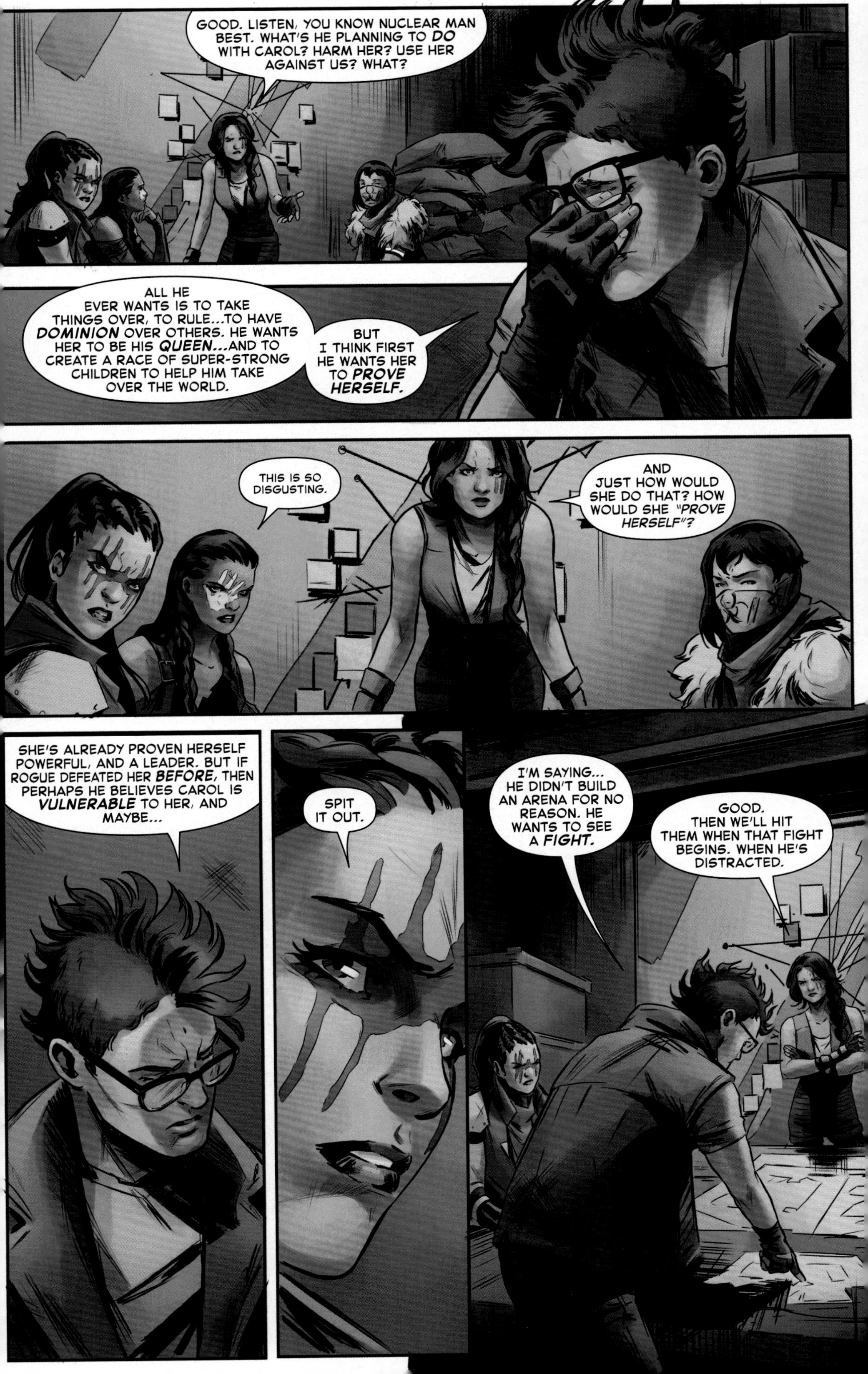
GOOD. LISTEN, YOU KNOW NUCLEAR MAN BEST. WHAT'S HE PLANNING TO DO WITH CAROL? HARM HER? USE HER AGAINST US? WHAT?
ALL HE EVER WANTS IS TO TAKE THINGS OVER, TO RULE...TO HAVE DOMINION OVER OTHERS. HE WANTS HER TO BE HIS QUEEN...AND TO CREATE A RACE OF SUPER-STRONG CHILDREN TO HELP HIM TAKE OVER THE WORLD.
BUT I THINK FIRST HE WANTS HER TO PROVE HERSELF.
THIS IS SO DISGUSTING.
AND JUST HOW WOULD SHE DO THAT? HOW WOULD SHE "PROVE HERSELF"?
SHE'S ALREADY PROVEN HERSELF POWERFUL, AND A LEADER. BUT IF ROGUE DEFEATED HER BEFORE, THEN PERHAPS HE BELIEVES CAROL IS VULNERABLE TO HER, AND MAYBE...
SPIT IT OUT.
I'M SAYING... HE DIDN'T BUILD AN ARENA FOR NO REASON. HE WANTS TO SEE A FIGHT.
GOOD. THEN WE'LL HIT THEM WHEN THAT FIGHT BEGINS. WHEN HE'S DISTRACTED.

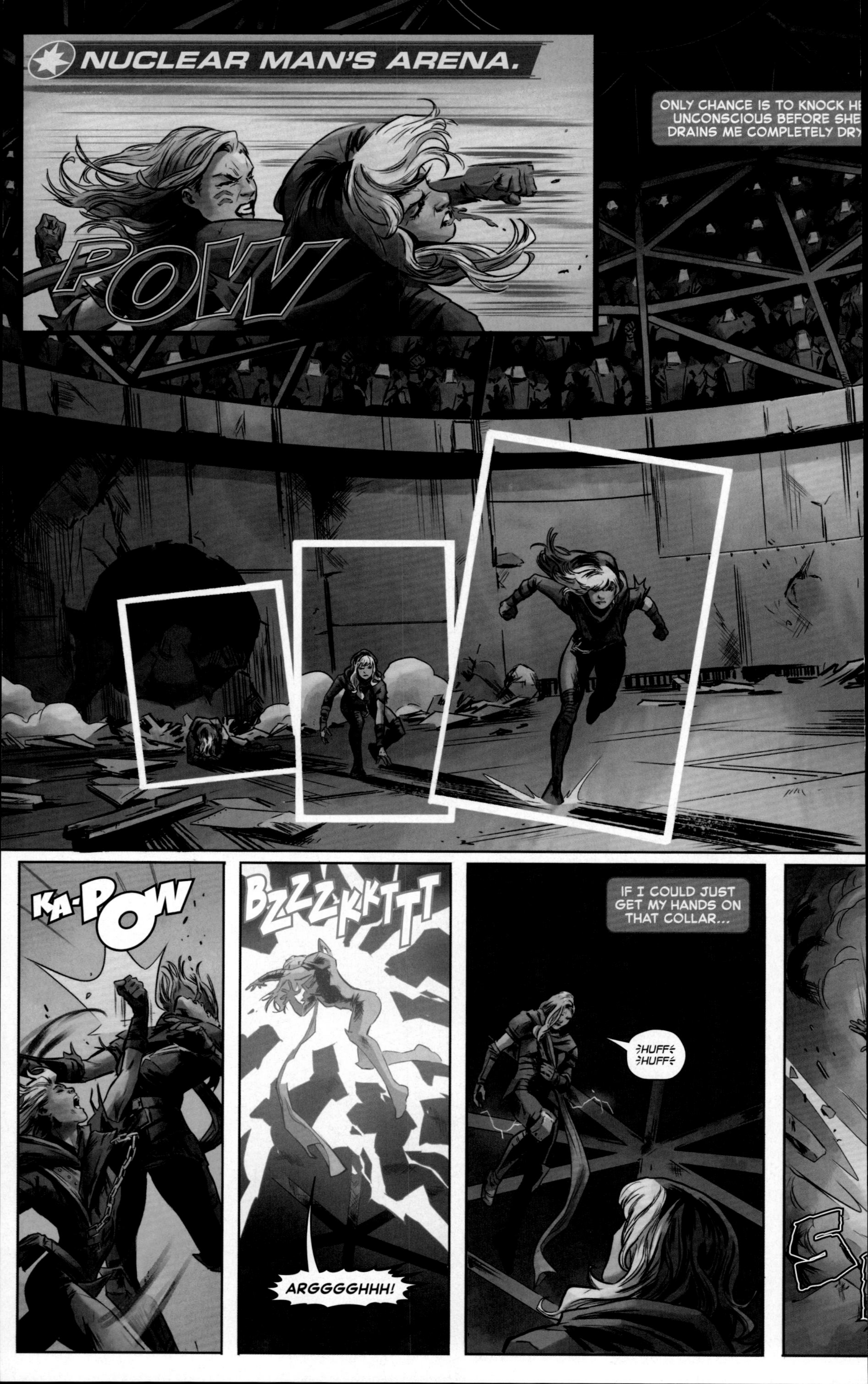
NUCLEAR MAN'S ARENA.
ONLY CHANCE IS TO KNOCK HE
UNCONSCIOUS BEFORE SHE
DRAINS ME COMPLETELY DRY
POW
KA-POW
BZZZ-KKTTT
ARGGGGHHH!
IF I COULD JUST GET MY HANDS ON THAT COLLAR...
HUFF HUFF

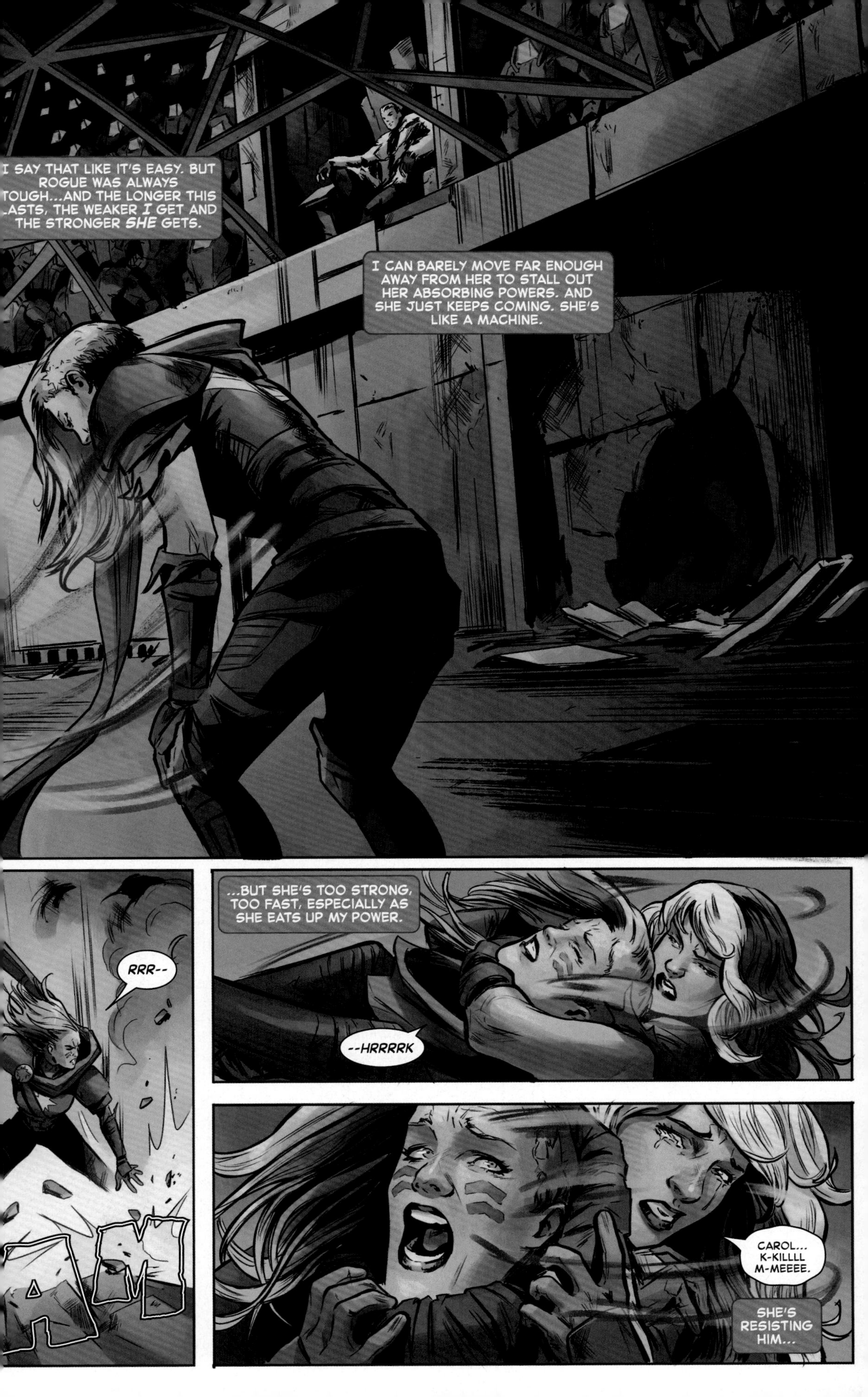
I SAY THAT LIKE IT'S EASY. BUT ROGUE WAS ALWAYS TOUGH...AND THE LONGER THIS LASTS, THE WEAKER I GET AND THE STRONGER SHE GETS.
I CAN BARELY MOVE FAR ENOUGH AWAY FROM HER TO STALL OUT HER ABSORBING POWERS. AND SHE JUST KEEPS COMING. SHE'S LIKE A MACHINE.
RRR--
...BUT SHE'S TOO STRONG, TOO FAST, ESPECIALLY AS SHE EATS UP MY POWER.
--HRRRRK
CAROL... K-KILLLL M-MEEEE.
SHE'S RESISTING HIM...

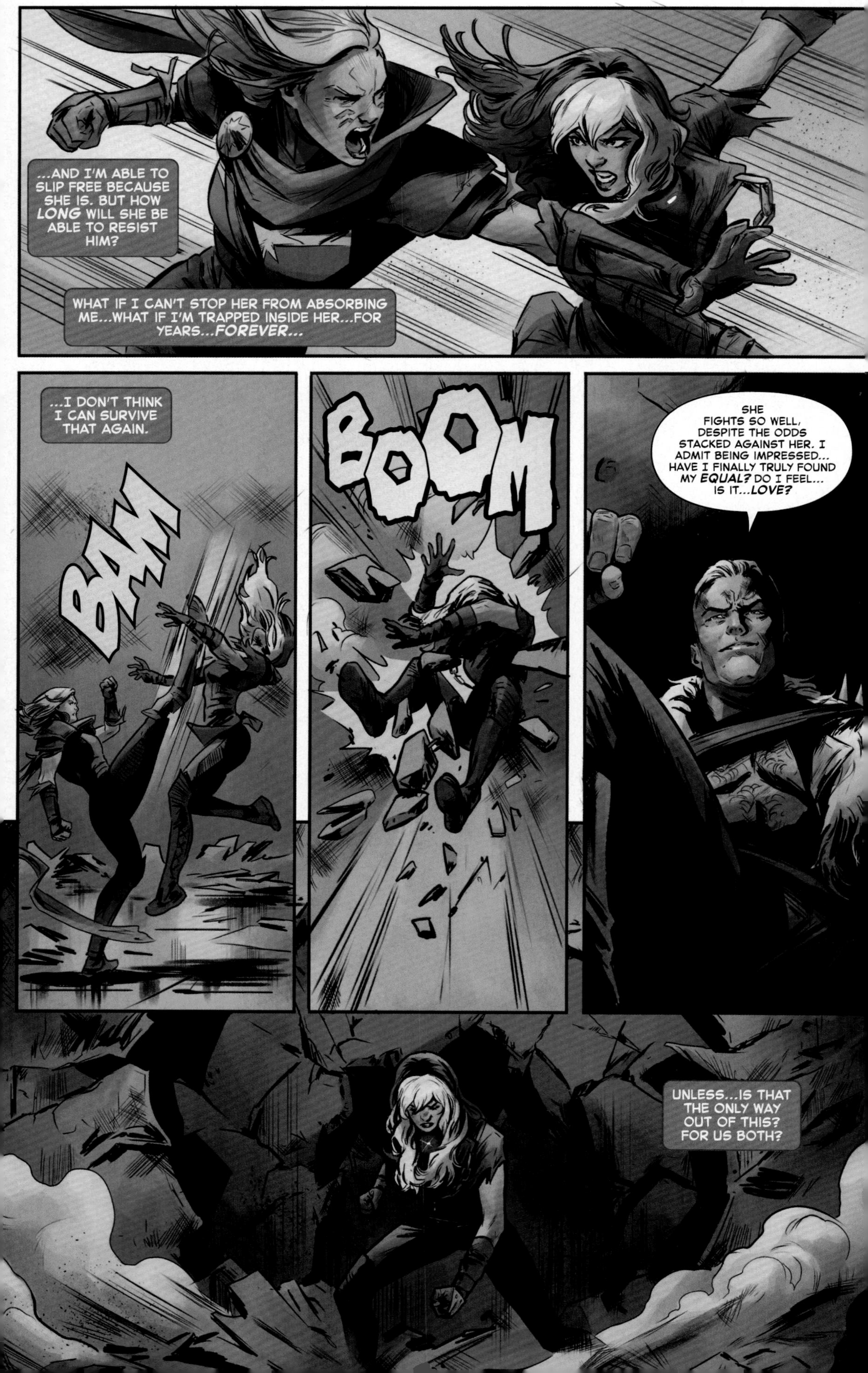
...AND I'M ABLE TO SLIP FREE BECAUSE SHE IS. BUT HOW LONG WILL SHE BE ABLE TO RESIST HIM?
WHAT IF I CAN'T STOP HER FROM ABSORBING ME...WHAT IF I'M TRAPPED INSIDE HER...FOR YEARS...FOREVER...
...I DON'T THINK I CAN SURVIVE THAT AGAIN.
BAM
BOOM
SHE FIGHTS SO WELL, DESPITE THE ODDS STACKED AGAINST HER. I ADMIT BEING IMPRESSED... HAVE I FINALLY TRULY FOUND MY EQUAL? DO I FEEL... IS IT...LOVE?
UNLESS...IS THAT THE ONLY WAY OUT OF THIS? FOR US BOTH?

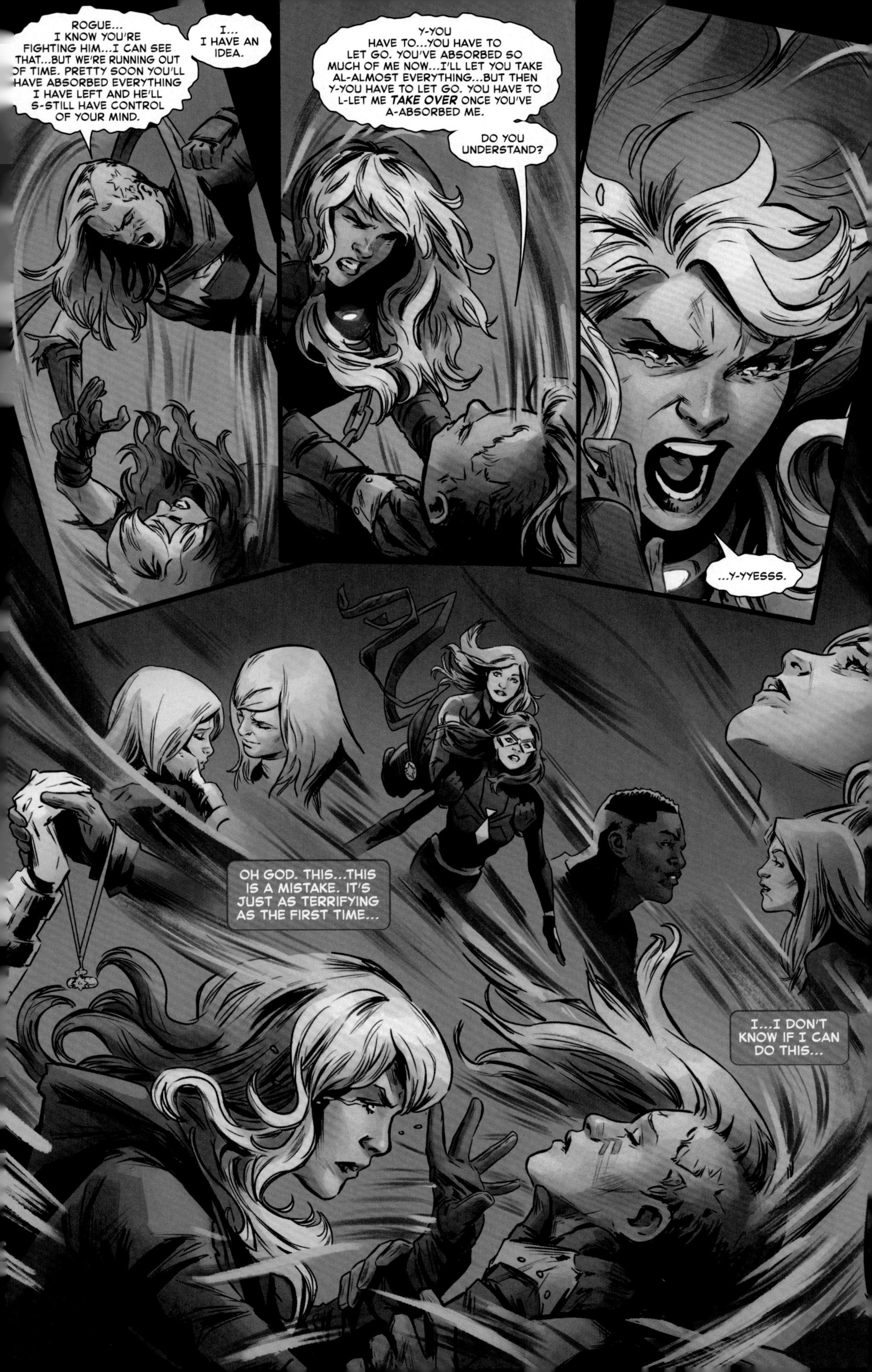
ROGUE... I KNOW YOU'RE FIGHTING HIM...I CAN SEE THAT...BUT WE'RE RUNNING OUT OF TIME. PRETTY SOON YOU'LL HAVE ABSORBED EVERYTHING I HAVE LEFT AND HE'LL S-STILL HAVE CONTROL OF YOUR MIND.
I... I HAVE AN IDEA.
Y-YOU HAVE TO...YOU HAVE TO LET GO. YOU'VE ABSORBED SO MUCH OF ME NOW...I'LL LET YOU TAKE AL-ALMOST EVERYTHING...BUT THEN Y-YOU HAVE TO LET GO. YOU HAVE TO L-LET ME *TAKE OVER* ONCE YOU'VE A-ABSORBED ME.
DO YOU UNDERSTAND?
...Y-YYESSS.
OH GOD. THIS...THIS IS A MISTAKE. IT'S JUST AS TERRIFYING AS THE FIRST TIME...
I...I DON'T KNOW IF I CAN DO THIS...

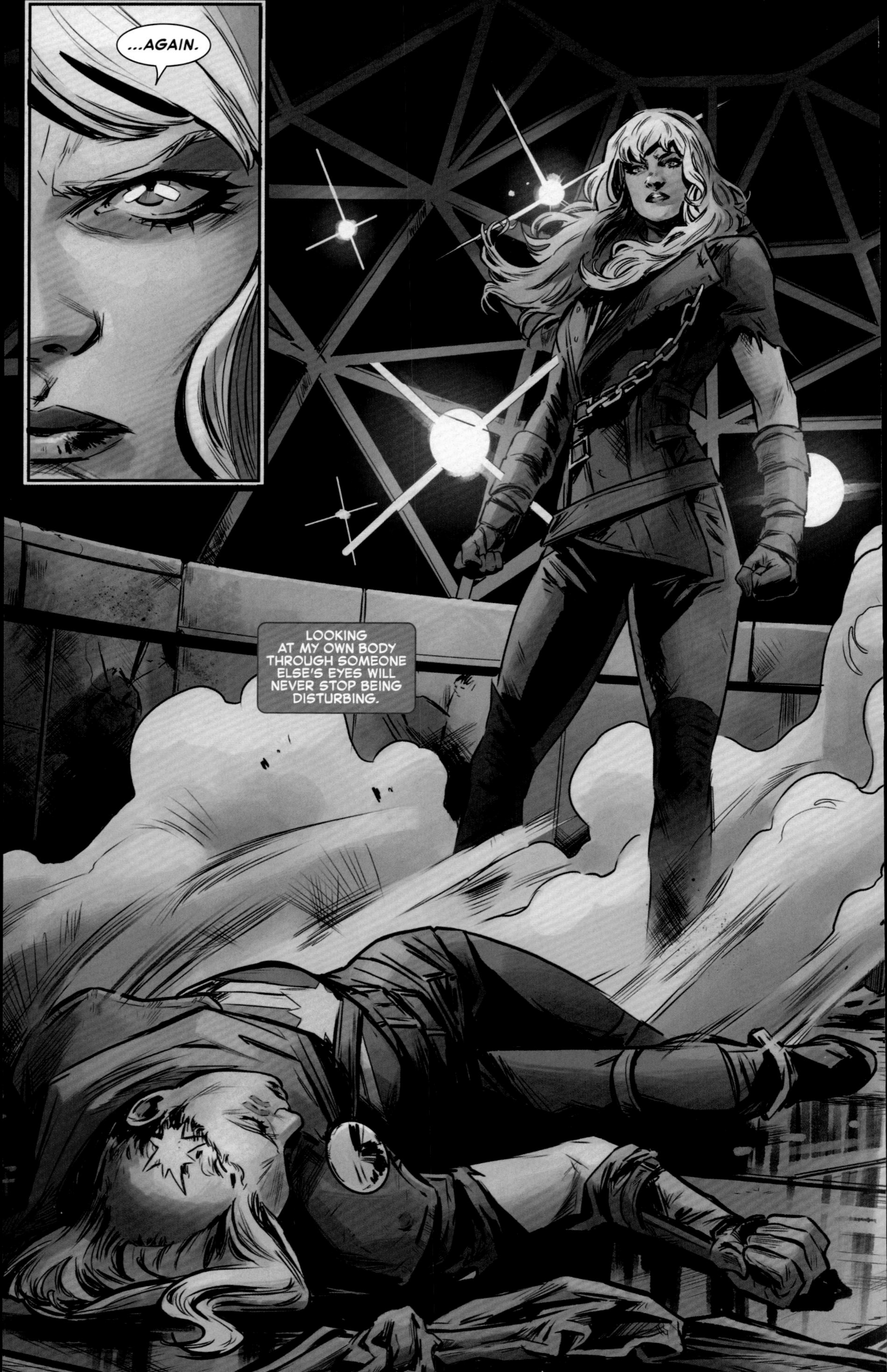
...AGAIN.
LOOKING AT MY OWN BODY THROUGH SOMEONE ELSE'S EYES WILL NEVER STOP BEING DISTURBING.

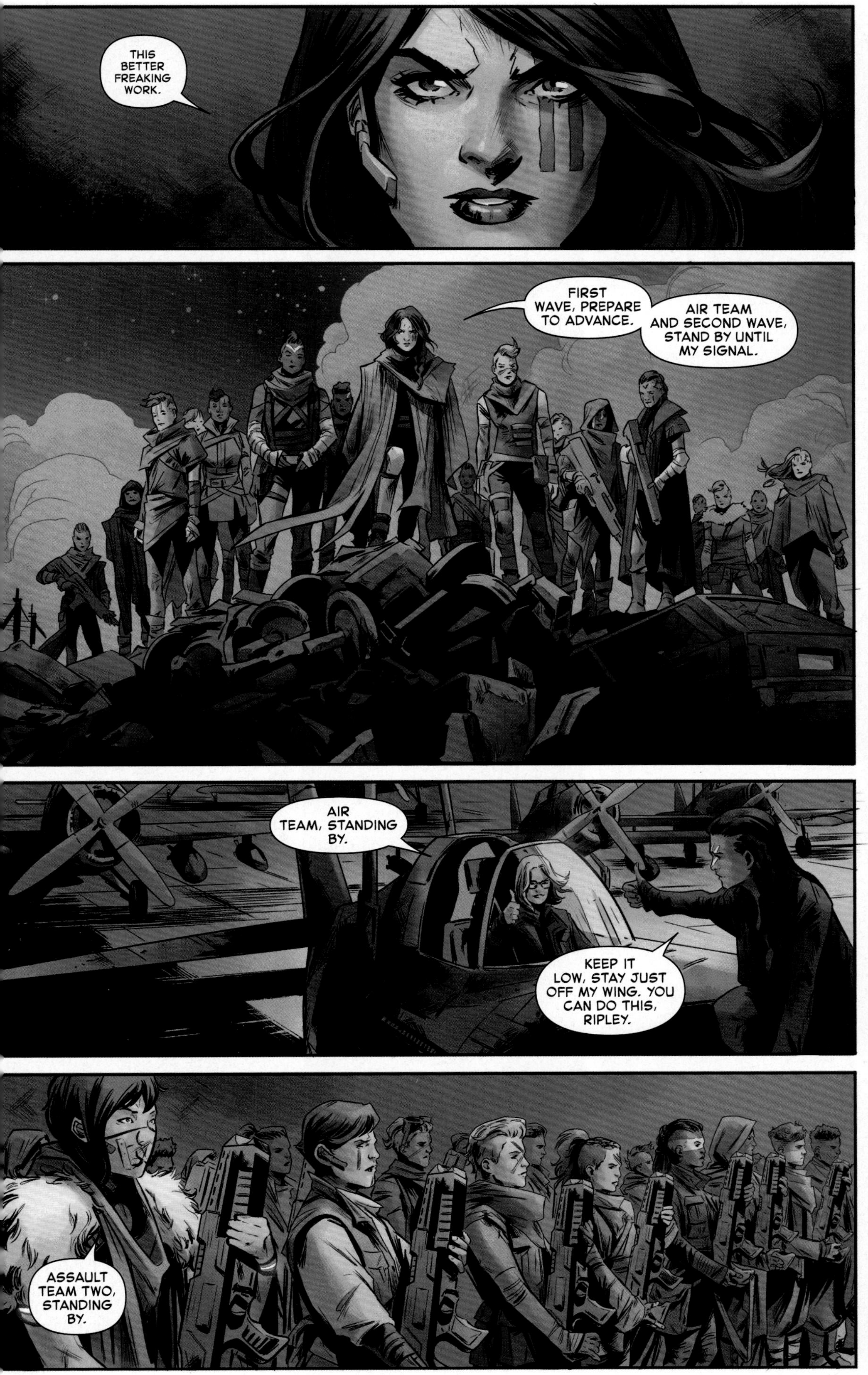
THIS BETTER FREAKING WORK.
FIRST WAVE, PREPARE TO ADVANCE.
AIR TEAM AND SECOND WAVE, STAND BY UNTIL MY SIGNAL.
AIR TEAM, STANDING BY.
KEEP IT LOW, STAY JUST OFF MY WING. YOU CAN DO THIS, RIPLEY.
ASSAULT TEAM TWO, STANDING BY.

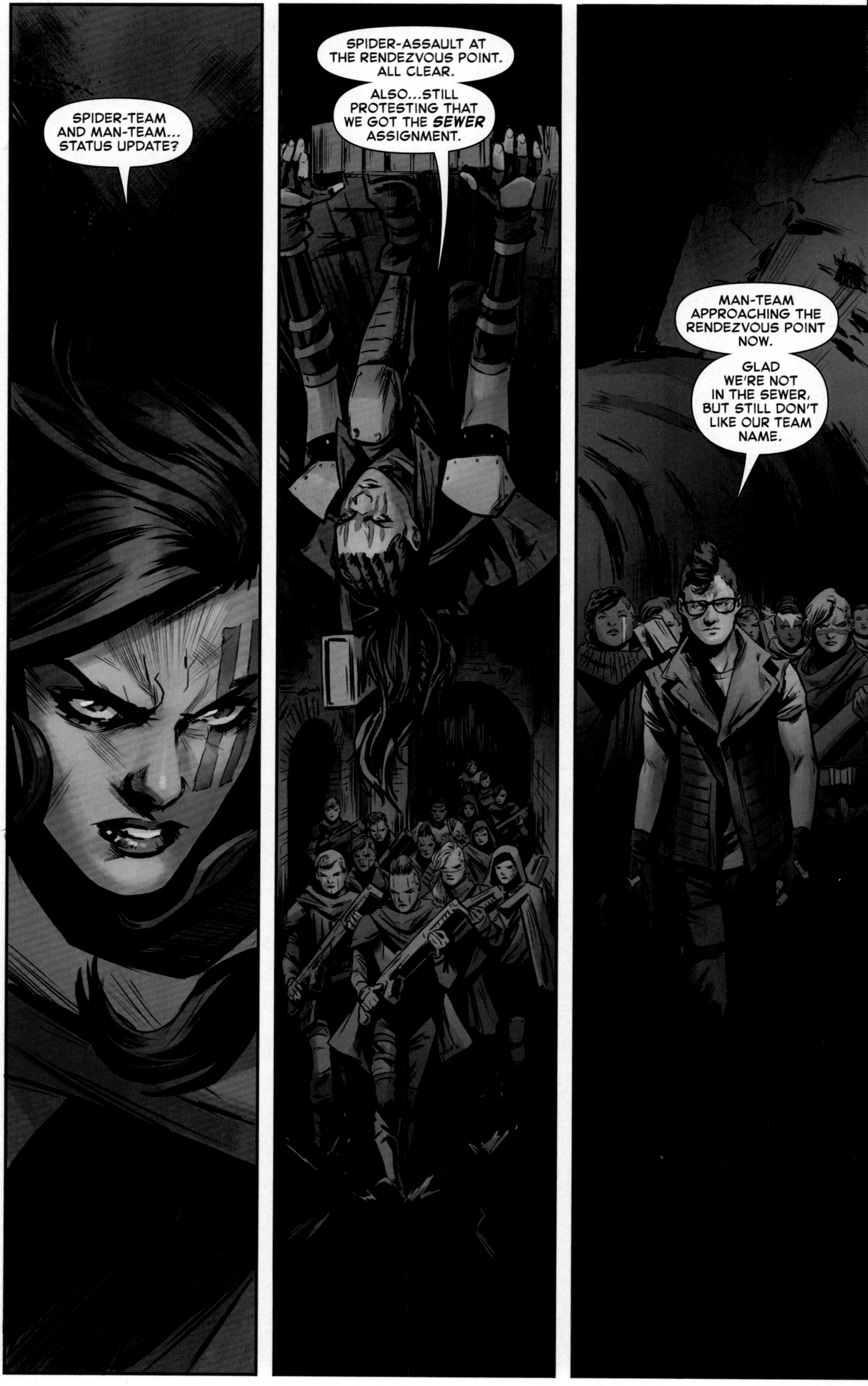
SPIDER-TEAM AND MAN-TEAM... STATUS UPDATE?
SPIDER-ASSAULT AT THE RENDEZVOUS POINT. ALL CLEAR.
ALSO...STILL PROTESTING THAT WE GOT THE *SEWER* ASSIGNMENT.
MAN-TEAM APPROACHING THE RENDEZVOUS POINT NOW.
GLAD WE'RE NOT IN THE SEWER, BUT STILL DON'T LIKE OUR TEAM NAME.

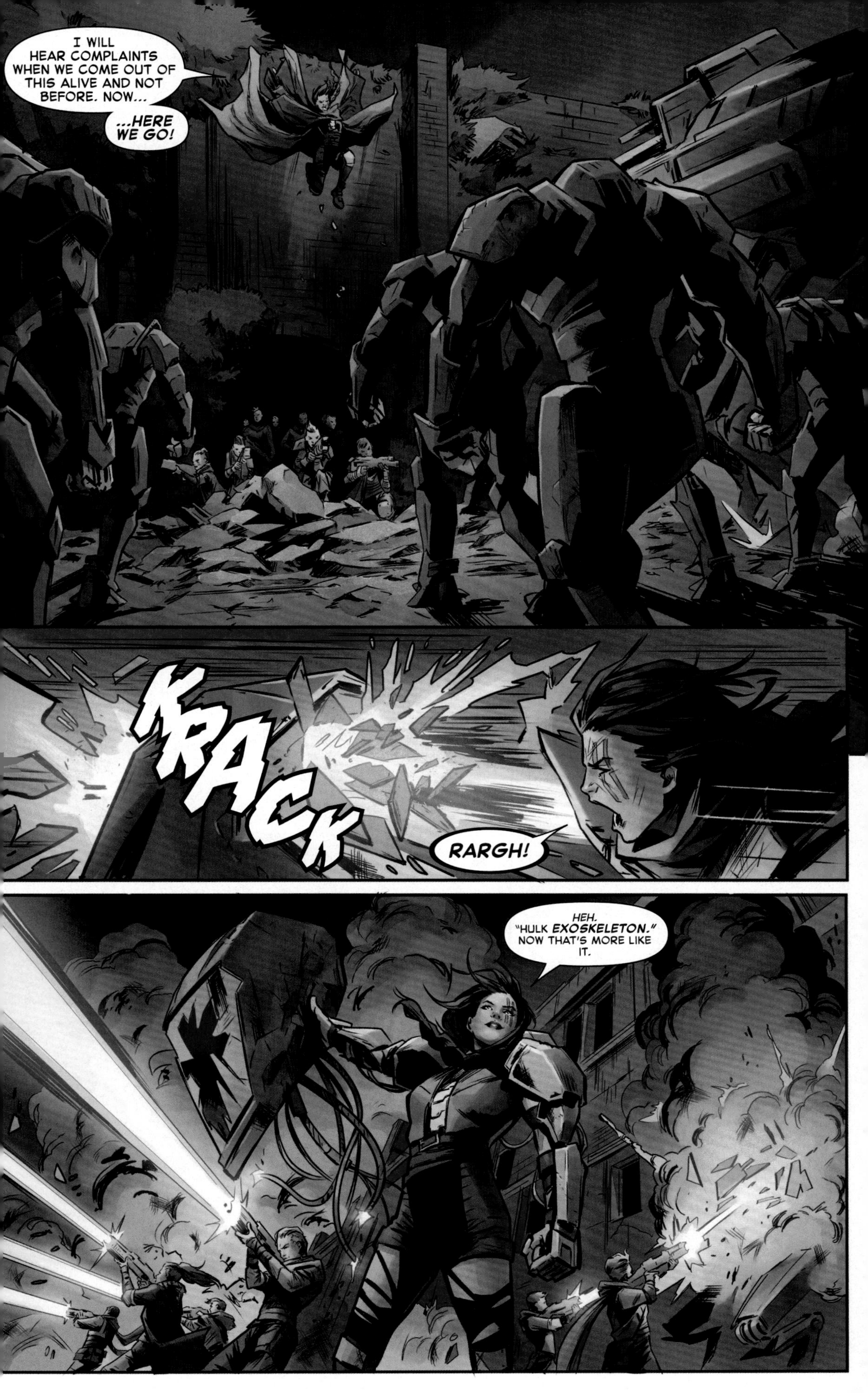
I WILL HEAR COMPLAINTS WHEN WE COME OUT OF THIS ALIVE AND NOT BEFORE. NOW...
...HERE WE GO!
KRACK
RARGH!
HEH. "HULK EXOSKELETON." NOW THAT'S MORE LIKE IT.

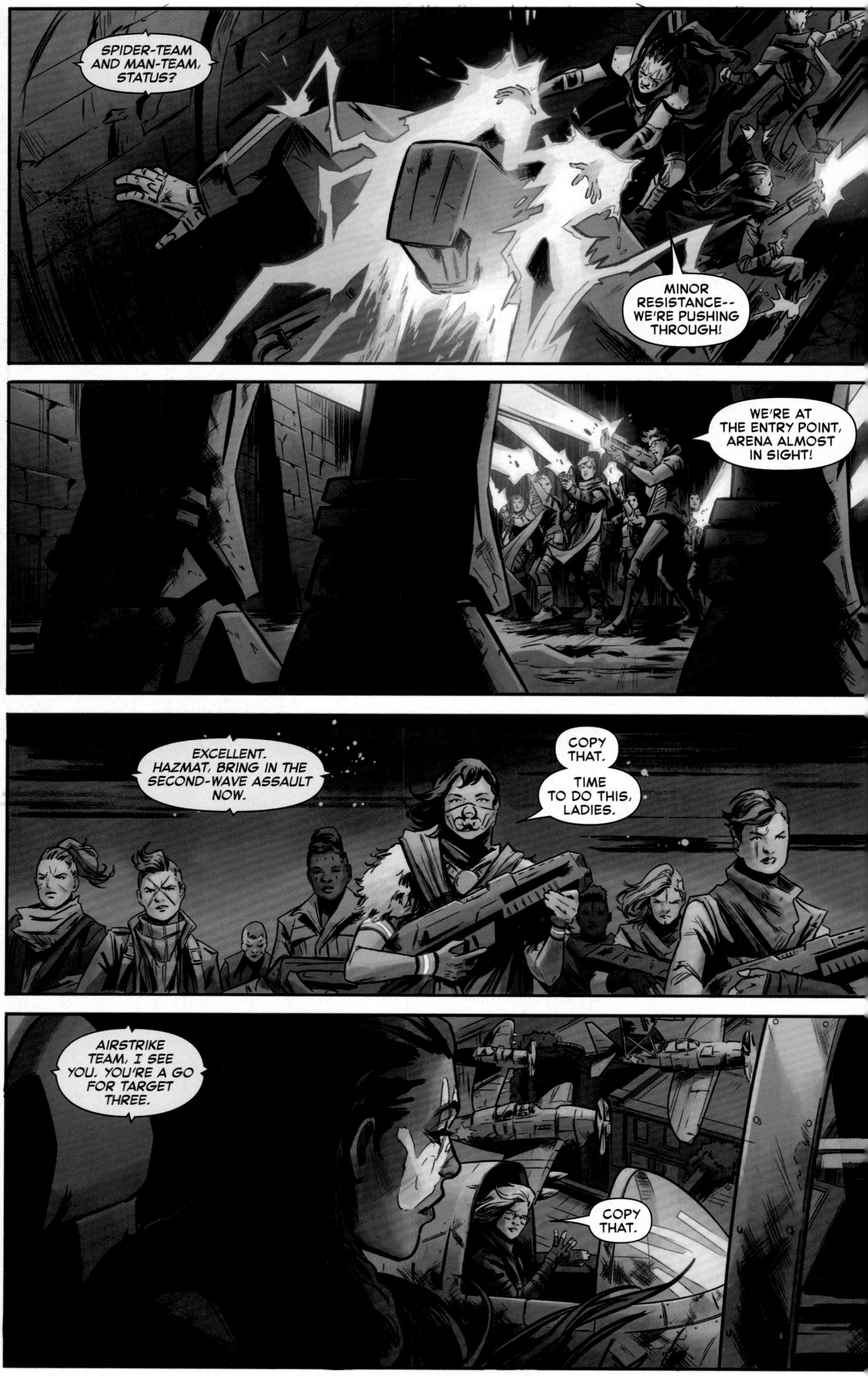
SPIDER-TEAM AND MAN-TEAM, STATUS?
MINOR RESISTANCE-- WE'RE PUSHING THROUGH!
WE'RE AT THE ENTRY POINT, ARENA ALMOST IN SIGHT!
EXCELLENT. HAZMAT, BRING IN THE SECOND-WAVE ASSAULT NOW.
COPY THAT.
TIME TO DO THIS, LADIES.
AIRSTRIKE TEAM, I SEE YOU. YOU'RE A GO FOR TARGET THREE.
COPY THAT.

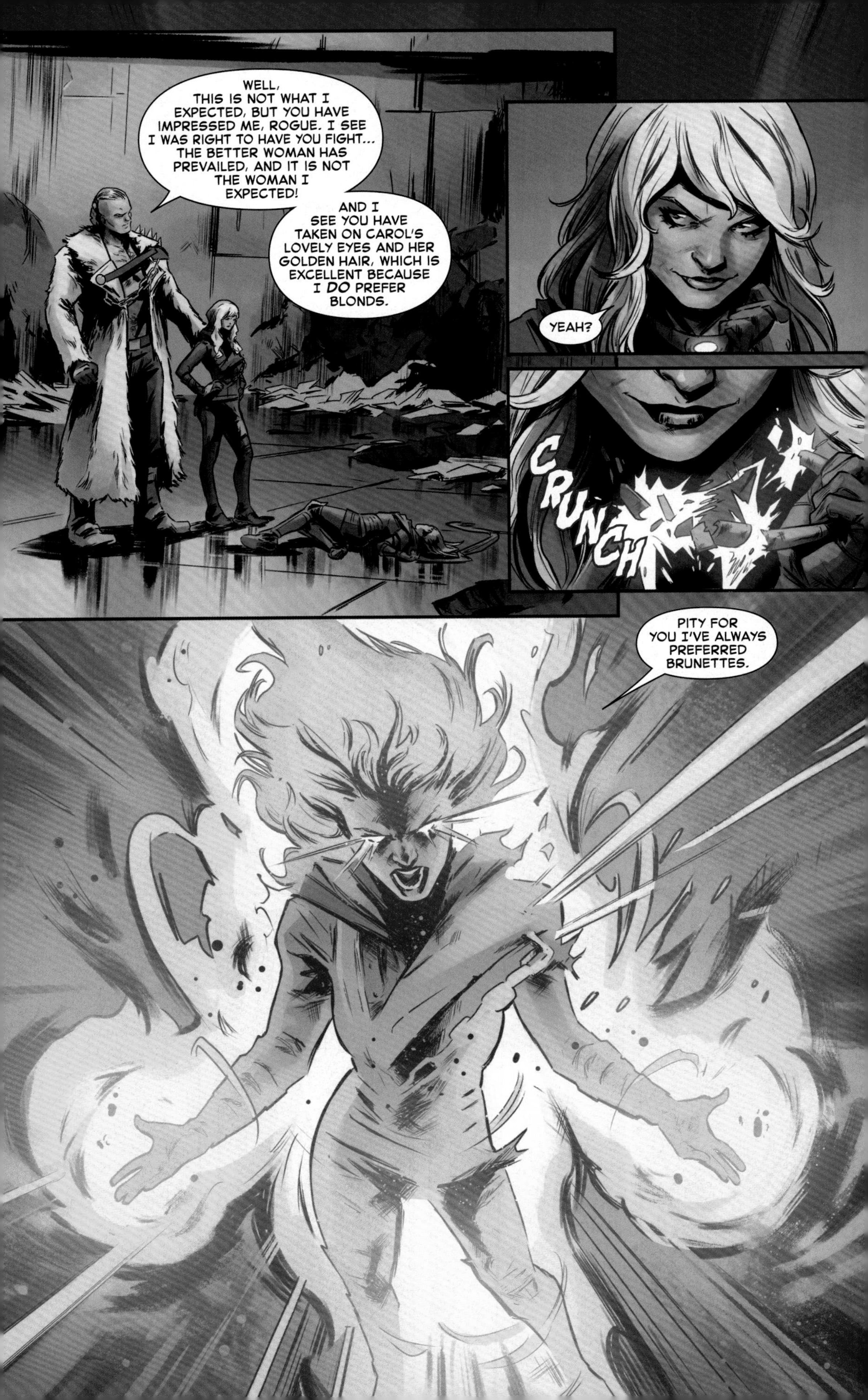
WELL, THIS IS NOT WHAT I EXPECTED, BUT YOU HAVE IMPRESSED ME, ROGUE. I SEE I WAS RIGHT TO HAVE YOU FIGHT... THE BETTER WOMAN HAS PREVAILED, AND IT IS NOT THE WOMAN I EXPECTED!
AND I SEE YOU HAVE TAKEN ON CAROL'S LOVELY EYES AND HER GOLDEN HAIR, WHICH IS EXCELLENT BECAUSE I *DO* PREFER BLONDS.
YEAH?
CRUNCH
PITY FOR YOU I'VE ALWAYS PREFERRED BRUNETTES.

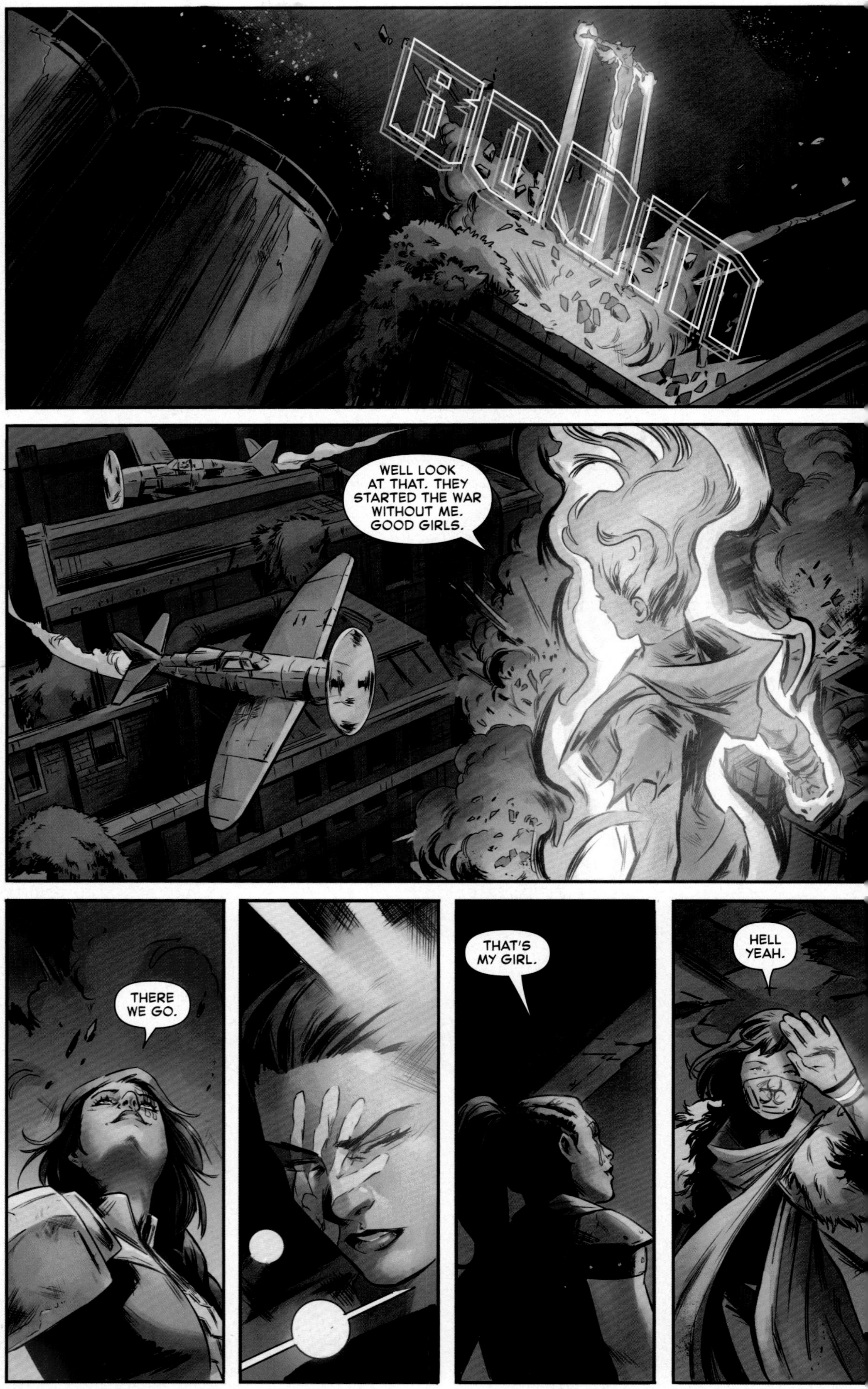
WELL LOOK AT THAT. THEY STARTED THE WAR WITHOUT ME. GOOD GIRLS.
THERE WE GO.
THAT'S MY GIRL.
HELL YEAH.

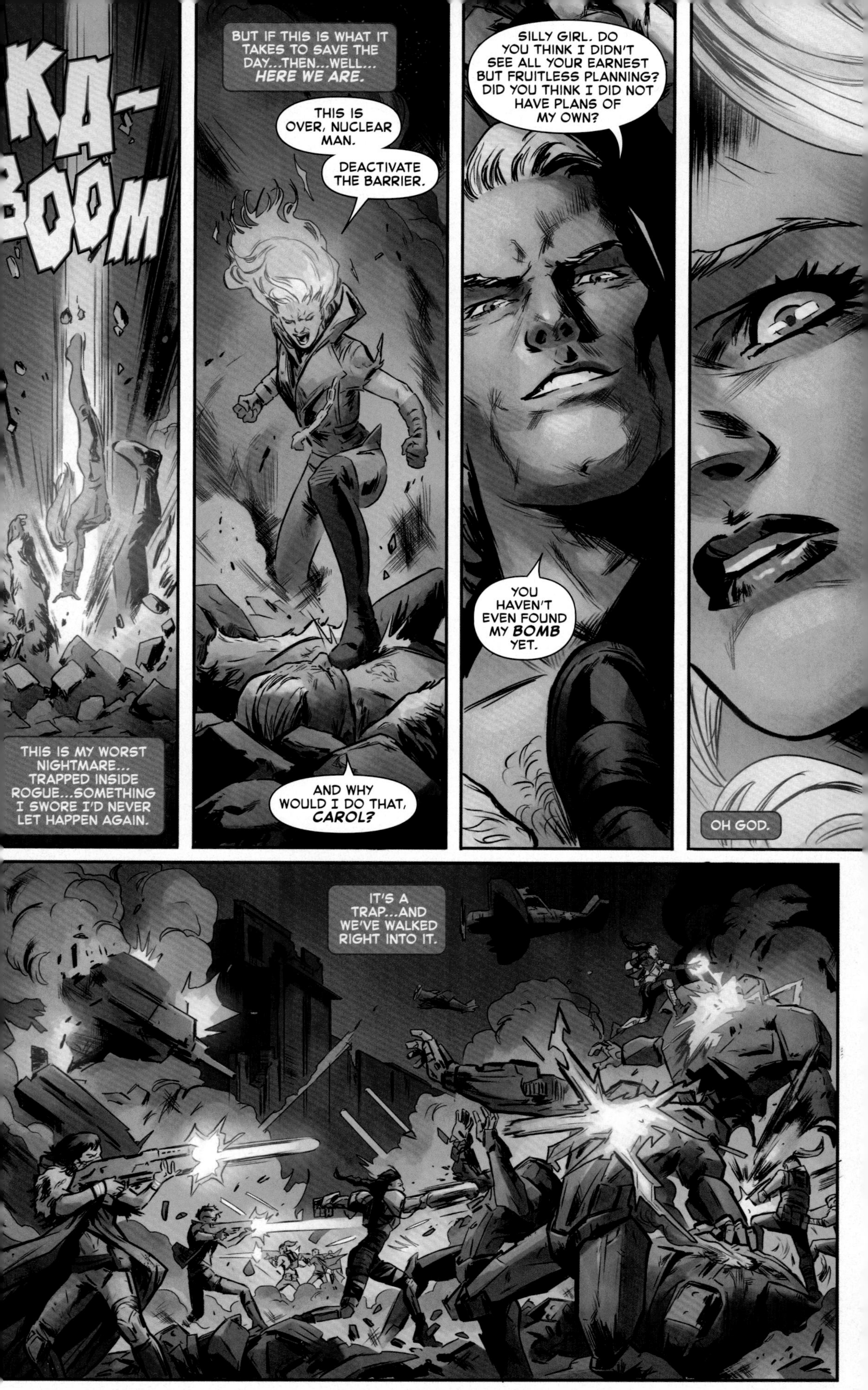
KA-BOOM
THIS IS MY WORST NIGHTMARE... TRAPPED INSIDE ROGUE...SOMETHING I SWORE I'D NEVER LET HAPPEN AGAIN.
BUT IF THIS IS WHAT IT TAKES TO SAVE THE DAY...THEN...WELL... HERE WE ARE.
THIS IS OVER, NUCLEAR MAN.
DEACTIVATE THE BARRIER.
AND WHY WOULD I DO THAT, CAROL?
SILLY GIRL. DO YOU THINK I DIDN'T SEE ALL YOUR EARNEST BUT FRUITLESS PLANNING? DID YOU THINK I DID NOT HAVE PLANS OF MY OWN?
YOU HAVEN'T EVEN FOUND MY BOMB YET.
OH GOD.
IT'S A TRAP...AND WE'VE WALKED RIGHT INTO IT.

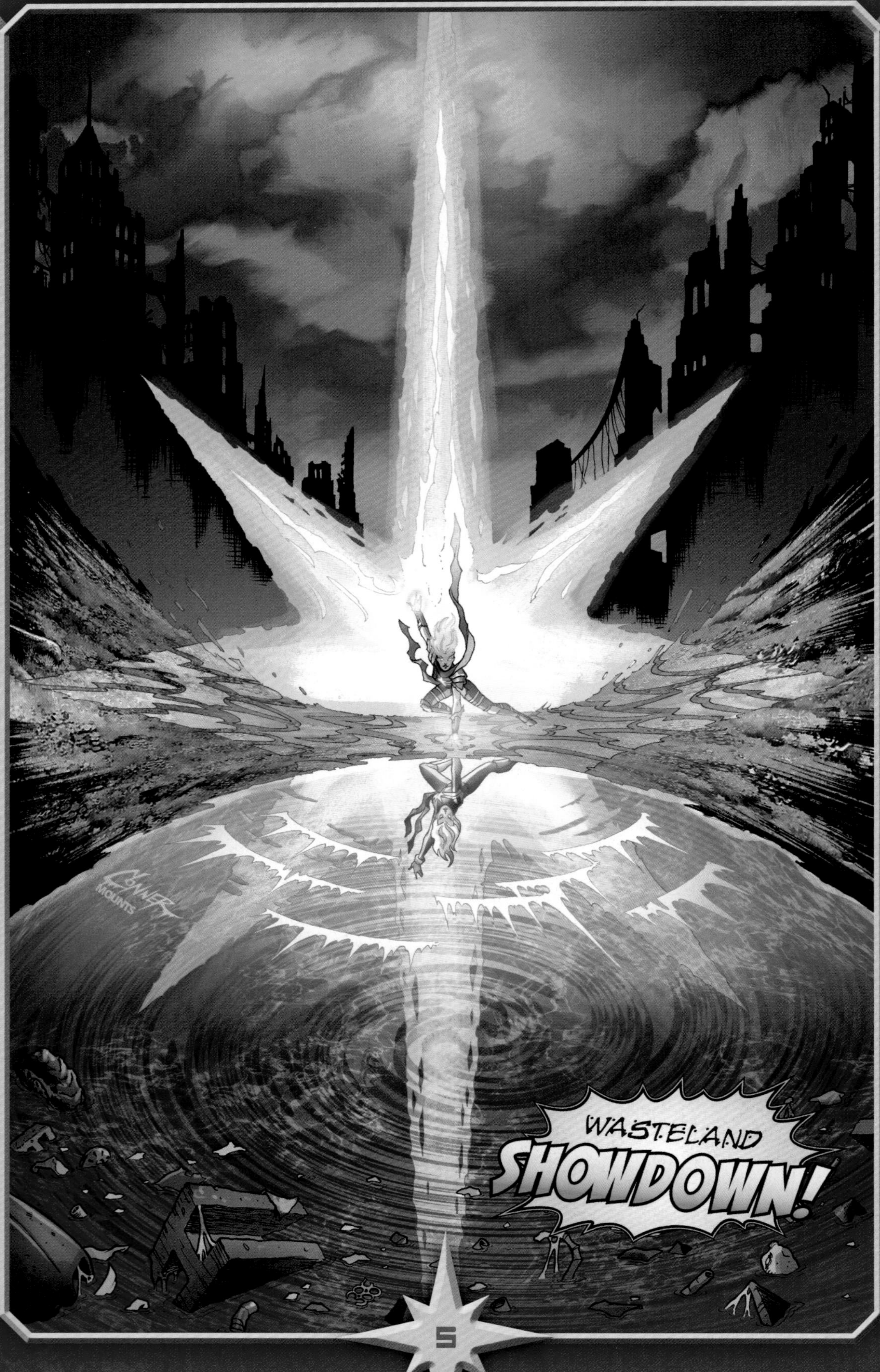
CONNER
MOUNTS
WASTELAND
SHOWDOWN!
5

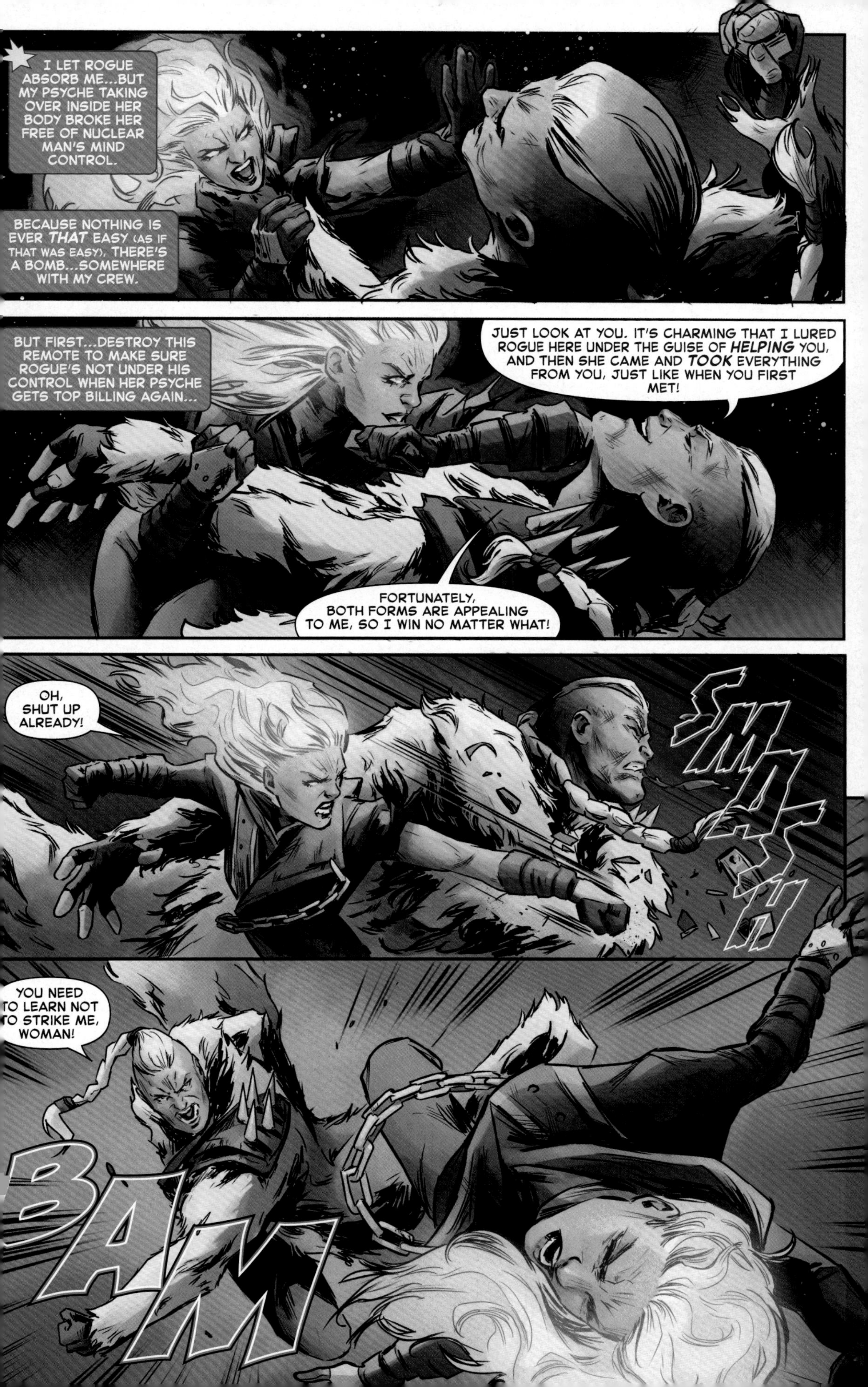
I LET ROGUE ABSORB ME...BUT MY PSYCHE TAKING OVER INSIDE HER BODY BROKE HER FREE OF NUCLEAR MAN'S MIND CONTROL.
BECAUSE NOTHING IS EVER *THAT* EASY (AS IF THAT WAS EASY), THERE'S A BOMB...SOMEWHERE WITH MY CREW.
BUT FIRST...DESTROY THIS REMOTE TO MAKE SURE ROGUE'S NOT UNDER HIS CONTROL WHEN HER PSYCHE GETS TOP BILLING AGAIN...
JUST LOOK AT YOU. IT'S CHARMING THAT I LURED ROGUE HERE UNDER THE GUISE OF *HELPING* YOU, AND THEN SHE CAME AND *TOOK* EVERYTHING FROM YOU, JUST LIKE WHEN YOU FIRST MET!
FORTUNATELY, BOTH FORMS ARE APPEALING TO ME, SO I WIN NO MATTER WHAT!
OH, SHUT UP ALREADY!
SMASHH
YOU NEED TO LEARN NOT TO STRIKE ME, WOMAN!
BAM

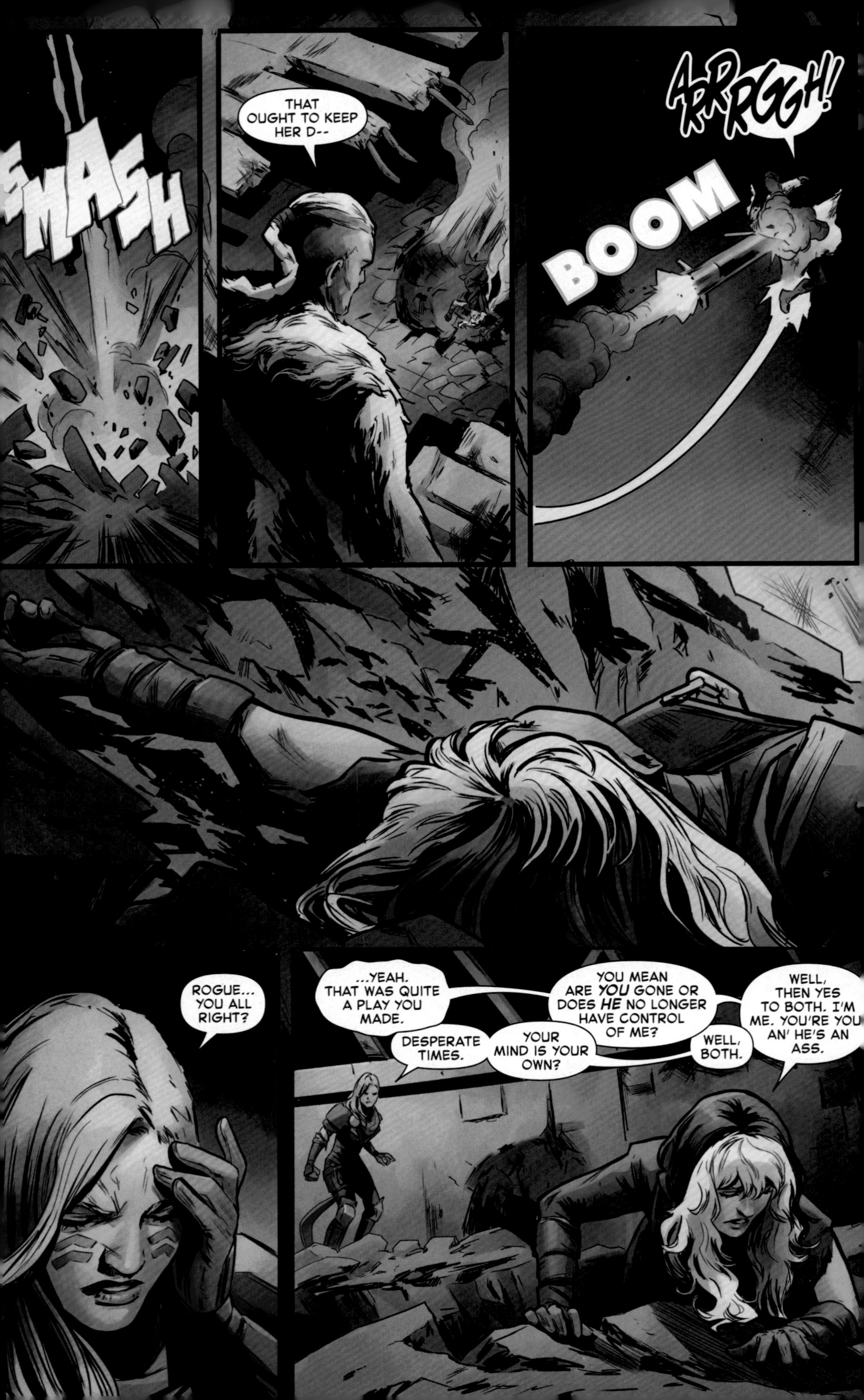
SMASH
THAT OUGHT TO KEEP HER D--
AARRGGH!
BOOM
ROGUE... YOU ALL RIGHT?
...YEAH. THAT WAS QUITE A PLAY YOU MADE.
DESPERATE TIMES.
YOUR MIND IS YOUR OWN?
YOU MEAN ARE YOU GONE OR DOES HE NO LONGER HAVE CONTROL OF ME?
WELL, BOTH.
WELL, THEN YES TO BOTH. I'M ME. YOU'RE YOU AN' HE'S AN ASS.

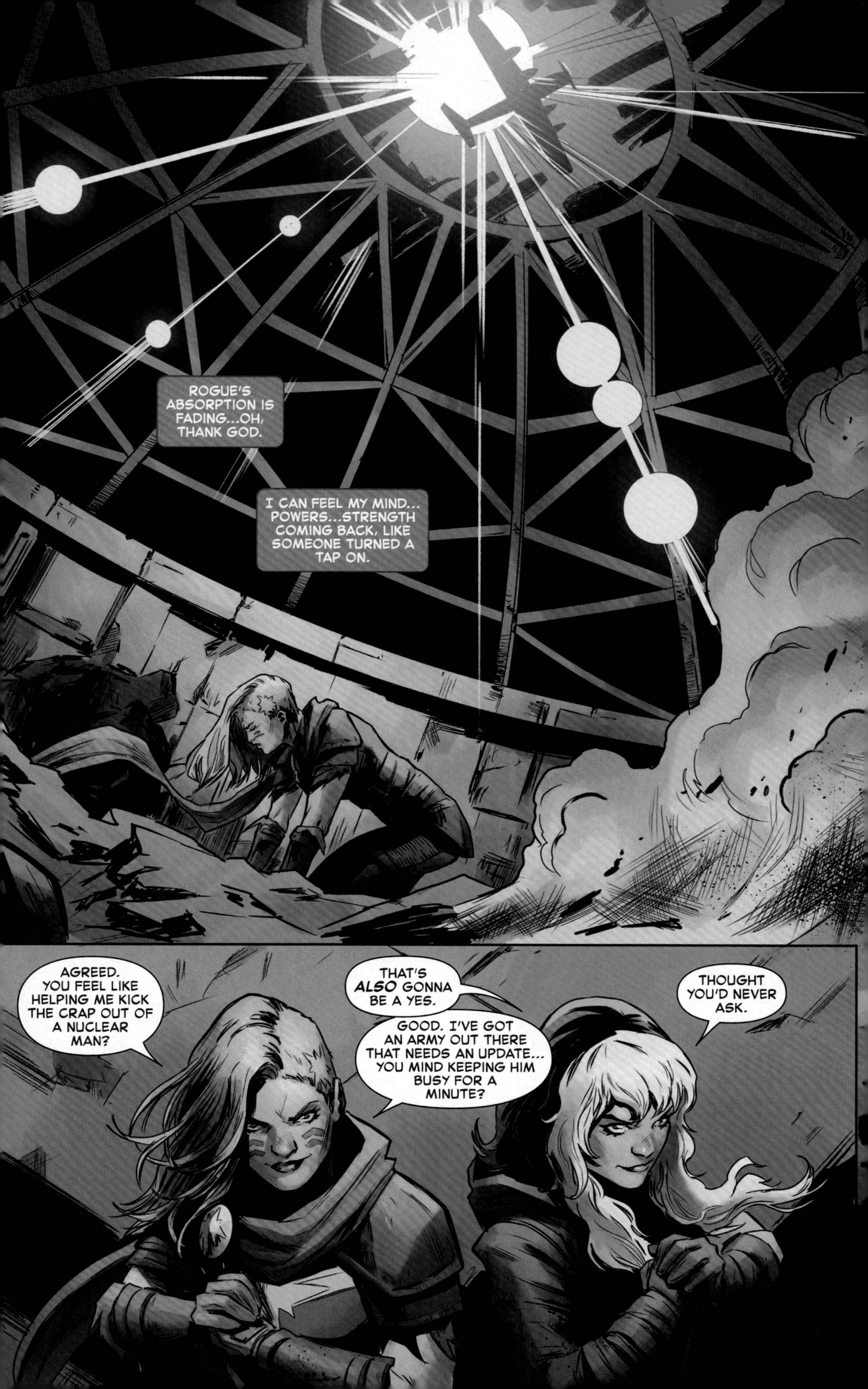
ROGUE'S ABSORPTION IS FADING...OH, THANK GOD.
I CAN FEEL MY MIND... POWERS...STRENGTH COMING BACK, LIKE SOMEONE TURNED A TAP ON.
AGREED. YOU FEEL LIKE HELPING ME KICK THE CRAP OUT OF A NUCLEAR MAN?
THAT'S ALSO GONNA BE A YES.
GOOD. I'VE GOT AN ARMY OUT THERE THAT NEEDS AN UPDATE... YOU MIND KEEPING HIM BUSY FOR A MINUTE?
THOUGHT YOU'D NEVER ASK.

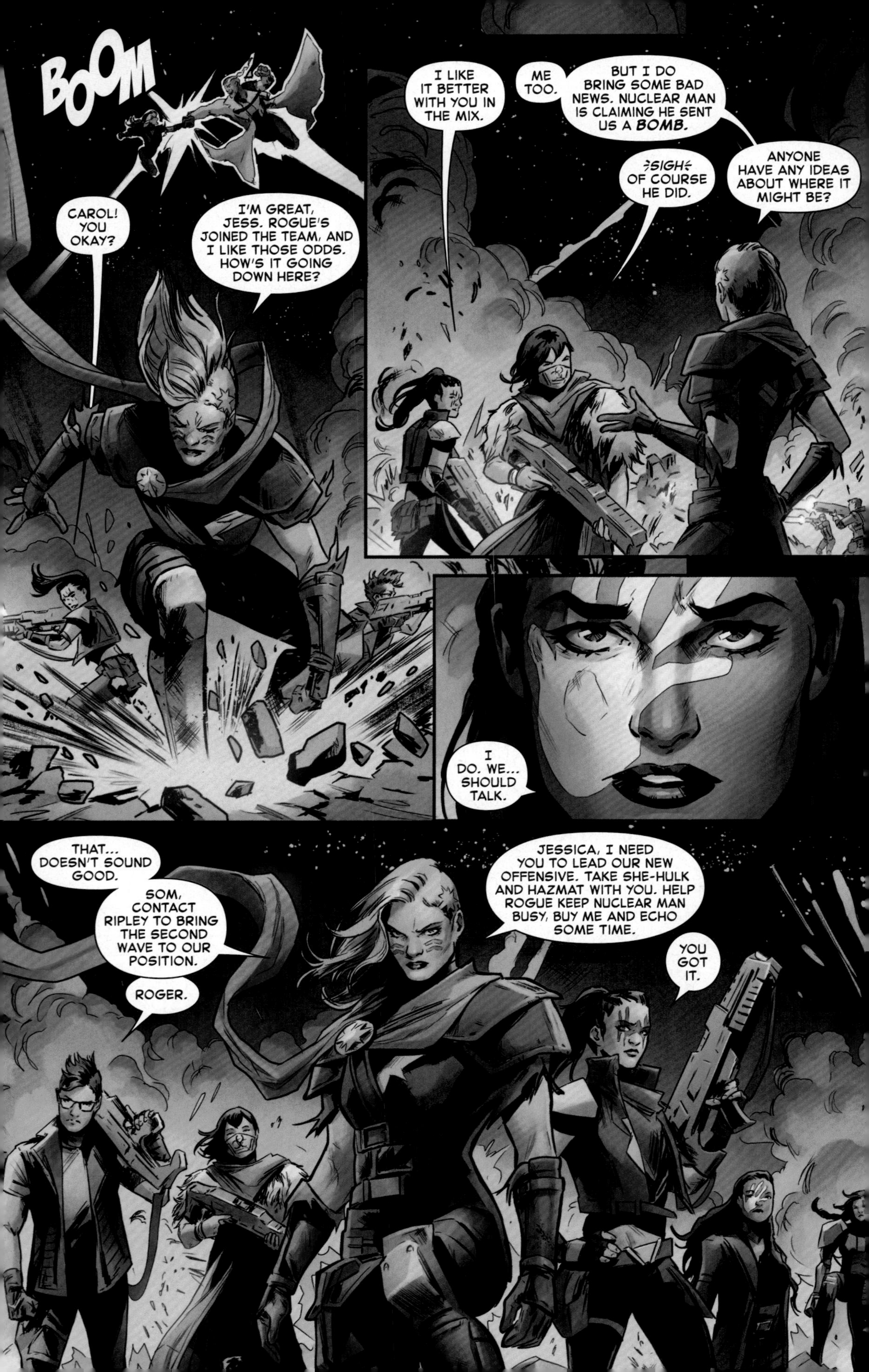
BOOM
CAROL! YOU OKAY?
I'M GREAT, JESS. ROGUE'S JOINED THE TEAM, AND I LIKE THOSE ODDS. HOW'S IT GOING DOWN HERE?
I LIKE IT BETTER WITH YOU IN THE MIX.
ME TOO.
BUT I DO BRING SOME BAD NEWS. NUCLEAR MAN IS CLAIMING HE SENT US A BOMB.
SIGH OF COURSE HE DID.
ANYONE HAVE ANY IDEAS ABOUT WHERE IT MIGHT BE?
I DO. WE... SHOULD TALK.
THAT... DOESN'T SOUND GOOD.
SOM, CONTACT RIPLEY TO BRING THE SECOND WAVE TO OUR POSITION.
ROGER.
JESSICA, I NEED YOU TO LEAD OUR NEW OFFENSIVE. TAKE SHE-HULK AND HAZMAT WITH YOU. HELP ROGUE KEEP NUCLEAR MAN BUSY, BUY ME AND ECHO SOME TIME.
YOU GOT IT.

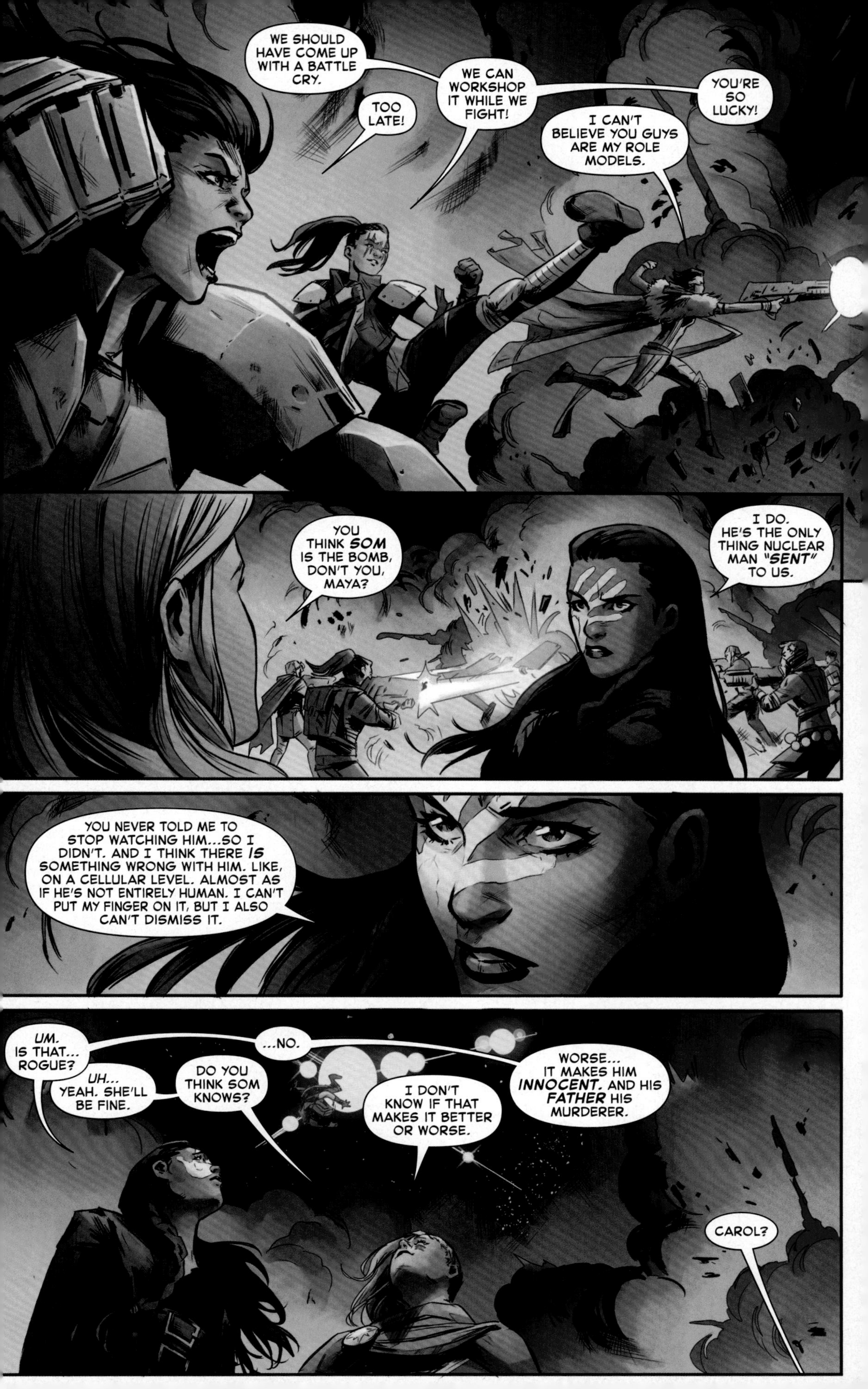
WE SHOULD HAVE COME UP WITH A BATTLE CRY.
TOO LATE!
WE CAN WORKSHOP IT WHILE WE FIGHT!
YOU'RE SO LUCKY!
I CAN'T BELIEVE YOU GUYS ARE MY ROLE MODELS.
YOU THINK SOM IS THE BOMB, DON'T YOU, MAYA?
I DO. HE'S THE ONLY THING NUCLEAR MAN "SENT" TO US.
YOU NEVER TOLD ME TO STOP WATCHING HIM...SO I DIDN'T. AND I THINK THERE IS SOMETHING WRONG WITH HIM. LIKE, ON A CELLULAR LEVEL. ALMOST AS IF HE'S NOT ENTIRELY HUMAN. I CAN'T PUT MY FINGER ON IT, BUT I ALSO CAN'T DISMISS IT.
UM. IS THAT... ROGUE?
UH... YEAH. SHE'LL BE FINE.
DO YOU THINK SOM KNOWS?
...NO.
I DON'T KNOW IF THAT MAKES IT BETTER OR WORSE.
WORSE... IT MAKES HIM INNOCENT. AND HIS FATHER HIS MURDERER.
CAROL?

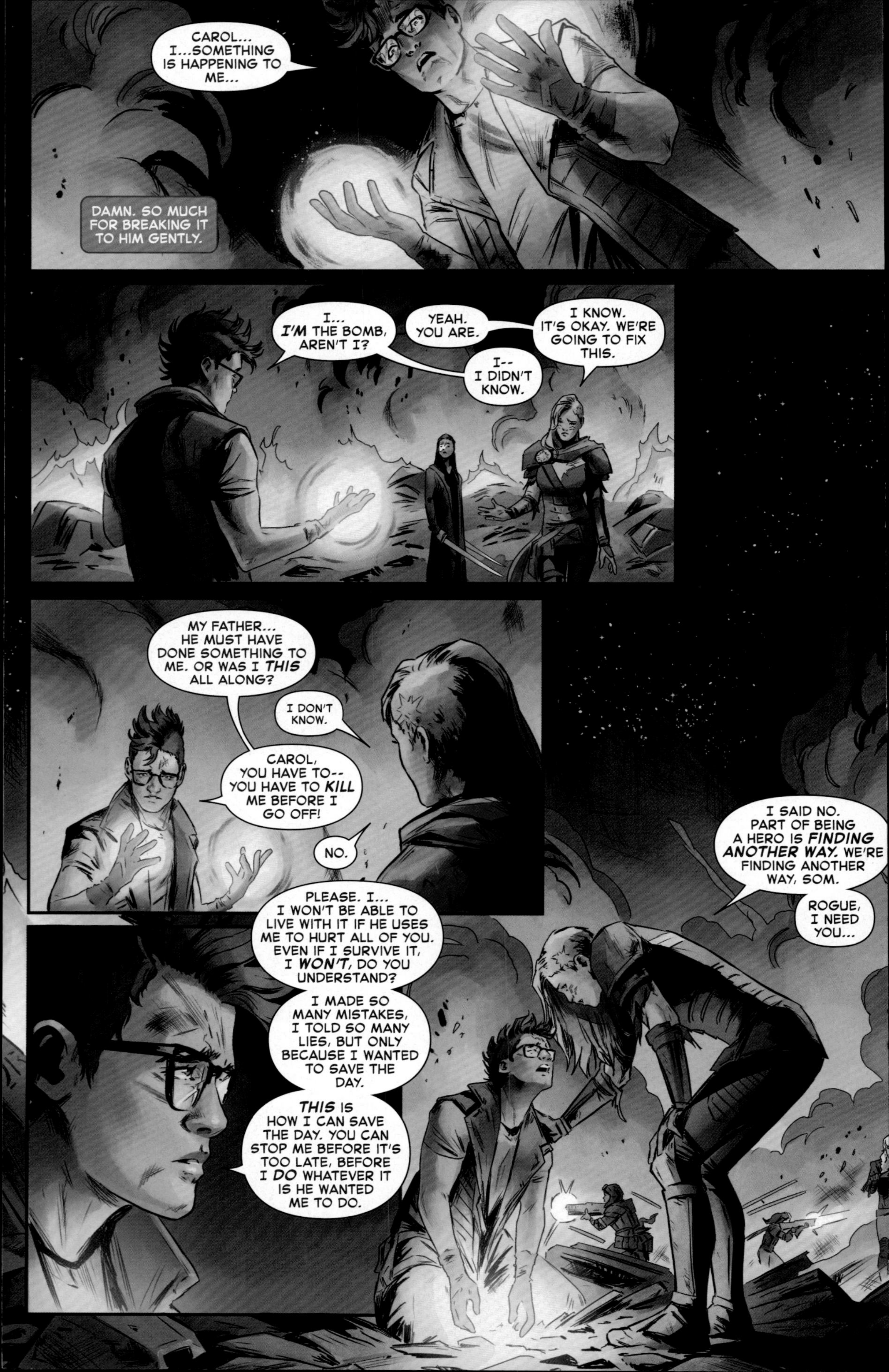
CAROL... I...SOMETHING IS HAPPENING TO ME...
DAMN. SO MUCH FOR BREAKING IT TO HIM GENTLY.
I... I'M THE BOMB, AREN'T I?
YEAH. YOU ARE.
I-- I DIDN'T KNOW.
I KNOW. IT'S OKAY. WE'RE GOING TO FIX THIS.
MY FATHER... HE MUST HAVE DONE SOMETHING TO ME. OR WAS I THIS ALL ALONG?
I DON'T KNOW.
CAROL, YOU HAVE TO-- YOU HAVE TO KILL ME BEFORE I GO OFF!
NO.
PLEASE. I... I WON'T BE ABLE TO LIVE WITH IT IF HE USES ME TO HURT ALL OF YOU. EVEN IF I SURVIVE IT, I WON'T, DO YOU UNDERSTAND?
I MADE SO MANY MISTAKES, I TOLD SO MANY LIES, BUT ONLY BECAUSE I WANTED TO SAVE THE DAY.
THIS IS HOW I CAN SAVE THE DAY. YOU CAN STOP ME BEFORE IT'S TOO LATE, BEFORE I DO WHATEVER IT IS HE WANTED ME TO DO.
I SAID NO. PART OF BEING A HERO IS FINDING ANOTHER WAY. WE'RE FINDING ANOTHER WAY, SOM.
ROGUE, I NEED YOU...

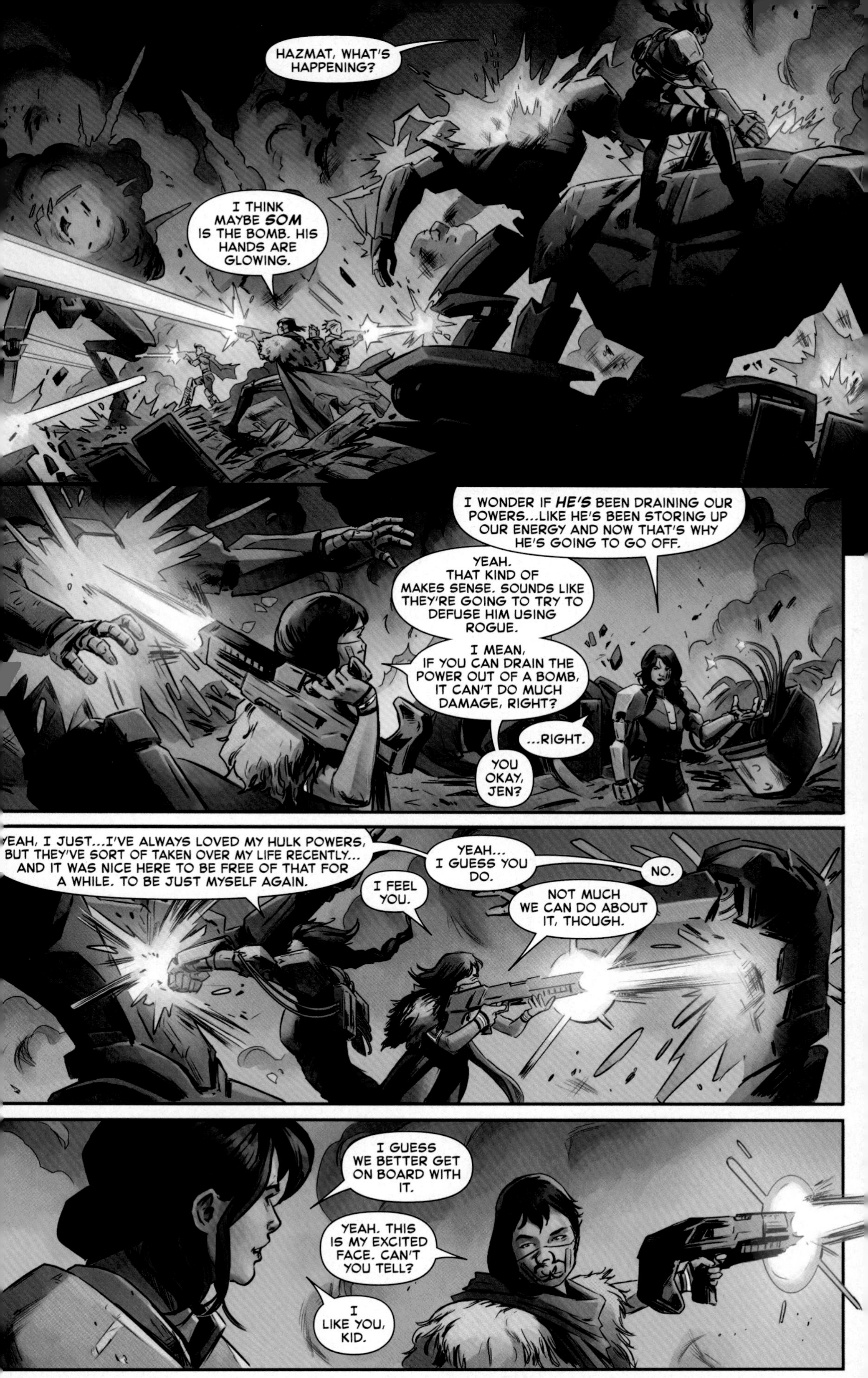
HAZMAT, WHAT'S HAPPENING?
I THINK MAYBE SOM IS THE BOMB. HIS HANDS ARE GLOWING.
I WONDER IF HE'S BEEN DRAINING OUR POWERS...LIKE HE'S BEEN STORING UP OUR ENERGY AND NOW THAT'S WHY HE'S GOING TO GO OFF.
YEAH. THAT KIND OF MAKES SENSE. SOUNDS LIKE THEY'RE GOING TO TRY TO DEFUSE HIM USING ROGUE.
I MEAN, IF YOU CAN DRAIN THE POWER OUT OF A BOMB, IT CAN'T DO MUCH DAMAGE, RIGHT?
...RIGHT.
YOU OKAY, JEN?
YEAH, I JUST...I'VE ALWAYS LOVED MY HULK POWERS, BUT THEY'VE SORT OF TAKEN OVER MY LIFE RECENTLY... AND IT WAS NICE HERE TO BE FREE OF THAT FOR A WHILE. TO BE JUST MYSELF AGAIN.
I FEEL YOU.
YEAH... I GUESS YOU DO.
NO.
NOT MUCH WE CAN DO ABOUT IT, THOUGH.
I GUESS WE BETTER GET ON BOARD WITH IT.
YEAH. THIS IS MY EXCITED FACE. CAN'T YOU TELL?
I LIKE YOU, KID.

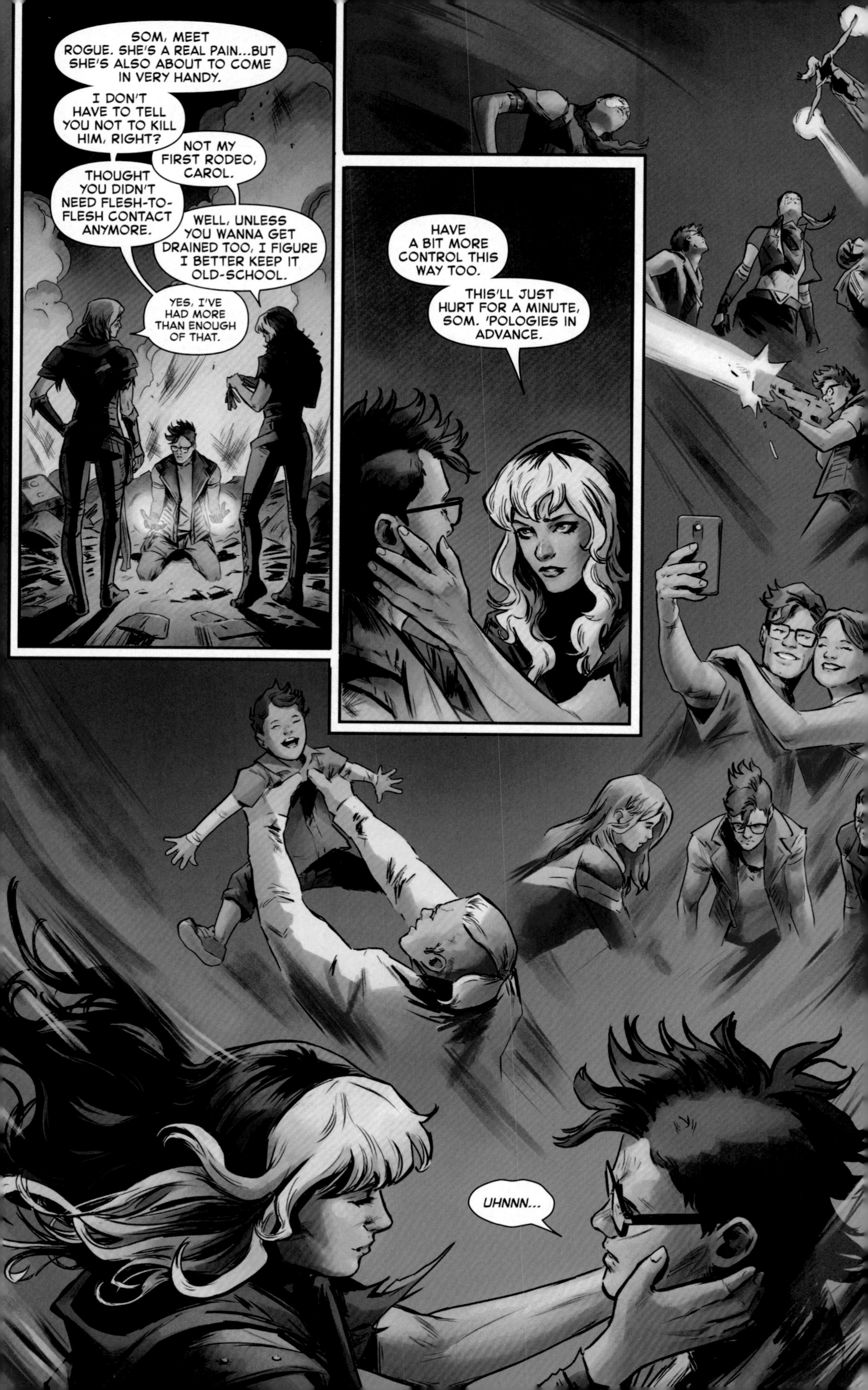
SOM, MEET ROGUE. SHE'S A REAL PAIN...BUT SHE'S ALSO ABOUT TO COME IN VERY HANDY.
I DON'T HAVE TO TELL YOU NOT TO KILL HIM, RIGHT?
NOT MY FIRST RODEO, CAROL.
THOUGHT YOU DIDN'T NEED FLESH-TO-FLESH CONTACT ANYMORE.
WELL, UNLESS YOU WANNA GET DRAINED TOO, I FIGURE I BETTER KEEP IT OLD-SCHOOL.
YES, I'VE HAD MORE THAN ENOUGH OF THAT.
HAVE A BIT MORE CONTROL THIS WAY TOO.
THIS'LL JUST HURT FOR A MINUTE, SOM. 'POLOGIES IN ADVANCE.
UHNNN...

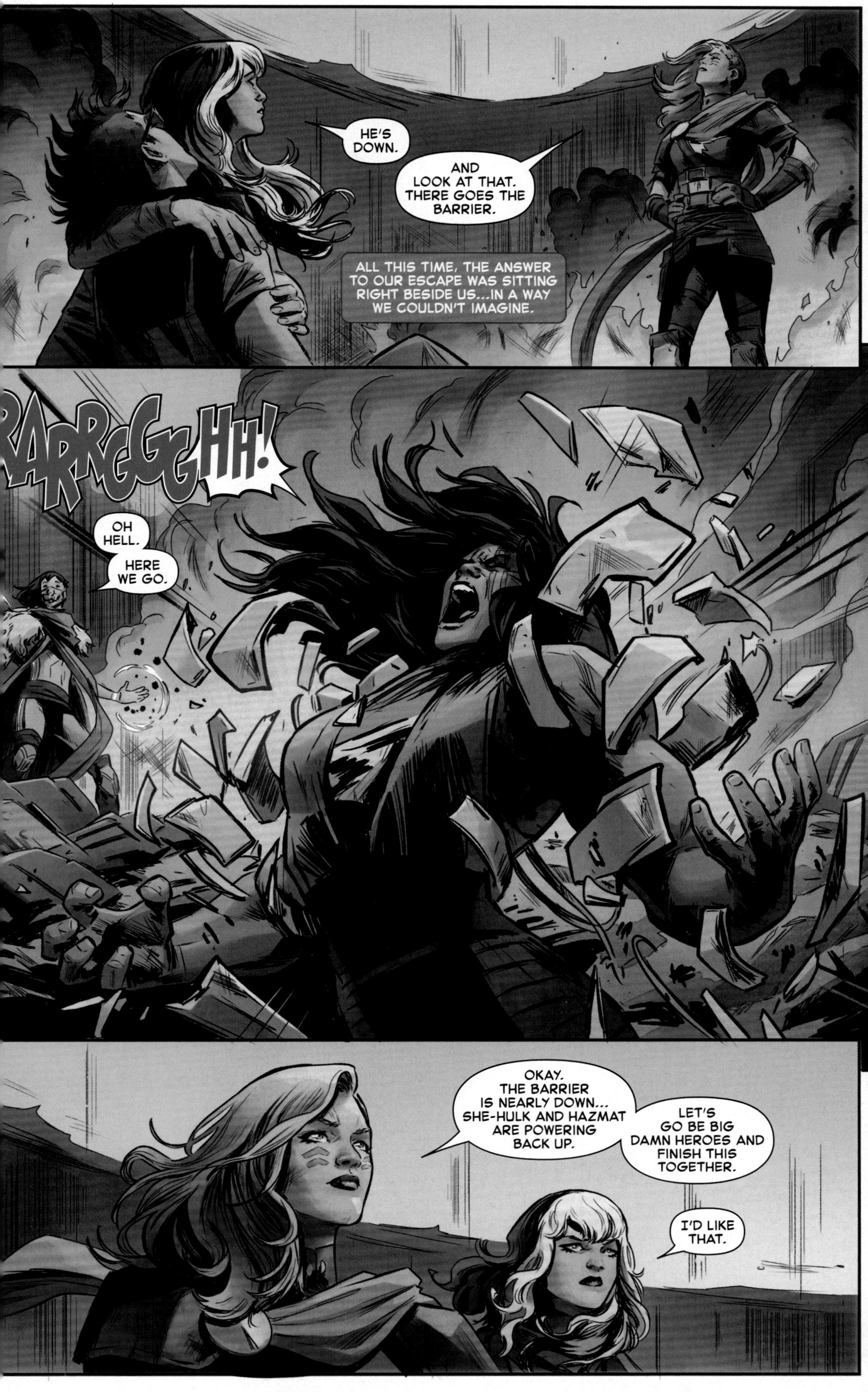
HE'S DOWN.
AND LOOK AT THAT. THERE GOES THE BARRIER.
ALL THIS TIME, THE ANSWER TO OUR ESCAPE WAS SITTING RIGHT BESIDE US...IN A WAY WE COULDN'T IMAGINE.
RARRGGGHH!
OH HELL.
HERE WE GO.
OKAY. THE BARRIER IS NEARLY DOWN... SHE-HULK AND HAZMAT ARE POWERING BACK UP.
LET'S GO BE BIG DAMN HEROES AND FINISH THIS TOGETHER.
I'D LIKE THAT.

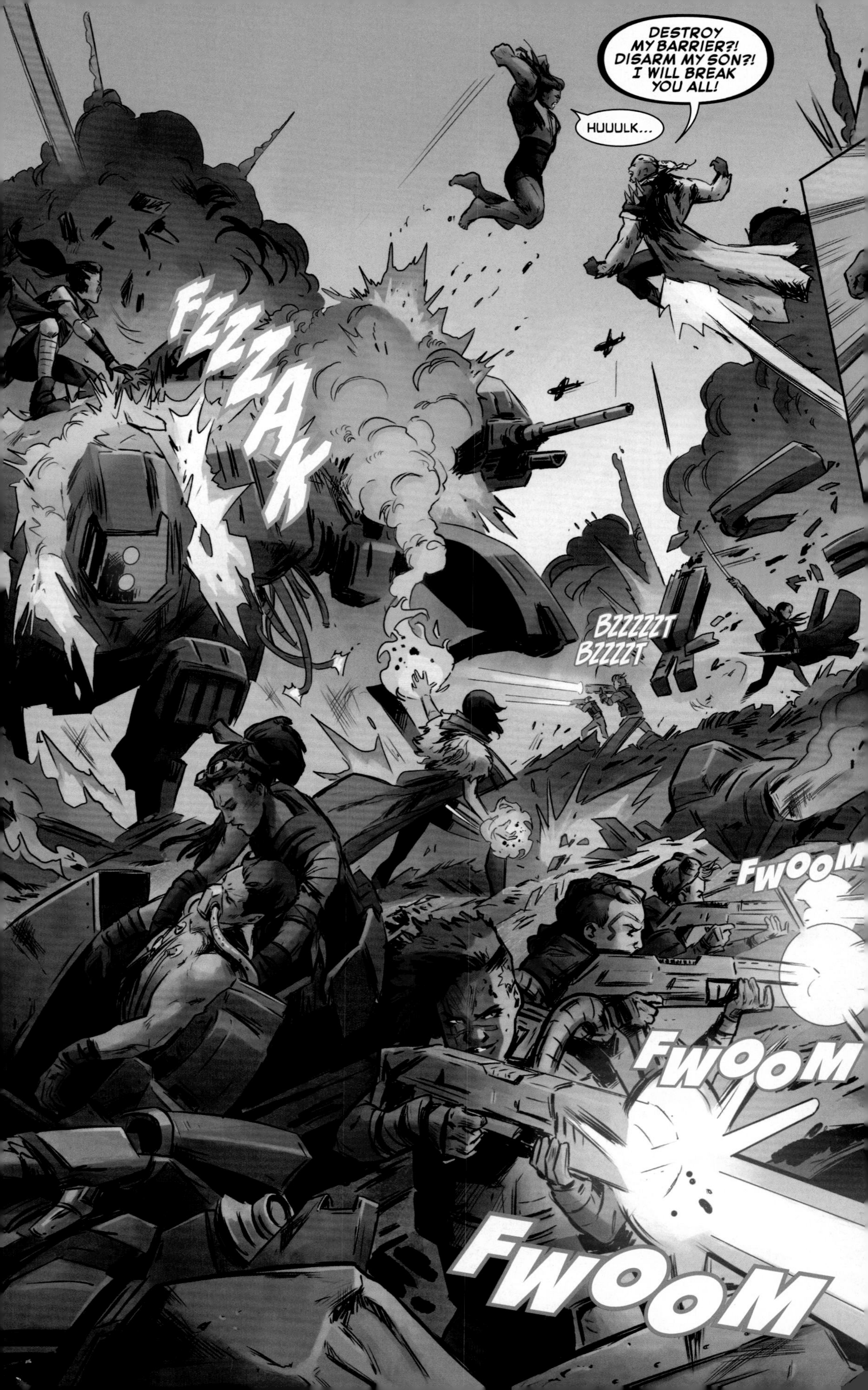
DESTROY MY BARRIER?! DISARM MY SON?! I WILL BREAK YOU ALL!
HUUULK...
FZZZZAK
BZZZZZT
BZZZZT
FWOOM
FWOOM
FWOOM

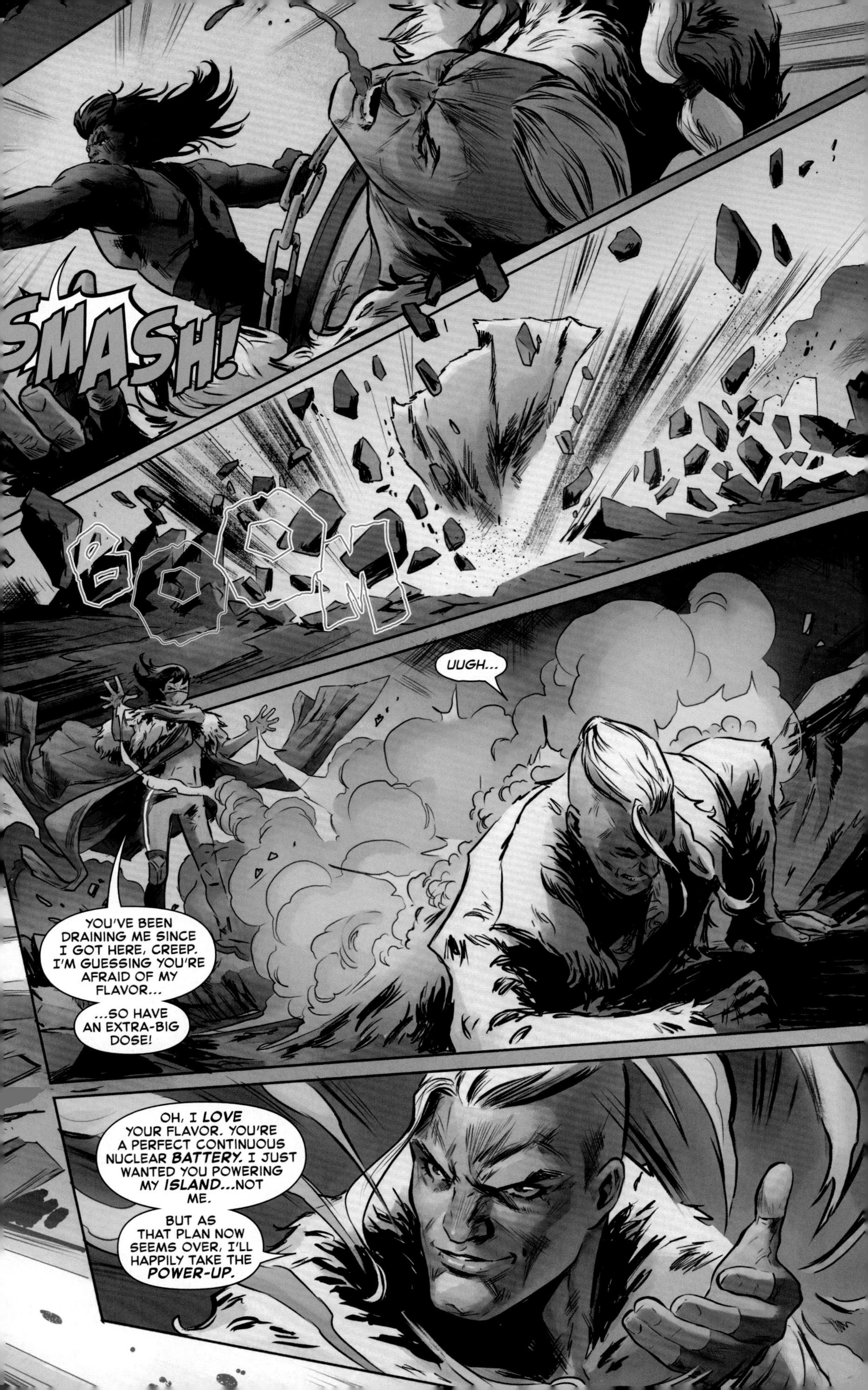
SMASH!
BOOM
UUGH...
YOU'VE BEEN DRAINING ME SINCE I GOT HERE, CREEP. I'M GUESSING YOU'RE AFRAID OF MY FLAVOR...
...SO HAVE AN EXTRA-BIG DOSE!
OH, I LOVE YOUR FLAVOR. YOU'RE A PERFECT CONTINUOUS NUCLEAR BATTERY. I JUST WANTED YOU POWERING MY ISLAND...NOT ME.
BUT AS THAT PLAN NOW SEEMS OVER, I'LL HAPPILY TAKE THE POWER-UP.

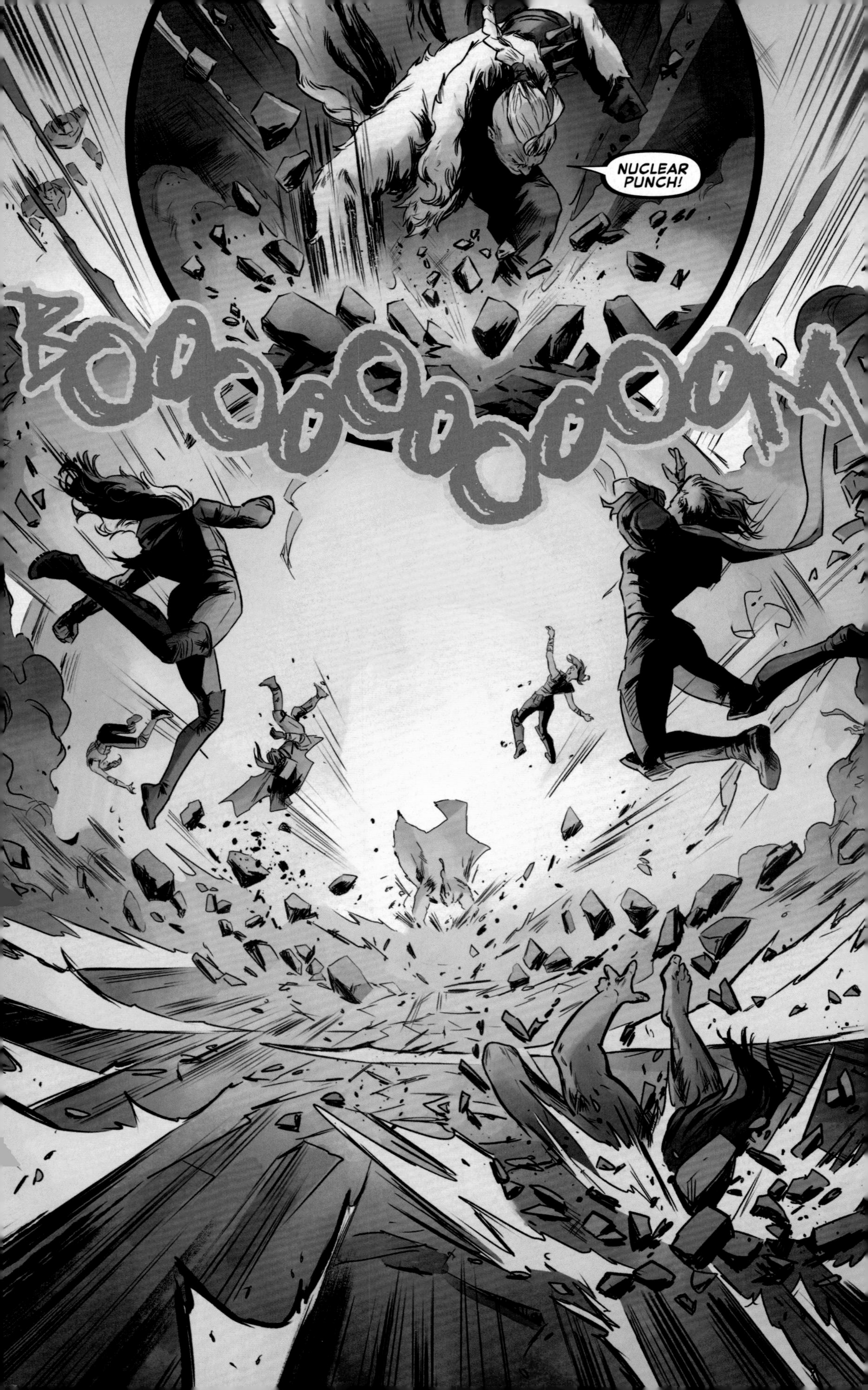
NUCLEAR PUNCH!
BOOOOOOOOOM

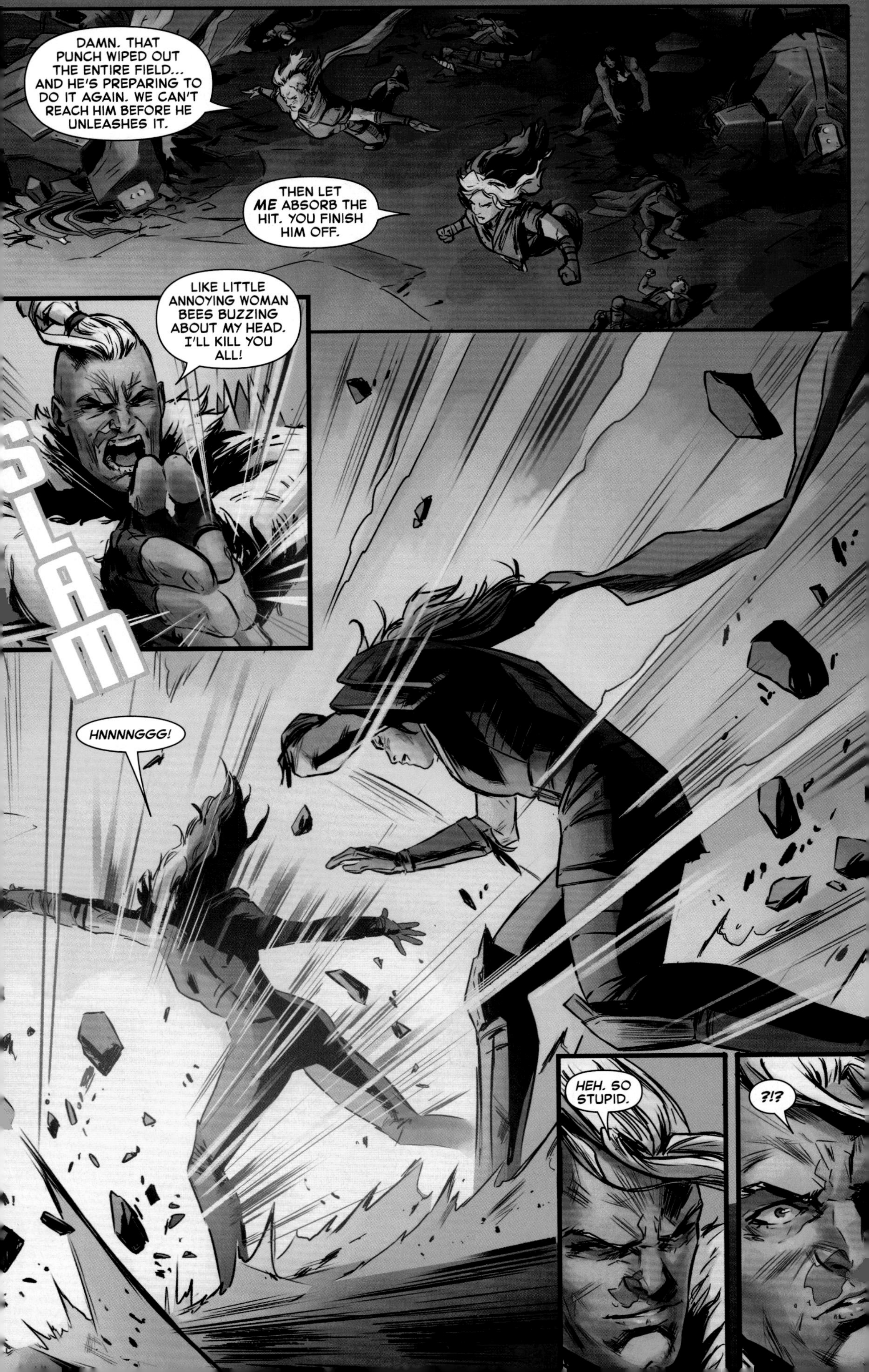
DAMN. THAT PUNCH WIPED OUT THE ENTIRE FIELD... AND HE'S PREPARING TO DO IT AGAIN. WE CAN'T REACH HIM BEFORE HE UNLEASHES IT.
THEN LET *ME* ABSORB THE HIT. YOU FINISH HIM OFF.
LIKE LITTLE ANNOYING WOMAN BEES BUZZING ABOUT MY HEAD. I'LL KILL YOU ALL!
SLAM
HNNNNGGG!
HEH. SO STUPID.
?!?

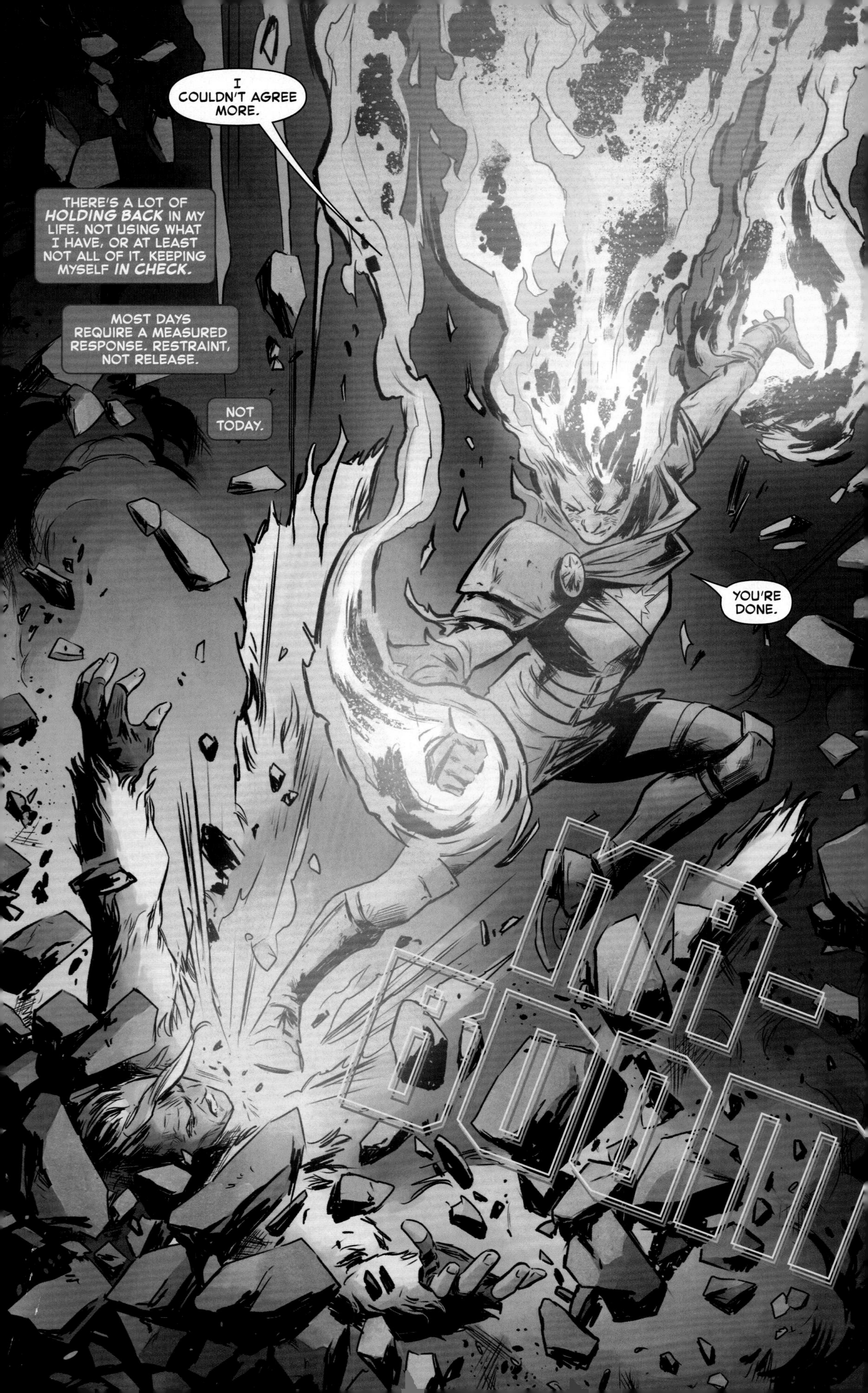
I COULDN'T AGREE MORE.
THERE'S A LOT OF **HOLDING BACK** IN MY LIFE. NOT USING WHAT I HAVE, OR AT LEAST NOT ALL OF IT. KEEPING MYSELF **IN CHECK.**
MOST DAYS REQUIRE A MEASURED RESPONSE. RESTRAINT, NOT RELEASE.
NOT TODAY.
YOU'RE DONE.

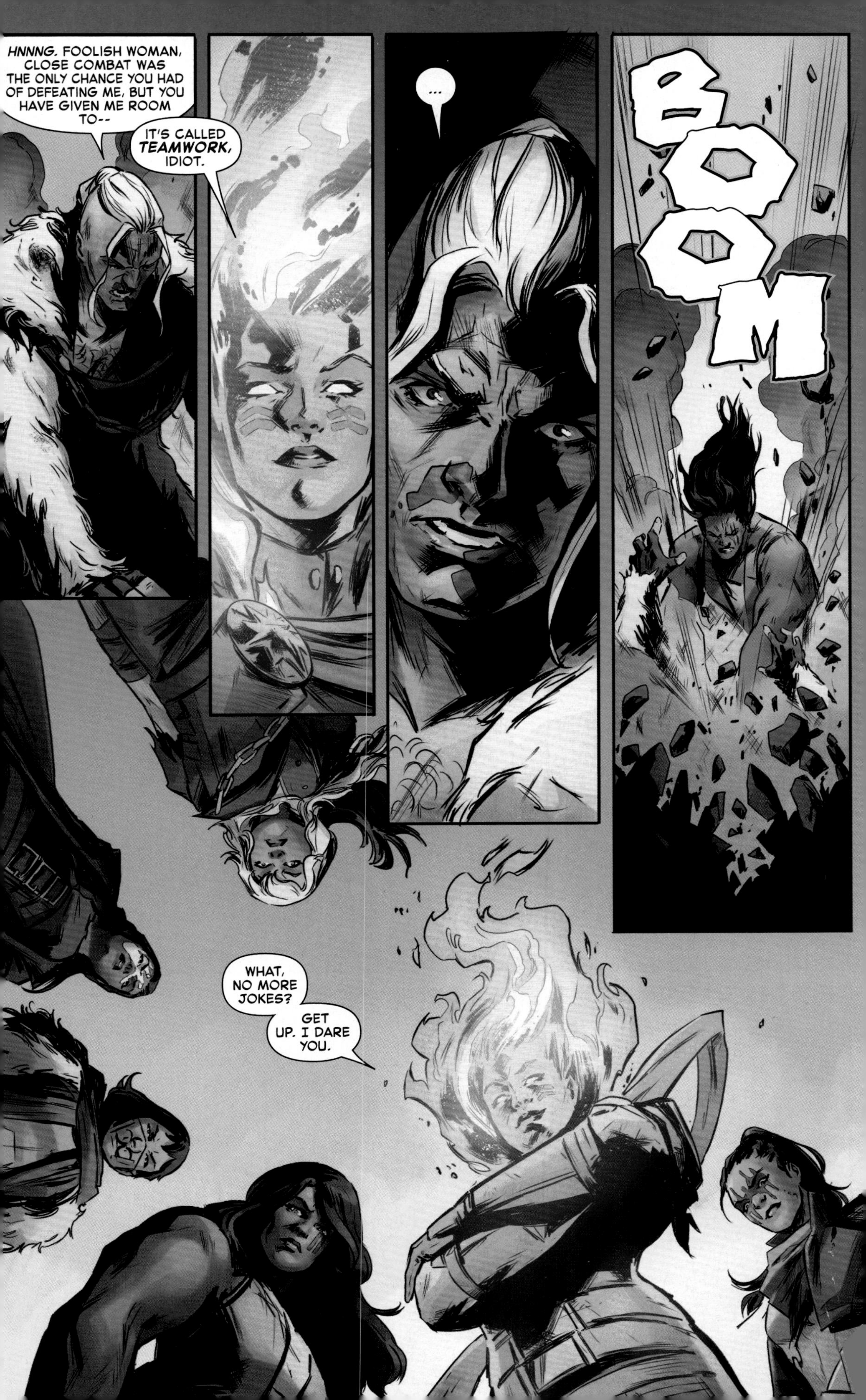
HNNNG. FOOLISH WOMAN, CLOSE COMBAT WAS THE ONLY CHANCE YOU HAD OF DEFEATING ME, BUT YOU HAVE GIVEN ME ROOM TO--
IT'S CALLED TEAMWORK, IDIOT.
...
BOOM
WHAT, NO MORE JOKES?
GET UP. I DARE YOU.

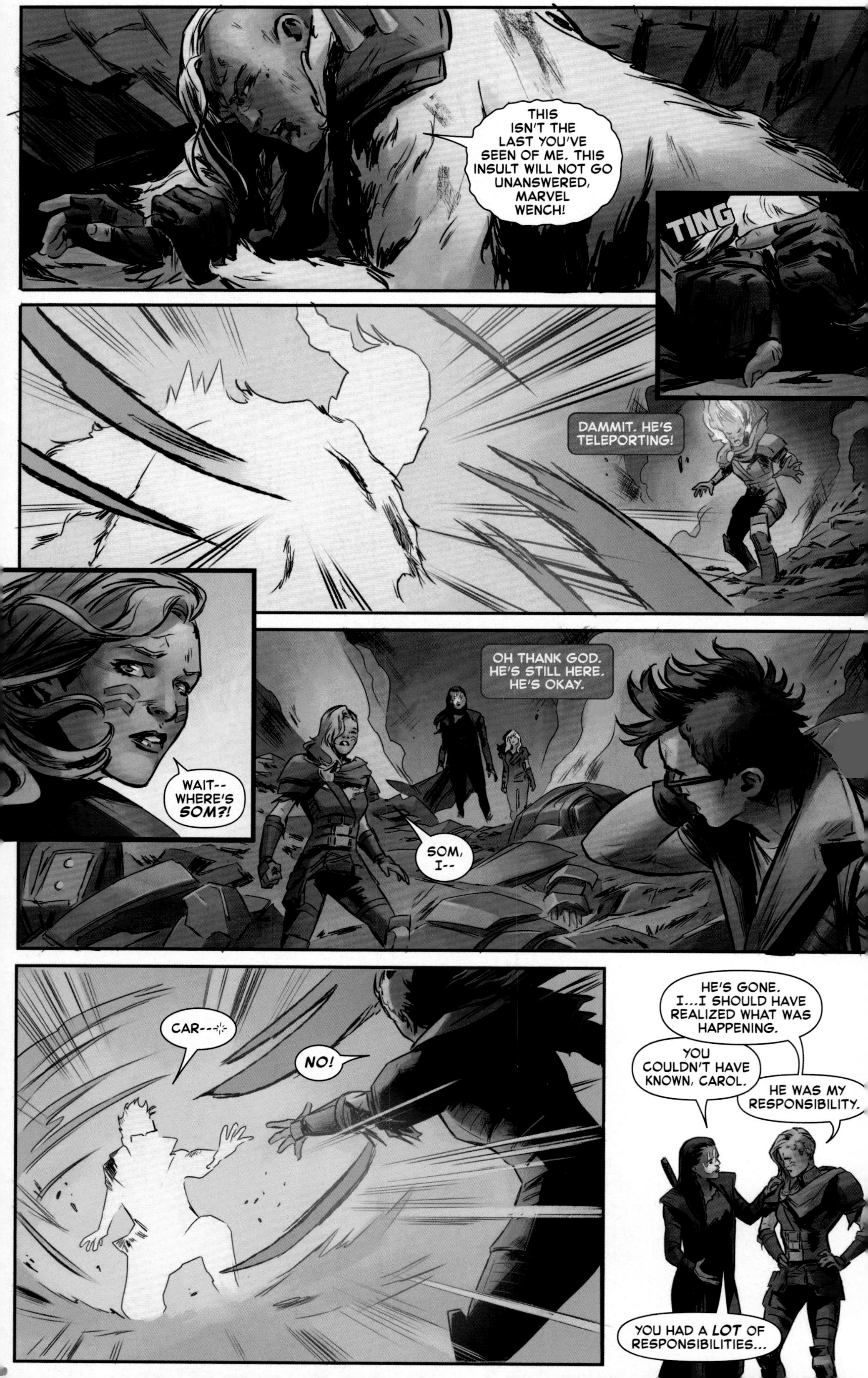
THIS ISN'T THE LAST YOU'VE SEEN OF ME. THIS INSULT WILL NOT GO UNANSWERED, MARVEL WENCH!
TING
DAMMIT. HE'S TELEPORTING!
WAIT-- WHERE'S SOM?!
OH THANK GOD. HE'S STILL HERE. HE'S OKAY.
SOM, I--
CAR--
NO!
HE'S GONE. I...I SHOULD HAVE REALIZED WHAT WAS HAPPENING.
YOU COULDN'T HAVE KNOWN, CAROL.
HE WAS MY RESPONSIBILITY.
YOU HAD A LOT OF RESPONSIBILITIES...

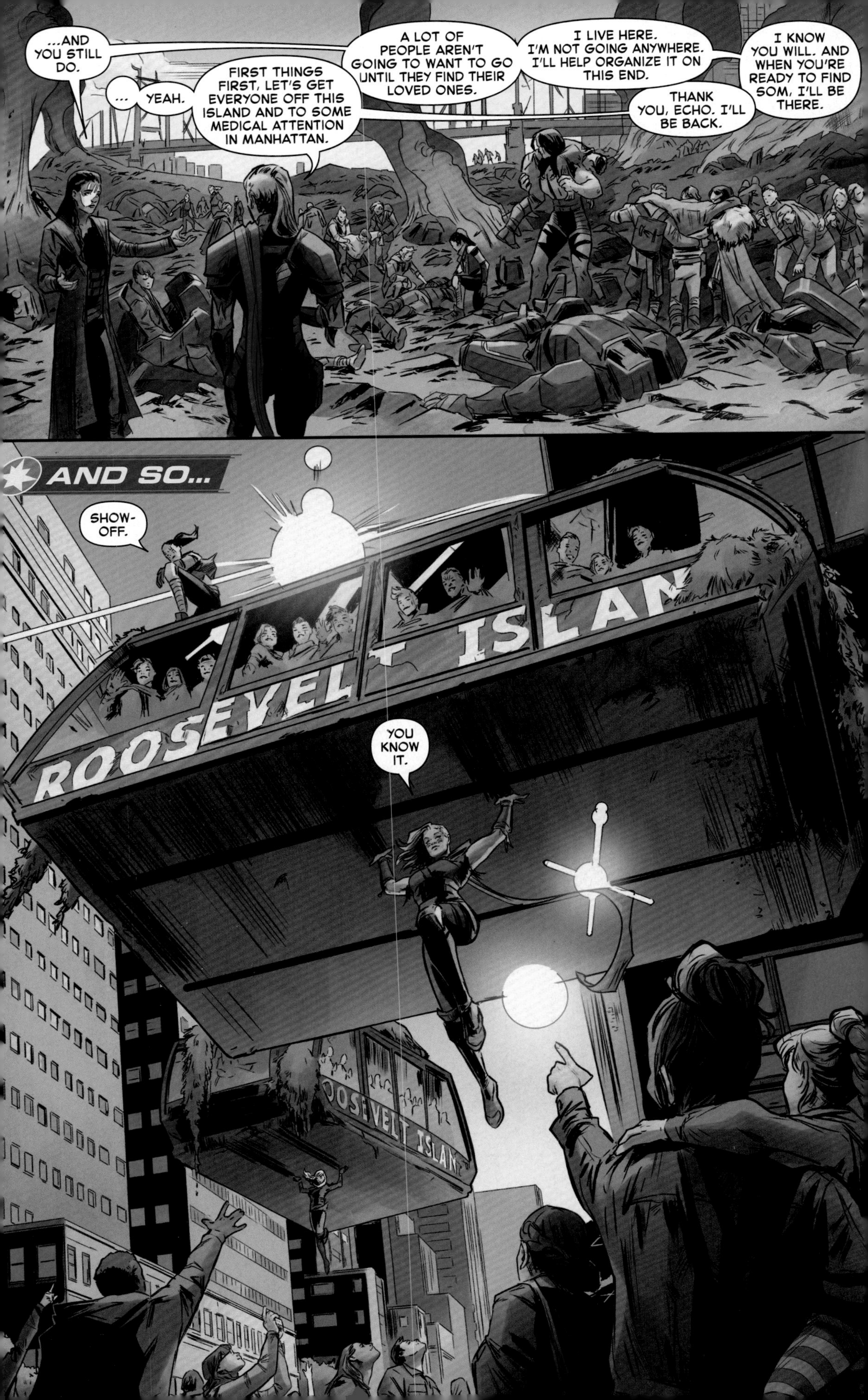
...AND YOU STILL DO.
...
YEAH.
FIRST THINGS FIRST, LET'S GET EVERYONE OFF THIS ISLAND AND TO SOME MEDICAL ATTENTION IN MANHATTAN.
A LOT OF PEOPLE AREN'T GOING TO WANT TO GO UNTIL THEY FIND THEIR LOVED ONES.
I LIVE HERE. I'M NOT GOING ANYWHERE. I'LL HELP ORGANIZE IT ON THIS END.
THANK YOU, ECHO. I'LL BE BACK.
I KNOW YOU WILL. AND WHEN YOU'RE READY TO FIND SOM, I'LL BE THERE.
AND SO...
SHOW-OFF.
ROOSEVELT ISLAN
YOU KNOW IT.
OOSEVELT ISLAN

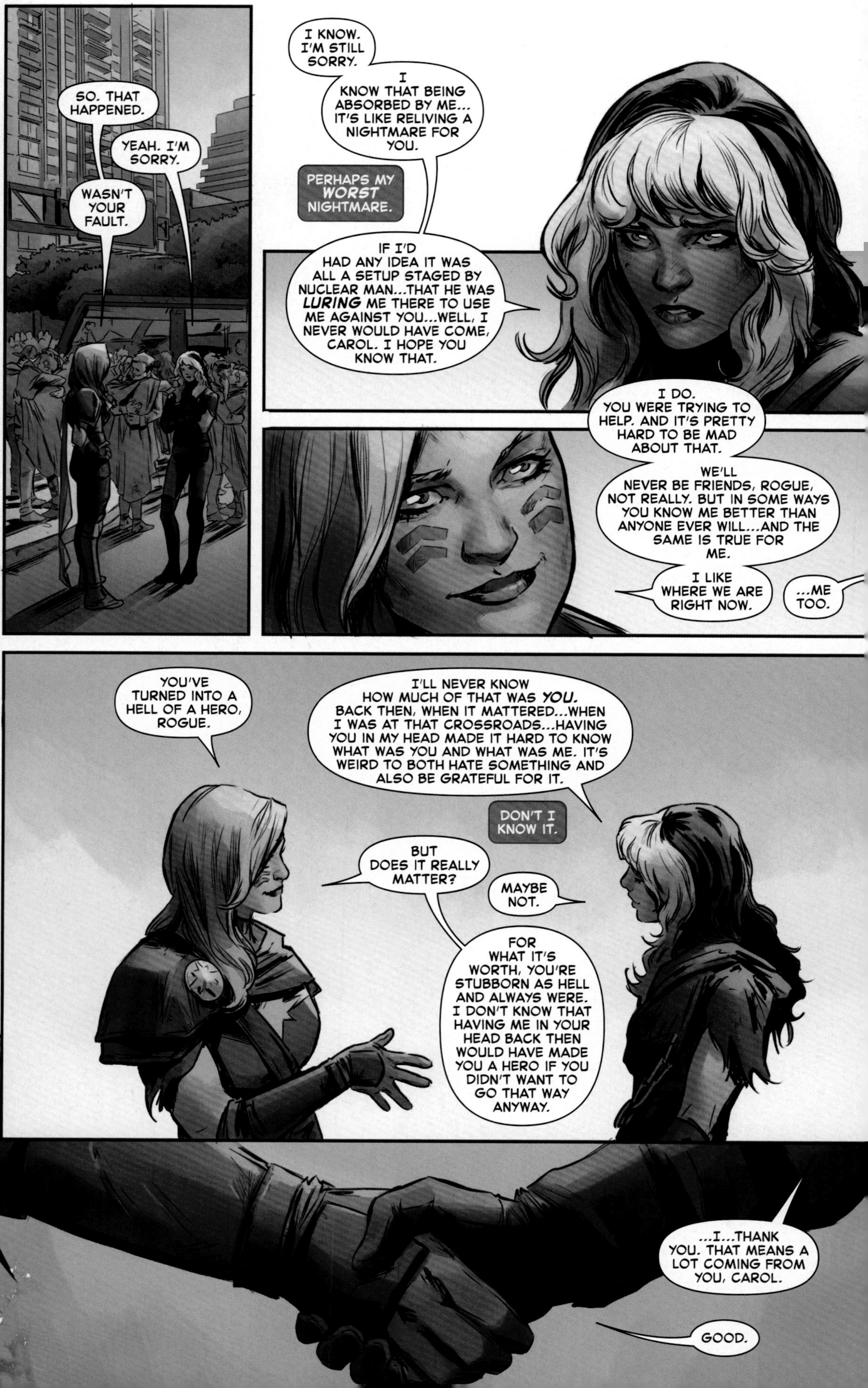
SO. THAT HAPPENED.
YEAH. I'M SORRY.
WASN'T YOUR FAULT.
I KNOW. I'M STILL SORRY.
I KNOW THAT BEING ABSORBED BY ME... IT'S LIKE RELIVING A NIGHTMARE FOR YOU.
PERHAPS MY WORST NIGHTMARE.
IF I'D HAD ANY IDEA IT WAS ALL A SETUP STAGED BY NUCLEAR MAN...THAT HE WAS LURING ME THERE TO USE ME AGAINST YOU...WELL, I NEVER WOULD HAVE COME, CAROL. I HOPE YOU KNOW THAT.
I DO. YOU WERE TRYING TO HELP. AND IT'S PRETTY HARD TO BE MAD ABOUT THAT.
WE'LL NEVER BE FRIENDS, ROGUE, NOT REALLY. BUT IN SOME WAYS YOU KNOW ME BETTER THAN ANYONE EVER WILL...AND THE SAME IS TRUE FOR ME.
I LIKE WHERE WE ARE RIGHT NOW.
...ME TOO.
YOU'VE TURNED INTO A HELL OF A HERO, ROGUE.
I'LL NEVER KNOW HOW MUCH OF THAT WAS YOU. BACK THEN, WHEN IT MATTERED...WHEN I WAS AT THAT CROSSROADS...HAVING YOU IN MY HEAD MADE IT HARD TO KNOW WHAT WAS YOU AND WHAT WAS ME. IT'S WEIRD TO BOTH HATE SOMETHING AND ALSO BE GRATEFUL FOR IT.
DON'T I KNOW IT.
BUT DOES IT REALLY MATTER?
MAYBE NOT.
FOR WHAT IT'S WORTH, YOU'RE STUBBORN AS HELL AND ALWAYS WERE. I DON'T KNOW THAT HAVING ME IN YOUR HEAD BACK THEN WOULD HAVE MADE YOU A HERO IF YOU DIDN'T WANT TO GO THAT WAY ANYWAY.
...I...THANK YOU. THAT MEANS A LOT COMING FROM YOU, CAROL.
GOOD.

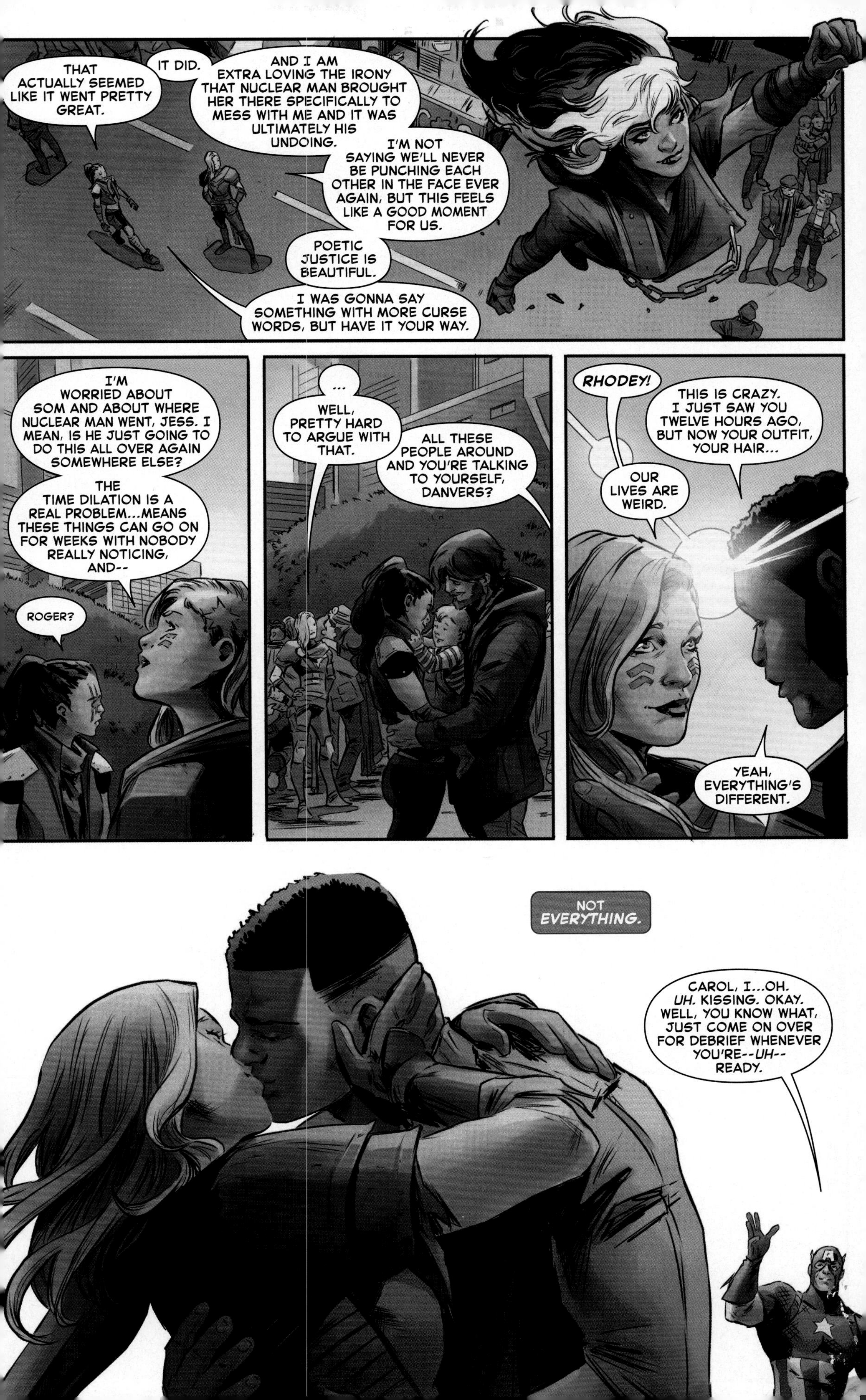
THAT ACTUALLY SEEMED LIKE IT WENT PRETTY GREAT.
IT DID.
AND I AM EXTRA LOVING THE IRONY THAT NUCLEAR MAN BROUGHT HER THERE SPECIFICALLY TO MESS WITH ME AND IT WAS ULTIMATELY HIS UNDOING.
I'M NOT SAYING WE'LL NEVER BE PUNCHING EACH OTHER IN THE FACE EVER AGAIN, BUT THIS FEELS LIKE A GOOD MOMENT FOR US.
POETIC JUSTICE IS BEAUTIFUL.
I WAS GONNA SAY SOMETHING WITH MORE CURSE WORDS, BUT HAVE IT YOUR WAY.
I'M WORRIED ABOUT SOM AND ABOUT WHERE NUCLEAR MAN WENT, JESS. I MEAN, IS HE JUST GOING TO DO THIS ALL OVER AGAIN SOMEWHERE ELSE?
THE TIME DILATION IS A REAL PROBLEM...MEANS THESE THINGS CAN GO ON FOR WEEKS WITH NOBODY REALLY NOTICING, AND--
ROGER?
...
WELL, PRETTY HARD TO ARGUE WITH THAT.
ALL THESE PEOPLE AROUND AND YOU'RE TALKING TO YOURSELF, DANVERS?
RHODEY!
THIS IS CRAZY. I JUST SAW YOU TWELVE HOURS AGO, BUT NOW YOUR OUTFIT, YOUR HAIR...
OUR LIVES ARE WEIRD.
YEAH, EVERYTHING'S DIFFERENT.
NOT EVERYTHING.
CAROL, I...OH. UH. KISSING. OKAY. WELL, YOU KNOW WHAT, JUST COME ON OVER FOR DEBRIEF WHENEVER YOU'RE--UH-- READY.

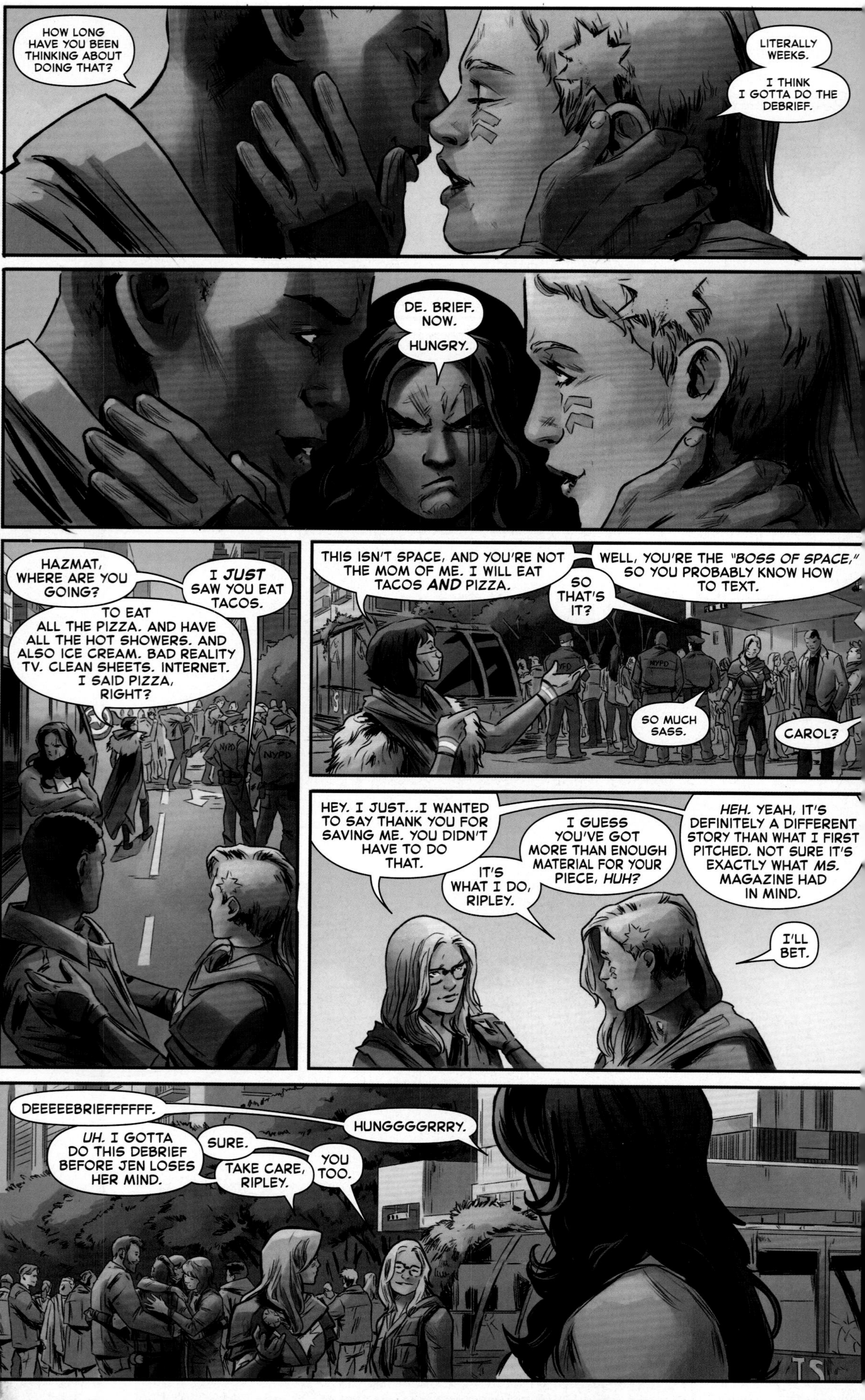
HOW LONG HAVE YOU BEEN THINKING ABOUT DOING THAT?
LITERALLY WEEKS.
I THINK I GOTTA DO THE DEBRIEF.
DE. BRIEF. NOW.
HUNGRY.
HAZMAT, WHERE ARE YOU GOING?
I JUST SAW YOU EAT TACOS.
TO EAT ALL THE PIZZA. AND HAVE ALL THE HOT SHOWERS. AND ALSO ICE CREAM. BAD REALITY TV. CLEAN SHEETS. INTERNET. I SAID PIZZA, RIGHT?
THIS ISN'T SPACE, AND YOU'RE NOT THE MOM OF ME. I WILL EAT TACOS AND PIZZA.
SO THAT'S IT?
WELL, YOU'RE THE "BOSS OF SPACE," SO YOU PROBABLY KNOW HOW TO TEXT.
SO MUCH SASS.
CAROL?
HEY. I JUST...I WANTED TO SAY THANK YOU FOR SAVING ME. YOU DIDN'T HAVE TO DO THAT.
IT'S WHAT I DO, RIPLEY.
I GUESS YOU'VE GOT MORE THAN ENOUGH MATERIAL FOR YOUR PIECE, HUH?
HEH. YEAH, IT'S DEFINITELY A DIFFERENT STORY THAN WHAT I FIRST PITCHED. NOT SURE IT'S EXACTLY WHAT MS. MAGAZINE HAD IN MIND.
I'LL BET.
DEEEEEBRIEFFFFFF.
HUNGGGGRRRY.
UH. I GOTTA DO THIS DEBRIEF BEFORE JEN LOSES HER MIND.
SURE.
TAKE CARE, RIPLEY.
YOU TOO.

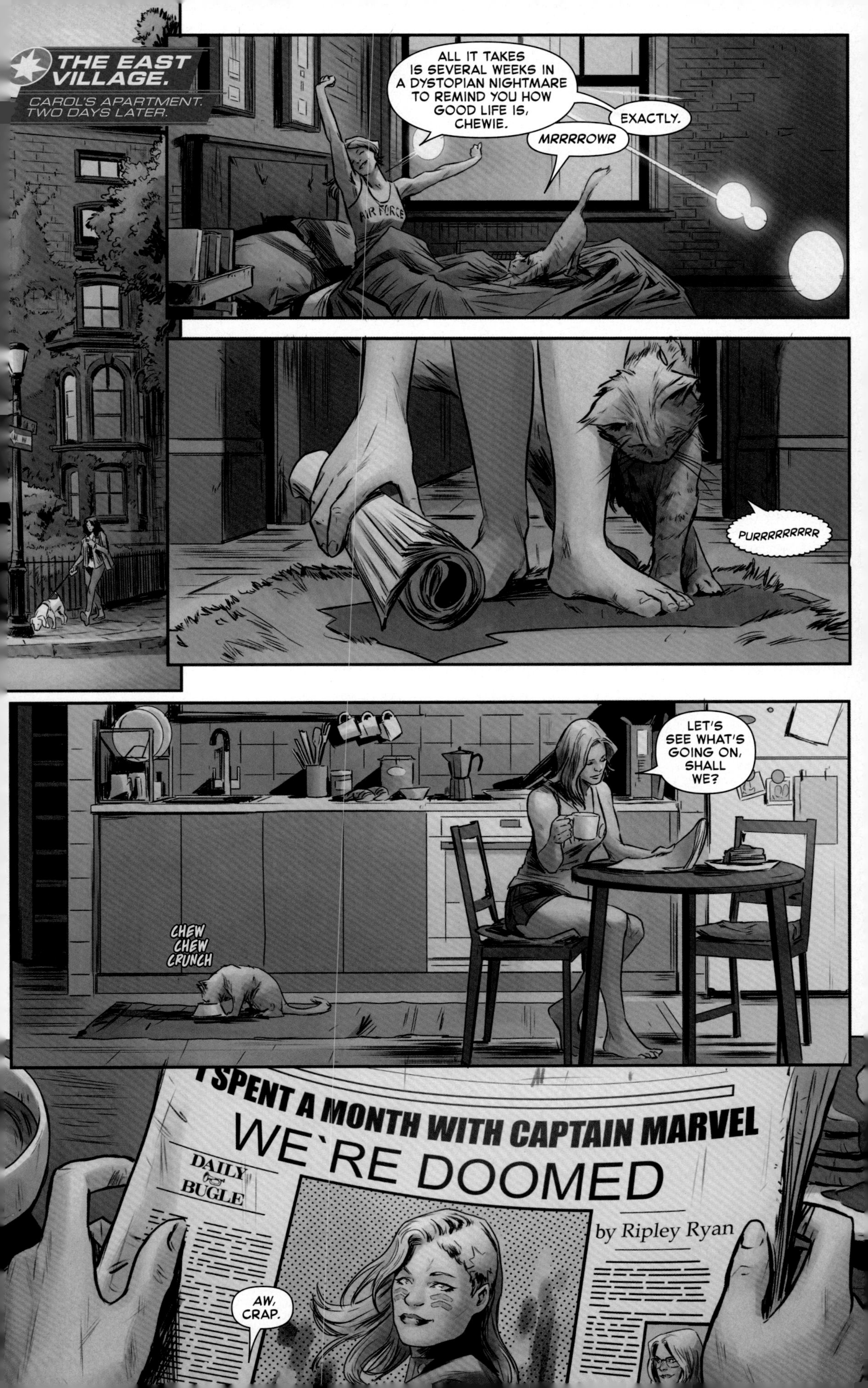
THE EAST VILLAGE.
CAROL'S APARTMENT. TWO DAYS LATER.
ALL IT TAKES IS SEVERAL WEEKS IN A DYSTOPIAN NIGHTMARE TO REMIND YOU HOW GOOD LIFE IS, CHEWIE.
MRRRROWR
EXACTLY.
PURRRRRRRRR
CHEW CHEW CRUNCH
LET'S SEE WHAT'S GOING ON, SHALL WE?
I SPENT A MONTH WITH CAPTAIN MARVEL
WE`RE DOOMED
DAILY BUGLE
by Ripley Ryan
AW, CRAP.

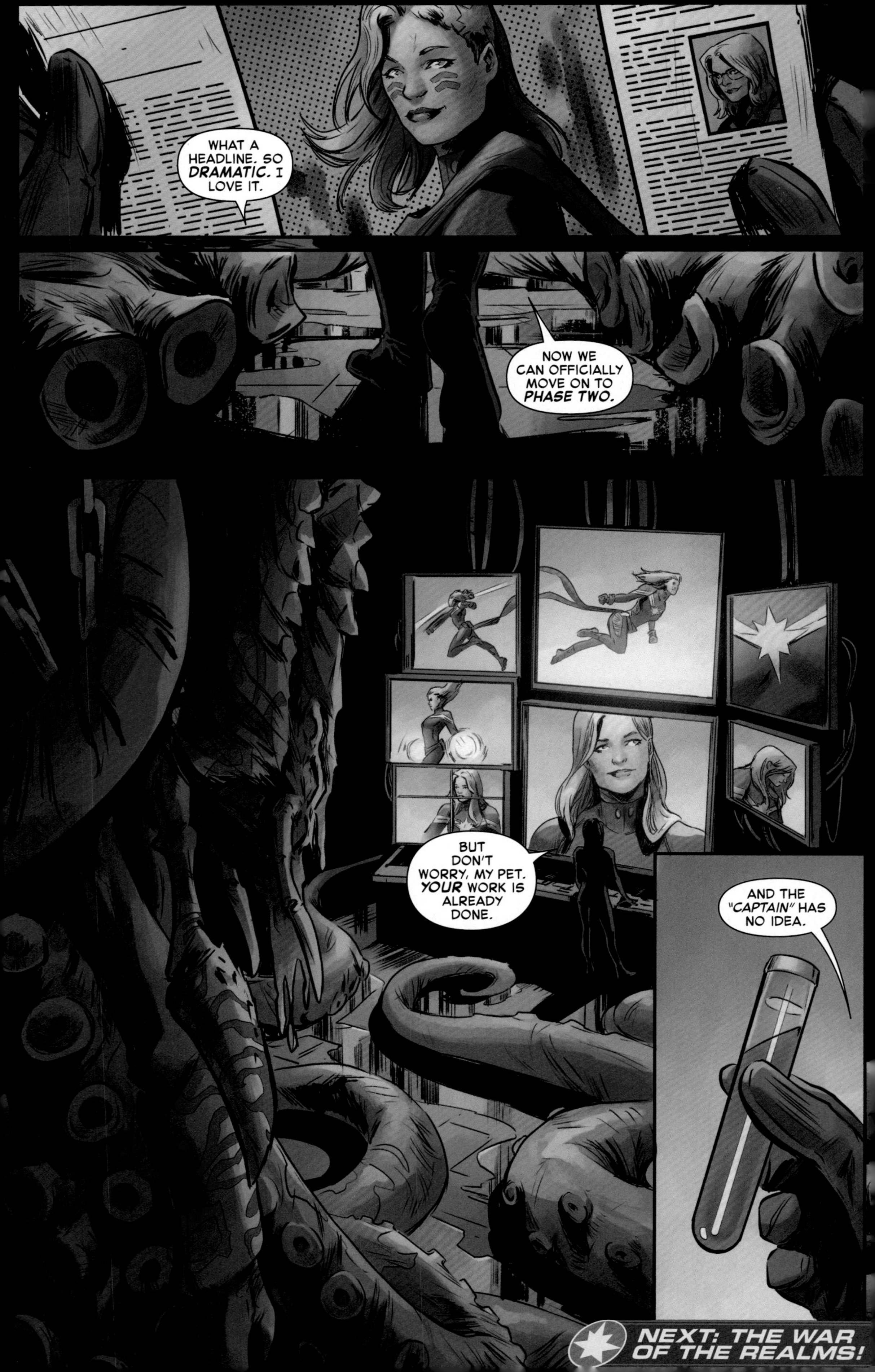
WHAT A HEADLINE. SO DRAMATIC. I LOVE IT.
NOW WE CAN OFFICIALLY MOVE ON TO PHASE TWO.
BUT DON'T WORRY, MY PET. YOUR WORK IS ALREADY DONE.
AND THE "CAPTAIN" HAS NO IDEA.
NEXT: THE WAR OF THE REALMS!

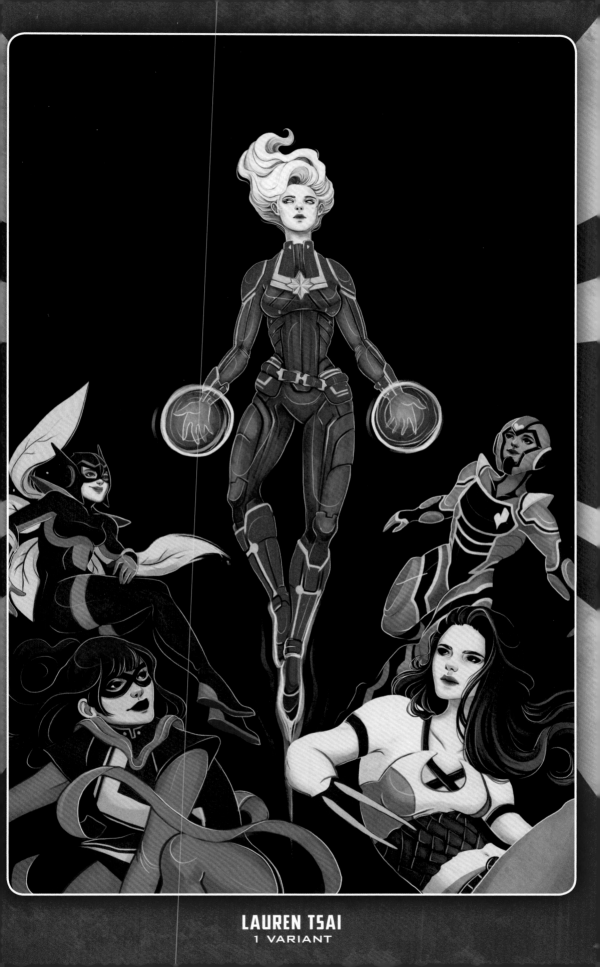

LAUREN TSAI
1 VARIANT

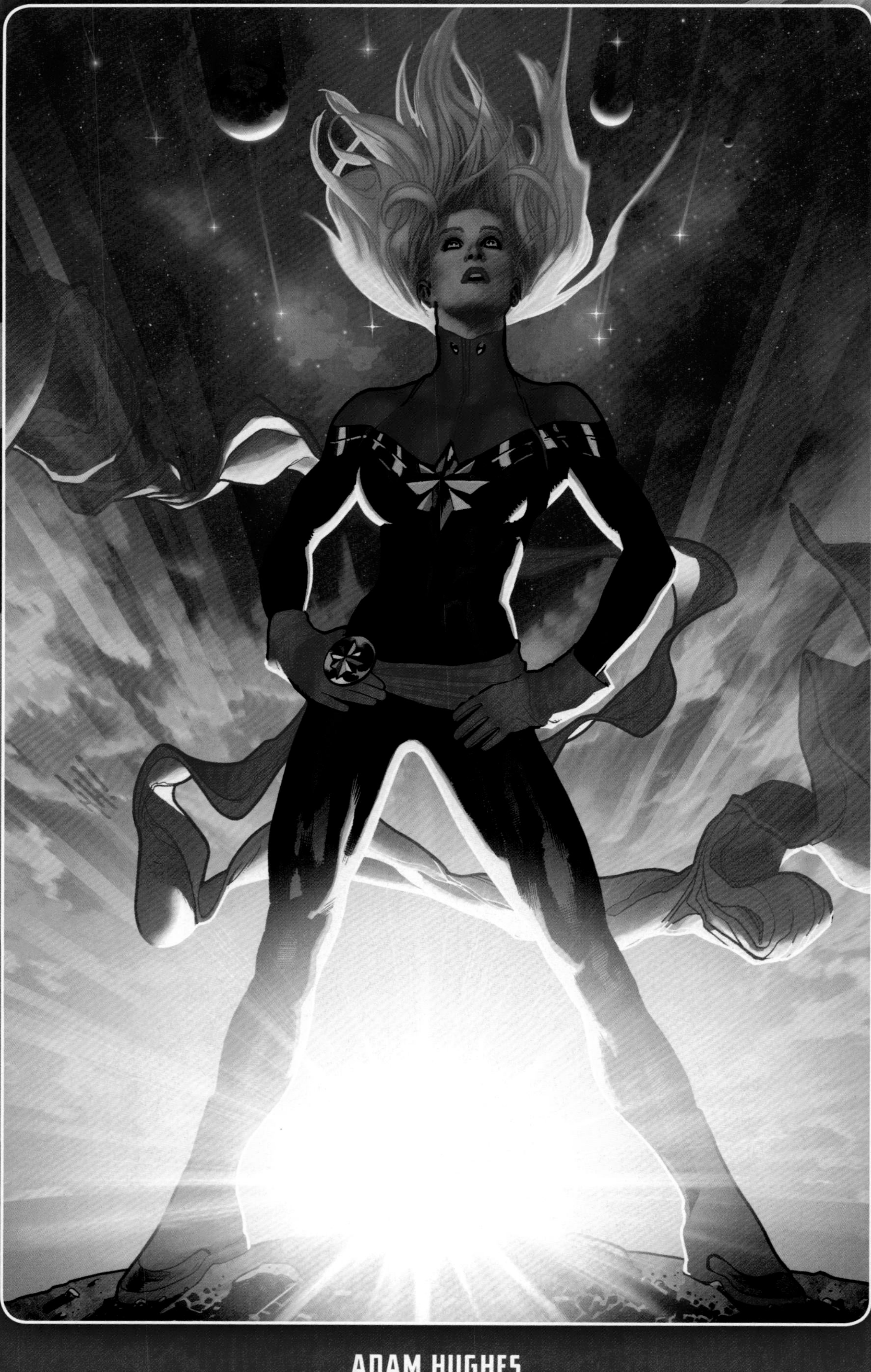

ADAM HUGHES
1 VARIANT

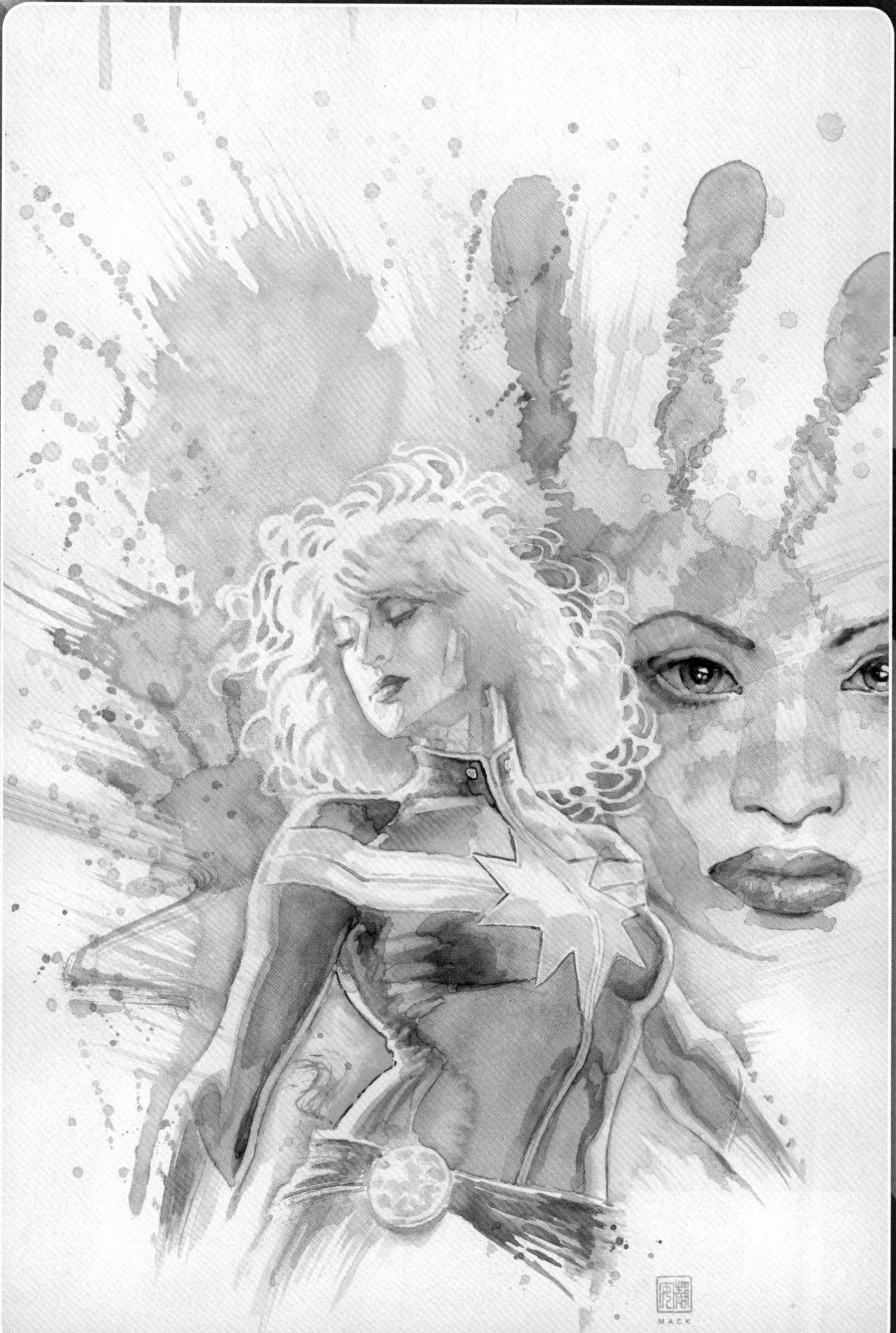
MACK

DAVID MACK
3 VARIANT

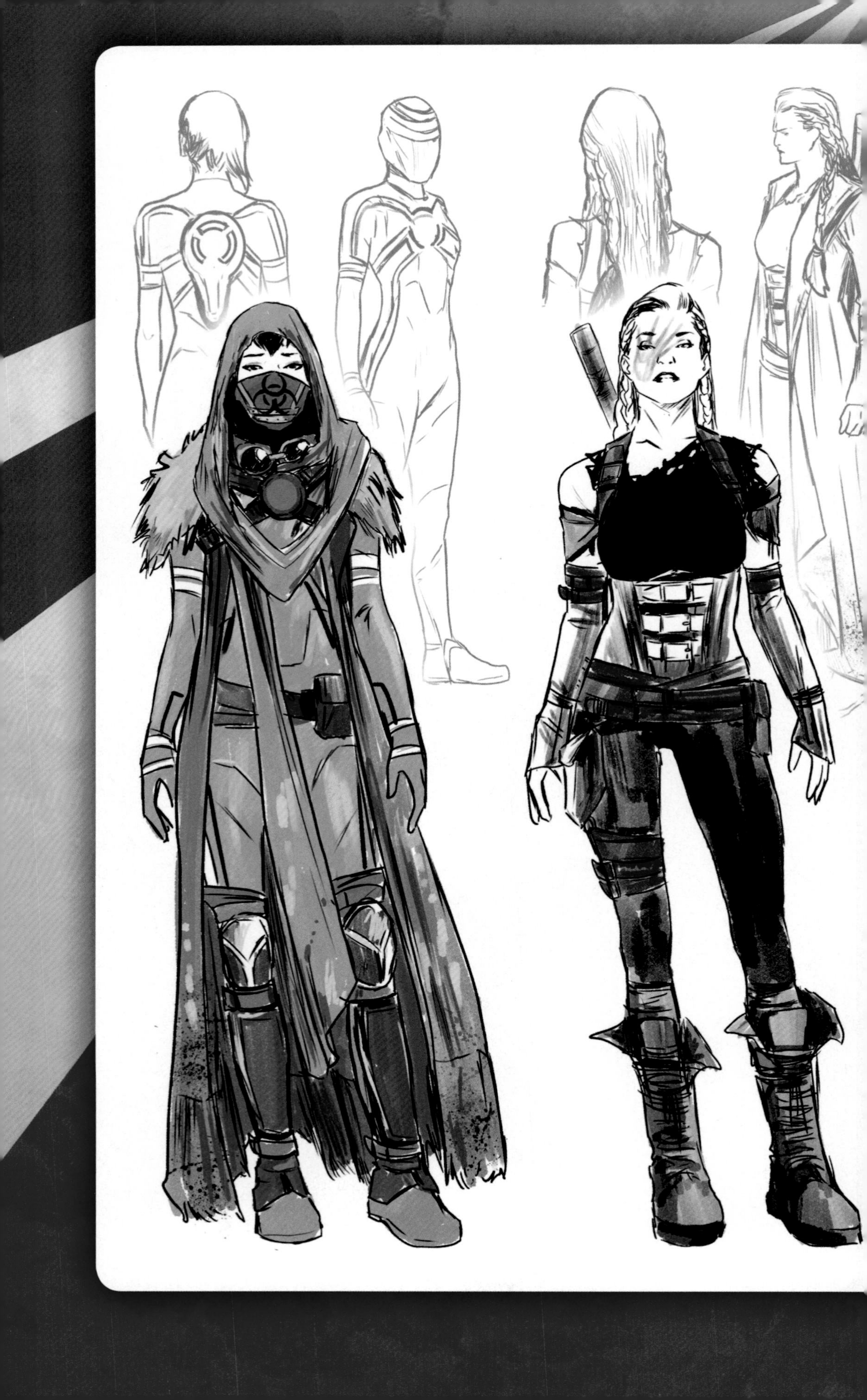

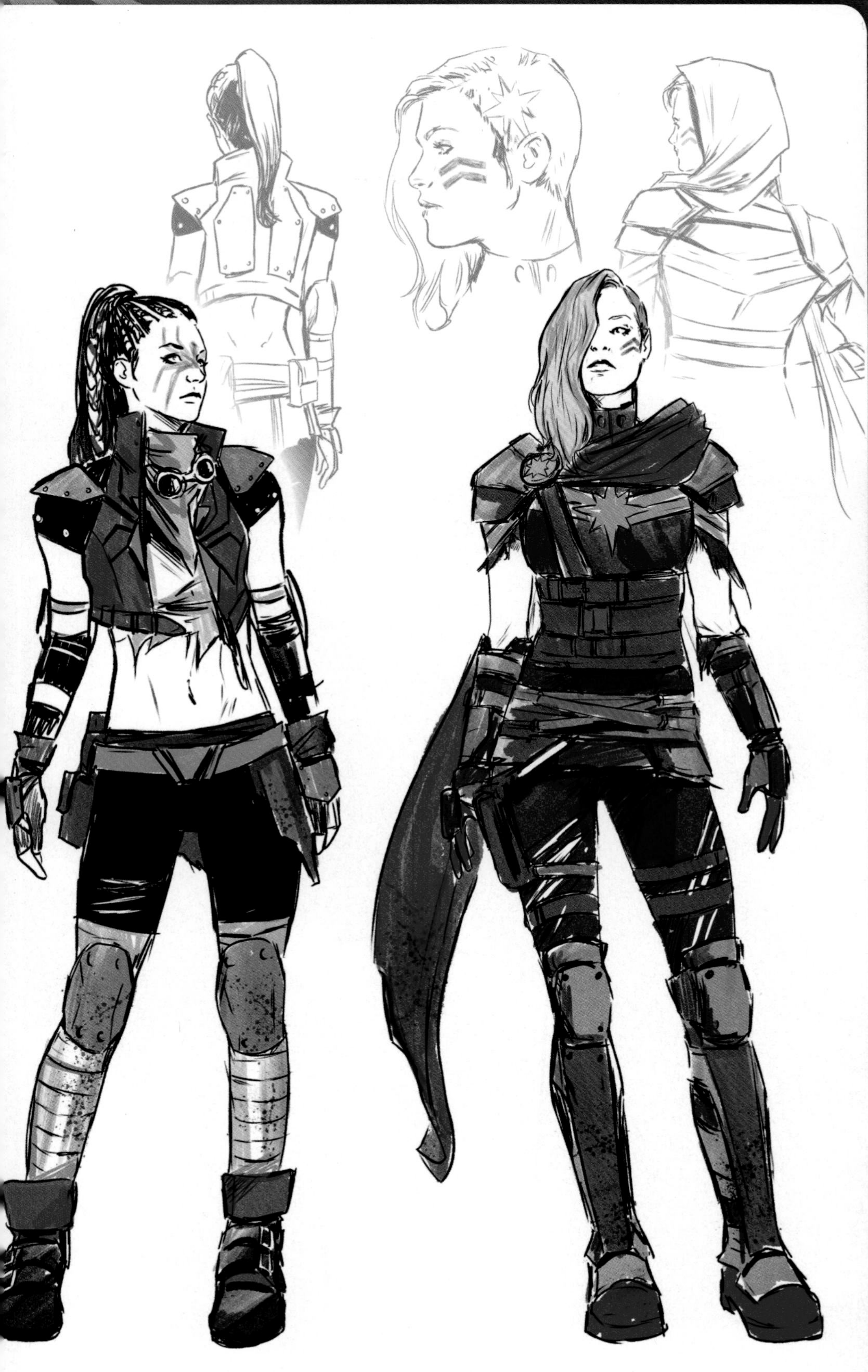

CARMEN CARNERO
2 DESIGN VARIANT

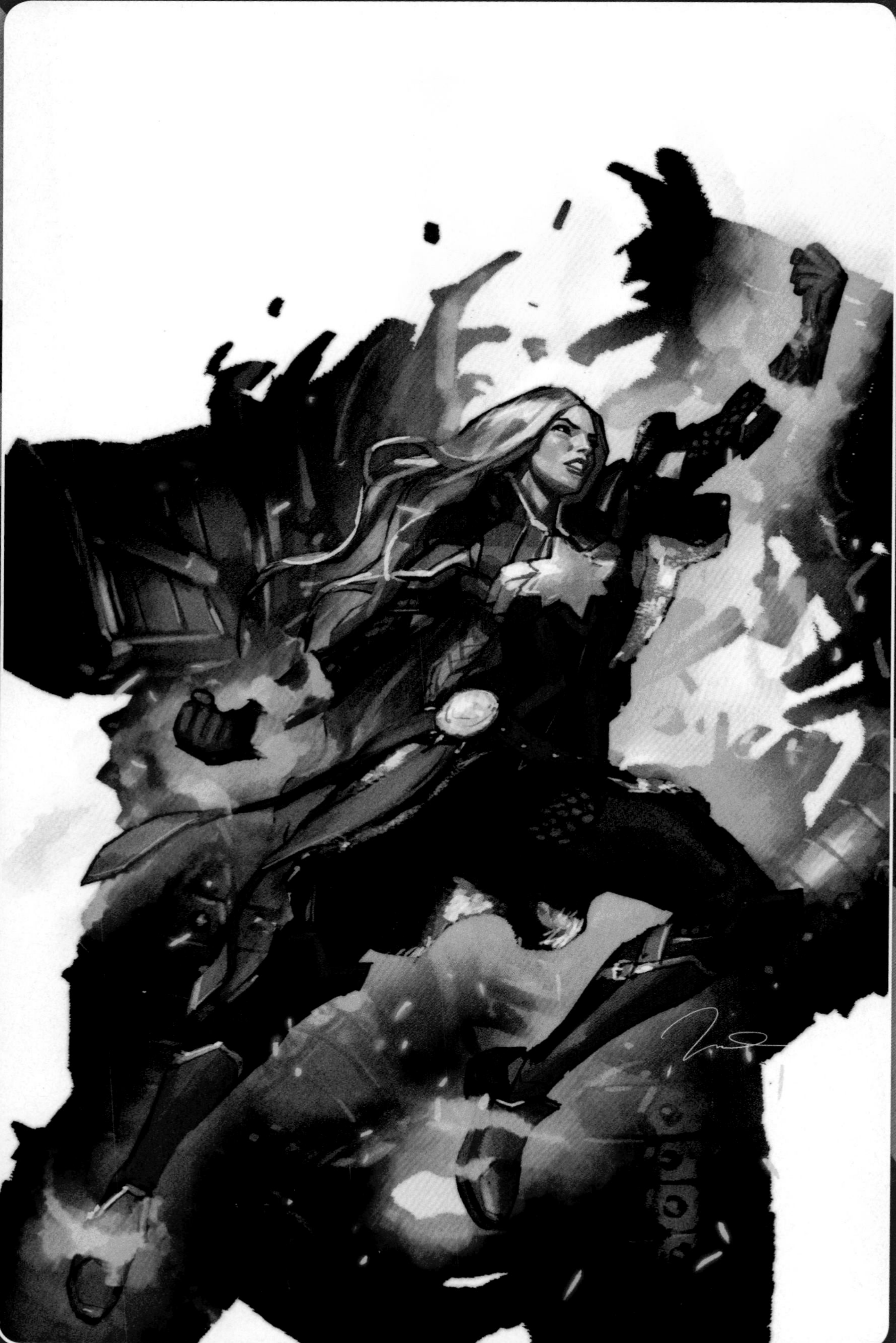

GERALD PAREL
4 ASGARDIAN VARIANT